Seasons on Ice

The Birth of Wisconsin Badgers Hockey

Craig P. Nelson

Piper Park Publishing—Madison, WI
ISBN: 979-8-9895478-0-7
Library of Congress Control Number: 2024900933
Title: *Seasons on Ice – The Birth of Wisconsin Badgers Hockey*
Author: Nelson, Craig P.,
Edited By: Harvey Nelson, Scott Sumbler and Brian Finch
Cover By: Sarah Knize Curzydlo
Paperback | 2024

Printed in the United States of America

Subjects: Wisconsin Badgers (Hockey team) -History.
| University of Wisconsin – Hockey – History | University of Wisconsin – Madison –
Hockey – History. | Hockey – Wisconsin – Madison – History.
| Hockey teams – Wisconsin – Madison – History.
| Hockey players – Wisconsin – Madison – History.

Description: Madison, Wisconsin. New Book Authors Publishing, [2024]

Dedication

Special thanks to the following important people and groups that contributed directly, and indirectly, to this book.

My parents Harvey and Phyllis Nelson for introducing me to the sport of ice hockey, for taking me to countless practices and games and for letting me accompany you to several Wisconsin Badgers hockey games at the Dane County Coliseum as a kid. For igniting my passions and inspiring me in so many ways. For allowing me to have so many opportunities in life. Love you.

My wife Stacey who strongly encouraged me to follow my dreams and write this book after I left corporate America. Your strengths and love are immeasurable. Love you.

My #1 son and pride of my life, Trent P. Nelson. I love you, son, more than life itself. You are incredibly intelligent, personable, resilient, courageous, humorous, strong and so talented. Keep chasing your dreams. The World is yours. You make me so proud each and every day. Love you.

Sister Kara K Nelson-Schwartz, love your wicked sense of humor. Thanks for being such an important and strong part of our family. Love you.

Bob & Susan Titus. Brian, Paula, Simon and Quinn Bjerketvedt. Love you.

My older brother Todd Michael Nelson, Trevor "Sam", "Trev Cat" Smeby, Karl Roeber, Timmy Venden, Eric "Wiley" Yandell, Billy "Jax" Jackson, Eric "Poy" Gensen, Cyrus "My Friend, My People" Irani, Milka "Silk" Miller and Kent Wosepka and the others. RIP. Until we meet again. Love you brothers.

Fellow Hockey enthusiasts and historians for their incredibly priceless contributions; Harvey Nelson, Brian Finch, Scott Sumbler, Frank Wilson, Mike Cowan and Steven D Schmitt. Love you guys!

My Grandpa, Elvin "Al" Nelson, who worked for the University of Wisconsin football program for over 40 years and helped to ignite my passion as a Badger fan. Love you grandpa. RIP. Go Badgers!

My totally awesome Akita named Suter that I miss every day. Such an amazing dog! RIP

MVPs Scott Doudna, Jason Goetz, Mark Engstrom, Randy Parent, Phil Stern, Jed Johnson, Thomas Murphy, Paul Hughes and Scott Severson. Much Love!

Seasons on Ice
The Birth of Wisconsin Badgers Hockey
By Craig P. Nelson
Cover Design by Sarah Knine Curnydle
1 1910 Murad Tobacco Sports Card
2 1910s Red Gym Postcard
3 Vintage Skates
4 Vintage Leather Hockey Gloves
5 Vintage Leather & Wire Eyeglasses Protector
6 January 1929, The Wisconsin Athletic Review
7 1928 Wan-Gard Hockey Stick
8 1910 Murad Tobacco B21 College Silk
9 Early 1900s Felt Wisconsin Pennant
10 1927-28 Wisconsin Badgers Team Photo
11 Captain Roy Kubista's Letterman Sweater
WISCONSIN

CONTENTS

ILLUSTRATIONS

ix

Foreword
William (Bill) Brophy

There are many people around Madison who like to gather with their hockey-loving friends, order their preferred beverage and tell stories about their favorite University of Wisconsin game or coach or player.

The old-timers will tell you about how they saw games at Hartmeyer Ice Arena on Madison's East Side. Then there are many who love to reflect on racing down to the beer garden between periods at the Dane County Coliseum only to return refreshed and ready to cheer on a third period rally at what was considered the Montreal Forum of college hockey. Many of the Coliseum crowd relish re-living the tales from the legendary "Water Bottle game" against North Dakota or have other memorable games.

For the last 25 years, hockey fans have been spoiled with the amenities of the Kohl Center on campus, but the stories and debates continue: Who was the best player to ever play for the Badgers?

Okay, the right answer is Mark Johnson, maybe the best college player of all-time.

But then who is the next best Badger player? Chris Chelios? Bert DeHate? Cole Caufield? Tony Granato? Theran Welsh? Mike Eaves? And pick your best goalie from Marc Behrend, Mike Richter, Jim Carey, Curtis Joseph and Brian Elliott. Let's order another round and may the debate continue.

Local fans can proudly tell you about Wisconsin's six national championships, the Badgers' success in the Western Collegiate Hockey Association over the years and how the current hockey life in the Big Ten has taken some getting used to.

But long before Bob Johnson and Jeff Sauer were coaching behind the Badger bench, the seeds were planted for interest in the University of Wisconsin hockey program when guys wearing horizontal stripes on their Wisconsin sweaters strapped on the skates and played on Lake Mendota.

Craig P. Nelson was a young fan at the Dane County Coliseum in the 1970's. He noticed that the Badger program cover during a game one season featured a former UW player from the 1920's. It piqued Nelson's interest about the players who wore the candy stripes and skated outdoors, but he discovered there was little written or spoken about those players or teams.

So, Nelson went to the way-back machine and discovered that, while the UW says the modern era of Wisconsin hockey began with the 1963-64 season, the origins of ice hockey actually began in the 1890's.

Because of the climate in Wisconsin in winter, ice hockey developed quite a following in Madison as a recreational activity. It grew into a varsity sport for the 1921-22 season when the Badgers fielded a team in the Western Intercollegiate Hockey League, which also had teams from the University of Michigan and the University of Minnesota.

Dr. A.C Viner was the first coach that season and his team went winless. But in subsequent seasons, coaches like Robert Blodgett, Kay Iverson, W.R. Bandow, John Farquhar, Spike Carlson and Art Thomsen kept the program alive.

Because of the economic crunch of The Depression, Wisconsin was forced to drop hockey as an intercollegiate sport when the 1933-34 season ended. Thomsen also coached the Wisconsin team in 1934-35 as well and he agreed to assist John Riley and was the co-coach of the Badgers for UW's re-birth into the hockey world for the 1963-64 season.

Decades later Nelson channeled his curiosity about the players in the old-time uniforms into a labor of love. After nearly seven years of research, he shines a light on the forgotten era of Badger hockey. This historical narrative was pieced together through information Nelson located in newspapers and school publications from the 1890s until the program was canceled in 1935.

"Seasons on Ice - The Birth of Wisconsin Badgers Hockey" examines a bygone era, introduces you to the characters who helped shape the program when the Badgers were playing Carleton College and the Janesville YMCA and shares a treasure trove of previously unseen photos from the Badger hockey team and their area opponents.

As Mike Hastings becomes the sixth coach in the modern history of the program and the school celebrates 75 seasons of Badger hockey in 2023-24, the casual Badger hockey fan now has a chance to peruse Nelson's collection of statistics, photos and stories and have an appreciation for the history of the program when games were contested in front of the Red Gym.

It is clear that, for over 100 years around Madison, Badger Bob was speaking long before his time as a coach when he invoked, "It's a great day for hockey."

Bill Brophy is the former sports editor at the Wisconsin State Journal who has been involved with the WCHA for nearly 50 years. He is currently a television analyst for college and high school sports and his work seen on Bally Sports, FS1 and NCAA.com.

Acknowledgements

University of Wisconsin Archives staff; David Null, Vicky Tobias, Katie Nash and Cat Phan. Their assistance, guidance and professionalism on my rookie pursuit of creating this book is immeasurable and greatly appreciated.

Thank you to the professionals outside of Wisconsin that were happy to help and also provided critically important assistance and information:

Mariel Carter, Adult Services Reference Librarian, Stephenson Public Library in Marinette, WI.

Erik Moore, Head, University Archives Co-Director, University of Minnesota Libraries.

Katie Blank, University/Digital Records Archivist, Marquette University, Raynor Memorial Libraries Special Collections & University Archives.

A phenomenal graphic artist who is a true blessing to me, Sarah Knize Curzydlo. saltyolivecreative.com

Much appreciation to Brian Bjerketvedt, a true multidisciplinary creative! hybridstudio.io

Special thanks to a life changing counselor and fantastic human being at Madison West, Mr. Dave Olson. As well as a brilliant Professor and wonderful man, C.C. Smith at UW-River Falls.

Michal Thomas for the outstanding Madison, Wisconsin climatology weather reports covering the 1910, 1920s and 1930s.

Fellow Wisconsin hockey enthusiasts, collectors and historians; Lon Bauer, Tim Satterthwaite, Matthew Wallock, Tom Grosse, Dave Vitale, Daniel Rung, Jim Gunderson, Mark Miller, Mark Kampa, Ron Hoffman, Kyle Oen, Greg Cascio and Michael Comins.

Huge thanks to the hockey families that influenced me and a ton of others in the sport of hockey around the city of Madison, the State of Wisconsin, the USA and even the World; the Johnsons, Suters, Mathers, Marshalls, Sauers, Flemings, Thomsens, Heidens, O'Briens, Schachtes, Heinrichs, Frantz, Byces and Andringas. And so many more…

The Wisconsin hockey reporters like Bill Brophy, Paul Braun, Mike Lucas, Andy Baggot, Brian Posick, Todd Milewski, Phil Mendel, Bob Leu and the others that have inspired me and brought us such amazing content over the decades.

Chapter One
The Creation of the Game

How the game of ice hockey came to evolve within the U.S. will never be clear. Like so many aspects of the history of this sport, there are countless theories. Most likely the natives, along with the countless people that immigrated to America from overseas, and the visitors to and from Canada, were concurrently playing variations of what would eventually become the new and exciting game of ice hockey. In the Midwest and along the East Coast it was the Europeans, Scandinavians and Natives who continued to play their traditional games on the many frozen lakes, ponds and rivers found during the winter months. There are records that indicate the game of hockey was played formally in the states as early as the 1890s. During these times the sport of ice hockey was in its infancy in North America.

For example, several East Coast Colleges and Universities were routinely playing ice hockey and eventually began to formalize the game as a recognized varsity sport at their higher learning institutions. In 1895, the college hockey teams at Yale and John Hopkins played two games that season. The following season Pennsylvania University, Yale, Columbia University and the Maryland Agricultural College had a hockey season. During the 1897-1898 season, Massachusetts Institute of Technology, Haverford and the Pennsylvania Dental College joined the other schools and were also actively playing organized hockey.

By 1898, Harvard, Yale, Brown and Columbia had formal ice hockey programs. The Skating Club of New York commissioned an Ice Hockey Champions trophy that would be handed out each season. Brown defeated the hockey teams at Harvard, Yale and Columbia to become the first collegiate hockey champion of 1898. The game of hockey continued to grow and increase in popularity year after year.

This game had traits of the Irish sport known as hurling, similarities to the Native American sport of lacrosse and a hint of the English sport of golf. It also had aspects similar to the games of Shinny, Shinty and ice polo among others. But this game was different and had a powerful attraction to both players and those that observed the activity. Ice hockey was truly a sport that no one could imagine would take root so strongly on the University of Wisconsin-Madison landscape and would quickly grow nationwide among many universities and colleges.

The Game of Hockey Migrates to the USA and UW

The University of Wisconsin Campus

In the Midwest, records at the University of Wisconsin cite a recreational club ice hockey team as early as the 1890s. On the UW campus, it likely began as a curiosity. The first pickup games of ice hockey on the Wisconsin campus began on the shores of Lake Mendota upon the natural ice-skating surface. Once the popularity of the sport distinguished itself as more than a temporary fad, a club hockey team formed at the University of Wisconsin in the 1890s. The eventual success of hockey at the University of Wisconsin was due in large part to the efforts and commitment of the coaches and skaters dedicated to the early UW club hockey teams.

In 1892, construction of the University of Wisconsin Armory and Gymnasium, better known as "the Red Gym," began on campus. It was completed in 1894 and was used primarily as a combination gymnasium and armory. The Red Gym resembles an ancient red brick castle and is located on the shores of Lake Mendota, adjacent to what is known today as the Memorial Library building across the street from the Memorial Union on the UW campus.

An original photo postcard from the 1930s showing the Gymnasium and Armory (aka Red Gym). It also shows the field across the street from the gym which is the area where the ice rink (Lower Campus Rink) was made for the Wisconsin hockey players and coaches to utilize for practices and games. The Memorial Library is adjacent to where the old campus rink used to be located.

Historical documentation shedding light on any of the UW club hockey teams from the 1890s until the late 1910s is extremely scarce and virtually nonexistent. In 1902, the Wisconsin Alumni magazine noted that there were plans designated to popularize the sport of ice hockey during the winter. An ongoing tradition for many decades was the Ice Fete, also known as the Winter Carnival, held on Lake Mendota behind the Red Gym. Promoted as a UW social event, the Ice Fete provided main attractions that specifically included hockey as well as curling, fancy skating and other ice-based events. As of 1905, the sport of organized ice hockey as a student activity on campus was not gaining any momentum beyond a winter curiosity. However, by the 1906-07 school year, the fraternities began forming competitive hockey schedules to be played at the rink on Lake Mendota. In addition, groups of students fortunate enough to own skates and hockey sticks were playing pickup games, further growing the popularity of this new winter sport.

The B33 University of Wisconsin hockey felt issued by Murad Tobacco.

The S21 University of Wisconsin hockey silk issued by Murad Tobacco.

The Murad Tobacco Company issued these college premiums packaged in their tobacco products between 1900 – 1910. They produced college felts, college silks and cards. These items were an attempt to market tobacco use among college students and fans of college athletics.

The fledgling University of Wisconsin hockey teams practiced their skating and played games on Lake Mendota. An area positioned near the rear of the Red Gym and the UW Boat House on Lake Mendota became the logical choice for hockey rinks, an eight-lap track for ice racing and a general skating area. A total of two designated hockey rinks were created on the lake by using a single row of boards to act as a border around the playing areas. Each rink was an impressive 64x128 feet. Eventually, there was also construction of a shelter that would act as a warming house and a place for skaters to rest and for everyone to escape the elements. It would also act as a protective barrier from the bone chilling wind that would race across Lake Mendota each winter. The annual costs for building and maintaining these designated skating areas were roughly $1,000. All of which was managed by the UW students and funded by season memberships in the skating club and admission fees for non-members.

Before 1910, the hockey matches consisted of two 30-minute halves and the goal area was simply two hockey sticks stuck into the ice. Continual repairs were required on these rinks since they were constantly exposed to the elements. Strong winds, snow, sleet and rain frequently pounded the rinks during the winter months and all too often left the ice surface unplayable.

By this time, tradition at the University of Wisconsin now had students constructing skating rinks behind the Red Gym on Lake Mendota after returning to campus from Christmas break. Several of the fraternities at the UW would form hockey teams and formal game schedules were finalized for matches upon the lake rink.

Joe Steinauer was a popular coach of the Wisconsin club hockey teams during this period. He is credited with ensuring the club program continued during these very early days at the UW. Coach Steinauer's efforts allowed players to consistently participate and thanks to his efforts, interest in the game was maintained at an admirable level even though conference play with other schools was still several years away.

Coach Joe Steinauer

Hockey on Campus at UW-Madison

World War I put a great strain on the momentum of the UW club hockey teams and was second only to the unfavorable weather challenges that were a constant antagonizing factor. Understandably, Mother Nature would prove to be the most feared opponent for the Wisconsin hockey program. For it was her that could and would, ruin many a game by making the ice-skating surface unplayable or nonexistent countless times during this original era of Wisconsin hockey. Countless games and ultimately seasons, had forced cancellations due to the unfavorable weather conditions during these decades.

On January 9, 1910, the UW Athletic department began construction of the hockey rink on the lower campus for the upcoming season. This was the first time it would be on campus rather than on Lake Mendota. A section of the ground was made level; the area was enclosed and framed up with hockey boards for the rink area while fire hydrants on Langdon Street were opened to cover the skating surface with the applications of water. With the weather cooperating and cold temps, additional layers of water were sprayed to thicken the ice for the skating surface. It would be fully operational and ready for skaters in late January 1910.

Wisconsin's Athletic department continued to put forth resources and funding to creatively maintain the Lower Campus Rink for the 1910-11 and 1911-12 school years as the sport of hockey continued to gain in popularity.

The Nitchi Cheeman Canoe Club hockey team, based in Madison, Wisconsin, was made up of hockey players attending school at the University of Wisconsin. In 1912, the University of Wisconsin club hockey players on Nitchi Cheeman were busy trying to establish an intercollegiate hockey league with other schools in the Midwest. At their February 19 meeting, F.C. Hutson, a senior at the UW, was elected as the captain of the Nitchi Cheeman Canoe Club's hockey team. W.C. Ketter was elected as the manager for the hockey team.

On February 24, 1912, the Nitchi Cheeman hockey club from the University of Wisconsin defeated the Madison high school hockey team 4-1 in what was described as, the first regular hockey game ever played on the University rink.

Games were arranged with teams like the Gordon Place Canoe Club out of Milwaukee. They were one of the oldest clubs in the state. The Gordons reigned as Milwaukee city hockey champions for several years.

It was March 2 1912, when players on the University of Wisconsin Badgers Nitchi Cheeman club hockey team played the first of two scheduled games against the Gordon Place Canoe Club on the Madison, Wisconsin campus rink. The Gordons were a highly talented hockey team. The UW team was at a disadvantage since they got a late start practicing hockey before the first scheduled games and because they were relatively new to the sport. Each game consisted of two 20-minute halves. Final score: Nitchi Cheeman 2, Gordon Place Canoe Club 5.

The second game between these two teams was played March 3 1912.

Final score: Nitchi Cheeman 1, Gordon 3.

Nitchi Cheeman Lineup: Alexander (Center), Merritt (Right Wing), King (Left Wing), Zander (Cover Point), Whipple (Point) and Roehm (Goalie). Spares: Phillips and Johnson. Referee: Coach John R. Richards.

The next weekend, March 8, the Nitchi Cheeman team from the University of Wisconsin played the hockey team from St. Johns Military Academy.

The weekend after, games were played Saturday March 16 and Sunday March 17. The Nitchi Cheeman hockey team traveled to Milwaukee for a pair of games against the Gordon Place Canoe Club hockey team.

The records do not reflect final scores for the games played against St. Johns Military Academy and Gordon Place Canoe this season.

The Nitchi Cheeman Canoe Club hockey team also handled the planning and preparations for the first annual 1912 winter Carnival at the University of Wisconsin. Events would include; hockey games, toboggan races and jumping, ice skating races and fancy skating among the featured events.

1912-13 UW Hockey Team

The players selected for the University of Wisconsin ice hockey team this season would be charged with representing the UW in several games that would soon be scheduled against their formidable opponents.

The Wisconsin skaters and personnel involved with the team were actively trying to lobby UW officials to add hockey as a minor sport at the University. Getting classified as a "minor" varsity sport was the first step on the path to eventually becoming a major or full-fledged "Varsity," sport.

One of the challenges that hockey continually faced was a dependable skating surface. On January 21, the University of Wisconsin Athletic Department started construction of a Lower Campus Rink. The boards that would make up the rink walls were put in place and the frozen ground was flooded. It would be completed in a few days and ready for skaters. The UW Athletic Department was also working on a decision to clear a place on Lake Mendota, behind the Red Gym, to create a secondary hockey rink.

This year the UW Athletic Department took over the planning and preparations for the second annual UW Winter Carnival. "Sheep" Alexander, who was the acting Chairman of the hockey committee arranged for the selection of two hockey teams from all available hockey skaters at the UW. The two teams would play a feature hockey game at the winter Carnival. The teams were also in consideration to play against a local high school team and some nearby adult teams.

Joe Steinauer was appointed by the Athletic Department to teach hockey classes on the Lower Campus Rink. Steinauer's hockey classes would count as a regular gym class. It was expected Steinauer would be appointed as head coach of the Wisconsin hockey team.

Although formal records remain incomplete, the basic architecture

of the primary and secondary UW hockey squads is known. A handful of men were involved in the early organized University of Wisconsin ice hockey team on campus for the 1912-13 hockey season. The coach, players and positions were as follows:
Joseph Steinauer, Coach

The First Team

Alfred Scheffer -   Center
Allan Briggs -   Right Forward
Frank Whipple -   Left Forward
George Stillman -   Rover
Arthur Alexander -   Cover Point
Hiram Roehm -   Goal
James Boucher -   Point

The Second Team

Clarence Boucher -   Center
Malcolm McFarlan -   Right Forward
Glenway Mason, Jr. -   Left Forward
James Bill -   Rover
Arthur Zander -   Point
Alvin Rowe -   Cover Point
Marshal Johnson -   Goal

The first and second team line-ups contain a total of seven players involved in the game at a time. This is consistent with the "Montreal Rules" (aka The McGill Rules) of ice hockey followed by ice hockey players from approximately 1877 until the hockey player positions were revised across North America in the early 1920s.

The position of "goal" would later be renamed "goalkeeper" or "goaltender." The "point" and "cover point" would change from a staggered positioning to side by side and would be renamed "right defense" and "left defense." Historically, the "center," "right forward," "left forward," and "rover" would change from being lined up as four across, to lined up as three across with the removal of the "rover" position. This would leave the "center," "right wing" and "left wing" we know today.

All of the planning and practices surrounding the Wisconsin hockey team this season were eventually for naught. As a result of unfavorable weather conditions during the short two to three months season every single scheduled game was unable to be played.

1912-13   Schedule and Results:
Coach Joe Steinauer

Date	Result	Opponent
	No Games Played	

1913-14 UW Hockey Team

The Wisconsin student hockey players and coach gathered again to play hockey at Wisconsin this season. Fortunately, the UW Club hockey team would exist for another year. While the weather was a little more accommodating than the previous season it was not without its occasional practice and game-wrecking attributes.

Under the expert guidance of Coach Steinauer, the returning veteran and freshman students that were around to play hockey on the Wisconsin campus would learn new strategies, practice standard play, and continue to get into game shape for any upcoming matches that would materialize. It was yet another important year building up the Wisconsin hockey program.

This was the same season that legendary player Hobey Baker would lead his Princeton University team to a national hockey championship. Experts would often proclaim Baker was the best hockey player to ever play the game. In his college playing career he only received one penalty (slashing) and had a fine reputation for his remarkable sportsmanship. After each game, win or lose, Baker would go into the opposing team's locker room and shake the hand of each player and thank them for playing. Many believe this is how the tradition of shaking hands-on ice immediately at the end of hockey games was formalized into a deep-rooted hockey tradition.

The Lower Campus Rink was flooded during the week of February 1. The rink also had the boards set up and a fence placed around the skating surface. Coach Joe Steinauer was working on organizing a UW hockey team. The annual Winter Carnival would again host a hockey game as one of the features for this event.

The University of Wisconsin hockey team traveled to Milwaukee to play the Milwaukee Town Club hockey team on February 22. The UW students showed great proficiency in the game of hockey under Coach Steinauer's direction. Wisconsin left town after accomplishing a 5-1 win over the Milwaukee hockey team. A rematch between these two teams was scheduled for Monday, February 23. Weather would prevent that game from happening.

Although the Wisconsin hockey team did not get in many practices or games, it was another crucial year keeping alive the hockey program at the University.

1913-14   Schedule and Results:
Coach Joe Steinauer
1-0-0 Overall

Date	Result	Opponent
February 22	Win 5-1	Milwaukee

1914-15 UW Hockey Team

Wisconsin's club hockey team was again comprised of an enthusiastic group of amateur hockey players. Coach Steinauer, who also had duties as the UW football trainer, was happy that a large number of potential candidates for the UW hockey team reported for initial informational meetings and practices to kick off the season.

Hockey players on this UW club team initially banded together as primarily a social organization among players who had a passion for the game of ice hockey. They were creative in lining up and scheduling games with similar hockey clubs at other schools. Competitors included small colleges, universities and recreational athletic hockey clubs. One of their formidable rivals involved fellow players at the historic Culver Military Academy. Culver routinely put together a very strong hockey team.

UW games continued to be played on the homemade rink located on campus. Players were responsible for construction and maintenance of this hockey rink to allow for practices and games. Without their participation in these roles, they would not have a rink. However, the always unpredictable forces of Mother Nature would not fully cooperate, especially in February when Madison experienced unusually warm weather and the Lower Campus Rink had to be closed.

A majority of the games this season (and for the next couple of years) would not be played on campus due to various factors that led to bad ice. Instead, the games and practices were forced back on to Lake Mendota where the ice was decent.

After another run of cold weather in March, the Athletic Department reopened the hockey rink on the Wisconsin campus. The ice surface was in the best shape of the season. Wisconsin's ice hockey team was thrilled to return to their training rink for practices and scrimmages.

The annual winter Carnival at the University of Wisconsin remained a popular event and hockey continued to be a highlight feature during the event.

1914-15 Wisconsin Hockey Club Team

A game against the St. John's Military Academy hockey team out of Delafield, Wisconsin was scheduled for Saturday, March 13. No records of such a game taking place exists and it is presumed the weather ruined this hockey game as well.

Fortunately, hockey would return the following season at the University of Wisconsin. Momentum continued for building a functional hockey program.

1914-15   Schedule and Results:
Coach Joe Steinauer

<u>Date</u>   <u>Result</u>   <u>Opponent</u>

No Games Played

1915-16 UW Hockey Team

The Wisconsin hockey team nearly disappeared entirely this season with the declaration of war in 1916. Most of the teams Wisconsin played hockey against faced the same dire circumstances. Many club hockey teams simply ceased to exist due to the extreme number of resources allotted to the war effort. A handful of UW students, and an educator or two acting as coach, did their best to ensure hockey survived at the University during this time while the nation was entering the first World War.

During the second week of January, the intramural hockey season began at the University of Wisconsin. The teams that made up the intra-college hockey league included; The Agrics, The Letters & Sciences, The Commerce Men and The Engineers. Approximately 40 college men signed up to participate in the campus league. From that group, the best skaters would be selected for the University of Wisconsin primary hockey team roster.

The University of Wisconsin Athletic Council had hockey on its agenda for the January 1916 meeting. Formal action to make hockey a varsity sport would be discussed considering teams had been formed annually on campus over the past several years and the game's continued increase in popularity. Sadly, there were not enough votes in favor of changing the status of hockey on campus at this time. For now, the team would still need to refer to themselves as an independent hockey team.

It was reported that over 80 University men participated in hockey during the 1915-16 season. Practices were scheduled to begin after the first semester examinations concluded at the UW. In mid-January city workers were constructing the skating area that would become the Lower Campus Rink. It would also be outfitted with sufficient artificial lighting so that skaters could work on their game well into the night. City of Madison workers were also responsible for removing snow from the ice-skating surface at the rink after winter storms.

<u>Wisconsin Ice Hockey Team</u>
Joe Steinauer   Head Coach
Gordon Grieve   Center
D. Dohr   Left Wing
H. Pribnow/C. Maedje   Right Wing
D.B. Kidder   Rover
W. Evans   Cover Point
R.C. Johnson (captain)   Point
G.F. Kritz   Goal

The intramural hockey league continued to grow in popularity. By mid-February, the league included over 60 hockey players. Players on campus were competing for the new Nelson Trophy. The coveted Trophy was presented to the University from Regent A.P. Nelson this season.

Again this year, the UW approved hockey classes that earned students required gym credits. A winter curriculum option students had utilized since 1913 at the University of Wisconsin. The Annual Winter Carnival, put on by the University of Wisconsin Athletic Department, returned again this year. Among all of the sport activities, hockey remained a highly entertaining game that many folks came out to watch.

The Wisconsin Badgers formal hockey team was able to play only one official hockey game this season. On February 22, they faced off against the St. John's Military Academy in Delafield, Wisconsin and dominated, pounding out a 3-0 victory.

Ice Hockey

First Row—Johnson, Evans, Kidder, Maedje
Second Row—Dohr, Kritz, Pribnow, Grieve

Wisconsin 3
St. John's Military Academy . . 0

The Team

Center . . . . G. Grieve
Left Wing . . . . D. Dohr
Right Wing . . . . . { H. Pribnow
{ C. Maedje
Rover . . . . D. B. Kidder
Cover Point . . . . . . W. Evans
Point . . . R. C. Johnson (Capt.)
Goal . . . . G. F. Kritz
Coach . . . . . . Joe Steinhauer

Winner of Inter-Mural Series—Commerce Team

The boys of winter would be back next season to restart hockey on the University of Wisconsin campus.

1915-16   Schedule and Results:
Coach Joe Steinauer
1-0-0 Overall

Date	Result	Opponent
February 22	Win 3-0	St. John's

1916-17 UW Hockey Team

Joe Steinauer continued his role as coach for the team and ambassador for the sport of hockey. The Director of Athletics and coach of the UW track team, Tom Jones, would also make an ideal supporter for the hockey team. He was a member of the Springfield, Massachusetts YMCA hockey team and played several games against opponents such as Harvard, Yale, Cornell and Princeton. It was Jones that brought forward the hockey agenda item again, proposing to promote hockey to the status of a varsity sport, to be discussed at the UW Athletic Council meeting.

A winter snowstorm January 12 left drifting snow over the playing surface. The UW Athletic Department allotted resources this year so employees would be able to maintain and repair the rink as needed. Many hoped the heightened attention toward the hockey facilities meant that the Athletic Council would finally agree to make hockey a varsity sport at the University.

By early January, two games against formidable opponents had already been scheduled. Robert "Bob" Johnson, who was captain of the 1915-16 team, arranged the hockey contests this season. Both games were scheduled to be played on the Lake Mendota rink that was just behind the Red Gym. On January 27, the Wisconsin team was scheduled to play a Chicago area team. Records show they were hoping to play the St. Johns Military Academy February 3 or 10. It is most likely this game was played February 3 as the latter date fell during the University's final examination period.

Members from last year's hockey team were responsible for the success of this year's team. Duties included setting up tryouts for the squad, scheduling practices and arranging games with teams from other colleges and universities. They were also encouraged to arrange a hockey tournament that the University of Wisconsin hockey team would host.

1916-17 Wisconsin Hockey Club Team

Coach Joe Steinauer was continually recruiting student hockey players to make sure practices and games would happen. He was often personally making repairs to ensure there was a decent rink for hockey activities even when the weather was interfering. Improvement plans at the ice rink for 1916-17 included the installation of additional lighting.

<u>Wisconsin Ice Hockey Team</u>

Joe Steinauer	Head Coach
Arnold Pribnow	Center
Robert Stanbury	Left Wing
E. Leonard Moran	Right Wing
Gilbert Grieve	Rover
Wilfred Evans	Cover Point
Hubert Fee	Point
Captain Johnson	Goal
C. Maedje	Backup Right Wing

A game was scheduled January 27 against the Northwestern University Dental School at the White City rink in Evanston, Illinois. It would be the first intercollegiate game played in Chicago in the past several years and it was also the first intercollegiate hockey game sanctioned by the UW Athletic Department.

Captain and starting goalie, "Bob" Johnson, had not yet announced his starting lineup as of January 24. He was still revising the roster. Johnson had a dozen qualified men that were proficient skaters including "Snook" Evans of Madison, Pribnow of Virginia, Minnesota, Moran and Fee from Superior, Wisconsin, along with Grieve, Maedje, Rogers, Kidder and Dohr. Captain Johnson would pick his final lineup the Thursday before the first game.

The Wisconsin Badgers hockey program got some long-awaited good news before their trip to Chicago. The UW Athletic Council met to discuss the status of Wisconsin hockey. Council members voted in favor of officially moving hockey to the status of a minor collegiate sport. A dozen or so hockey players at the Council meeting erupted in celebration and cheers when the formal vote results were announced. But the battle was not over.

Even though voting by the Athletic Council gave way to approval, the UW Athletic Board had not yet officially recognized hockey as a minor sport since the vote results had not yet acquired formal faculty sanction. Faculty sanction is one of the mandatory requirements for athletic teams that wish to be recognized as a minor or major sport. As a result, the UW hockey club was not allowed to represent the University as an officially recognized team. At this time the hockey club was still required to refer to themselves as an independent hockey team. The Northwestern hockey team was in the exact same predicament. Neither team was permitted to represent themselves as a varsity team for their respective colleges.

Wisconsin and Northwestern matched up evenly for this game which started at 8 p.m. Saturday January 27. Bad luck struck the Badgers early in the game when forward Gil Grieve broke his shoulder on a hard check. This ended his night. Grieve was replaced by Maedje. At the end of the first half the score was tied 1-1.

The Badgers were able to score early in the second half to take a 2-1 lead. The Wildcats countered and it was 2-2 at the end of the second half, so the game went into a sudden death five-minute overtime period. Both the UW and NU scored early in the extra OT period to make the score 3-3. Northwestern scored with just 30 seconds left in OT for a one-goal advantage and won the game 4-3.

Wisconsin Lineup: Kidder (Center), Grieve (Right Wing), Pribnow (Left Wing), Evans (Cover Point), Fee (Point), Moran (Rover) and captain Johnson (Goal). Spare: Maedje.

A tentatively scheduled game in early February the against St. John's Military Academy never came to fruition February 3. Instead, the Wisconsin hockey team scheduled a much-anticipated rematch against Northwestern University. On Saturday February 17 the Wildcats arrived in Madison for a rematch against the mighty Badgers. This game was a featured event at Wisconsin's annual Winter Ice Carnival and began as scheduled at 2:30 p.m. on Lake Mendota.

Both teams were equally aggressive on offense and stingy on defense. They also had to battle a constant, unusually strong wind howling across Lake Mendota that was relentless during the entire match. Northwestern worked hard to take a 2-1 lead on the Wisconsin team, but the Badgers never quit battling. After the first UW goal by E.L. Moran, Rob Stanbury was able to tie the score at 2-2.

Late in the second half Moran added his second goal of the day to give Wisconsin a 3-2 lead. It would be the game winning goal for the home team. After the game, several of the Northwestern players complained that the low side boards of the homemade rink on Lake Mendota were way too low when compared with what they were used to for side boards and this was a great disadvantage for them. The Wisconsin players and spectators celebrated the big 3-2 victory throughout their Winter Ice Carnival.

Wisconsin Lineup: Grieve (Center), Dohr (Right Wing), Pribnow (Left Wing), Evans (Cover Point), Fee (Point), Moran (Rover) and captain Johnson (Goal). Spares: Maedje, Stanbury and Van Ever.

Aside from the daily hockey practices, the Wisconsin team set up an intra-squad scrimmage game Thursday, February 22 at 3 p.m. The game was open for anyone interested in attending to watch the action. Coach Steinauer and captain Johnson were serious in their preparations for their next opponent. They knew the team of skilled hockey players hand-picked from the best available men in the Milwaukee metro area would be stiff competition. But the Wisconsin men remained optimistic and trained hard for the game.

The afternoon of Sunday, February 24 offered a special hockey game for all of those in attendance. An admission charge of 25 cents was required from spectators in order to help defray costs of the event. It was played at their traditional home rink behind the Red Gym on Lake Mendota because the rink on campus was again having too many issues to handle the match.

The Wisconsin Badgers hosted the Milwaukee All-Stars hockey team. This team was comprised of the finest skaters from the greater Milwaukee area. Not only were they considered the best hockey players from Cream City, they were also very confident they would get an easy win in Madison. They were wrong.

A 2:30 p.m. start time gave way to a fast hockey game that the fans enjoyed watching. The score was 0-0 after the first half but the action was fast-paced and exciting. Midway through the second half, Wisconsin's E.L. Moran scored to give the Badgers the lead. Moran's goal would end up being the game winning goal. It was a huge 1-0 win for the home team and they took great joy in sending home the defeated "All-Star" visitors from the Milwaukee hockey team.

Wisconsin Lineup: Grieve (Center), Pribnow (Right Wing), Stanbury (Left Wing), Evans (Cover Point), Fee (Point), Moran (Rover) and captain Johnson (Goal). Spares: Maedje, Dohr and Van Ever.

On March 3, the Northwestern University Dental School hockey team hosted Wisconsin for one more game in Evanston, Illinois at the White City rink. Previously, these teams had each won a game against the other. It was decided that this match would decide the intercollegiate championship between the two schools. Although the

Wildcats had the home crowd and their school band on hand to cheer them on, a contingent of 40-plus loyal Wisconsin fans showed up to cheer on the Badgers.

Grieve had recovered better than expected from his broken shoulder suffered in late January during their first game against Northwestern. He was expected to play in this game. The score was 2-2 after the first half. By this point the teams were familiar with one another and the game was tight. The Badgers played furiously in the final minutes of the second half and scored three goals before the clock expired, winning 5-3. Highly skilled UW right winger E.L. Moran recorded a hat trick (3 goals) in this match. Pribnow and Grieve also scored for the victors. It was a big win for a young program and their first intercollegiate championship.

Wisconsin Lineup: Pribnow (Center), Moran (Right Wing), Stanbury (Left Wing), Evans (Cover Point), Fee (Point), Grieve (Rover) and captain Johnson (Goal). Spares: Maedje, Dohr and Van Ever. Referee: Allen from Winnipeg.

At the conclusion of this season, an article in a local Madison newspaper incorrectly stated that the University of Wisconsin Athletic Board handed out six letterman "W's" representing players that earned a formal varsity letter award ("W") for themselves due to their play in the sport of hockey. It was reported that, although hockey was not a formal varsity sport, the UW Athletic Board awarded the "W's" due to the success of the hockey team this season. The hockey players reported to have received this award were; captain R.C. Johnson, G. Grieve, W. Evans, R. Pribnow, H. Fee and E.L. Moran. The players awarded numerals, for contributing in an assistant JV type role, were; D. Dohr, C. Maedje and H. Stanbury.

One day later, the same newspaper printed a retraction about the hockey awards. The players were not given "W's" as varsity awards. Rather, they were given hockey sweaters with a design featuring crossed hockey sticks design in place of where the "W" letters go on the letterman sweaters of formal Wisconsin players in other recognized varsity sports. Six players received these commemorative hockey sweaters. However, Dohr, Maedje and Stanbury did receive sweaters with numerals indicating their graduating class year in recognition of their backup role for the hockey team this season.

In February, the University of Wisconsin Athletic Council voted to recognize hockey as a formal sport, but that would not be official until it garnered the faculty vote. This is what led to the confusion and caused the newspaper to report in error that hockey players were presented with varsity awards for their accomplishments this season.

As stated earlier, the UW Athletic Council forwarded the question of whether hockey should be a varsity sport to the UW Student Life and Interests committee. The Committee presented the proposal to make hockey a varsity sport to the UW Faculty for ratification, the final step in the formal process. As a result of the progress of the proposal, UW professor J.F.A. Pyre agreed to bring up the consideration for hockey to be a varsity sport at the upcoming meeting of the Big Nine faculty representatives. At this point the classification and fate of the sport of hockey at the University of Wisconsin was dependent upon the action of the faculty. To this end, the Wisconsin faculty would not take any action or make any determination, until the faculty representatives considered the sport of hockey and passed by majority recommending that it should be a regular conference activity and official winter sport at the University.

At the end of season hockey team meeting, Harry Pribnow was elected captain of the team for next season. Pribnow was a contributing member of the hockey team for the past two seasons. E.L. Moran, a regular player on this season's team, was elected manager. Both would be strong contributors to the 1917-18 hockey team.

The Badgers ended the fantastic season with a winning record comprised of three wins against only one loss. They also recorded an intercollegiate championship by defeating Northwestern. It was a huge success for the independent Wisconsin Badgers hockey program. They took another important step toward becoming a formally recognized minor sport at the University.

1916-17   Schedule and Results:
Coach Joe Steinauer
Intercollegiate Champions
3-1-0 Overall

Date	Result	Opponent
January 27	Loss 4-3	@Northwestern
February 17	Win 3-2	Northwestern
February 24	Win 1-0	Milwaukee
March 3	Win 5-3	@Northwestern

Only 18 men or so, were available to keep the UW hockey club program going this season because it was at the height of World War I. Those men fond of hockey and fortunate enough to be on campus at this time when our nation was at war made a point to practice and actively play upon the Lake Mendota ice frequently. They were encouraged under the watchful eye of Coach Joe Steinauer. He was an intelligent hockey coach that was able to motivate the players to compete hard. He was also quick with his wit and able to make the players laugh often. It helped keep the men focused away from the horrors of the war that was impacting their family, friends and neighbors. It was a necessary distraction and made the sport of ice hockey that much more magical to those skating on the Madison Lake. It was a much-needed escape.

Popularity in the sport of ice hockey skyrocketed this year as a result of World War I and the UW's decision to close both gyms. The closures were due to the imminent need to minimize the consumption of coal that was required to heat the various buildings on campus. With the gyms closed, students became much more active with outdoor activities and ice hockey quickly became one of the most popular sports among students. Ice hockey would become a wonderful spectacle.

The UW Athletic Council recommended to the faculty that ice hockey be adopted as a regular minor varsity sport at the school. Wisconsin faculty were keenly aware that students had taken a deliberate and increased interest in ice hockey at the University. And Wisconsin officials wanted to capitalize on the tremendous benefits of ice hockey for the students and for the school. Unfortunately, hockey would not get serious consideration as a "Minor" sport until the 1919-20 season since faculty sanction was not accomplished.

In a focused effort to increase training and preparation for UW students to participate in organized athletics, the UW Athletic Department elected to give curriculum required gymnastic and scholastic credits for men playing hockey and students taking skating classes. A secondary goal was to build up the popularity of ice hockey and to ensure Wisconsin could contribute qualified players to a UW hockey team roster and be able to compete with other schools that fielded ice hockey teams. These coordinated efforts worked and created a greater increase in participation and a heightened popularity in the sport of hockey. It also solidified the inception and acceptance of ice hockey as a minor sport at the University of Wisconsin.

This season, Wisconsin's hockey rink upon Lake Mendota was monster sized and measured 325' x 223.' By design, the overall rink was made extra-large with the designated hockey game section placed at one end. Last winter it was deemed far too inconvenient to have the hockey game playing portion in the center of the skating area that was used by countless Wisconsin students and general skating enthusiasts from the City of Madison. Understandably, skating enthusiasts frequently took over every possible open ice portion of the skating surface as skating continued to increase in popularity and it was an enormous hassle trying to clear the masses off the Wisconsin hockey team practice and game "only" portion of the skating surface.

By mid-January, the hockey rink upon Lake Mendota was welcoming all type of hockey players and general skaters. It was announced that the rink would not just be for Wisconsin students. Citizens of the city of Madison were invited to enjoy the skating amenities. By late January, hundreds of grade school children were skating on the rink every day.

Coach Steinauer also made certain that a heated warming house was erected next to the Lake Mendota rink so that skaters could get their hockey gear on, or simply escape the elements and warm up. The UW Athletic Department also had designated staff that were in charge of snow removal and ice repair.

This seasons Wisconsin Badgers hockey team would be a strong one since it had several returning players. Captain E.L. Moran was helping to organize all of the players. Other players returning included: Stanbury, Dohr, Sturtevandt and Fee. These men would be the core of the team. Although Harry Pribnow had been elected captain of the team for this season, E.L. Moran was promoted to the rank of team captain and would lead the team on the ice. Before coming to the University of Wisconsin hockey team, Moran played for both the Superior and Duluth hockey clubs. It was not disclosed why Harry Pribnow would not fulfill the captaincy for the Badger hockey team this season.

An early photo below depicting the Wisconsin hockey team shows less than a dozen hockey players standing with their coach in front of a warming house constructed on Lake Mendota. These warming houses were crucial and allowed participants to take a break from the bitter cold elements of the winter months. Such creature comforts also attracted skaters to the sport of hockey.

In 1917, "blue lines" were introduced onto the hockey surface. Before this addition, forward passing was not allowed in the game of ice hockey. After the blue lines were universally accepted, forward passing was also now allowed and became an integral and exciting part of ice hockey. It was also during this year when the NHL was formed. Hockey pioneers, Frank and Lester Patrick, devised the concept that had hockey games played with three 20-minute periods. They also implemented intermissions between periods. These breaks were beneficial for the ice to be cleaned as needed and the players could get a necessary rest from the action. In the NHL setting, the Patrick brothers also knew the break between periods would benefit sales at concessions stands. Not all hockey teams in the states embraced the notion of three periods of play at the same time. It took a while before the concept was fully implemented.

Players take a break near the warming house on Lake Mendota.

Long before whistles were a part of standard officiating equipment, referees and goal judges were using hand bells to signal goals, penalties and other situations that warranted a quick stop in play.

Wisconsin's hockey captain E.L. Moran had negotiated tentative hockey games with opponents that included Culver Military

Academy, St. John's Military Academy, Northwestern University Dental School and a Milwaukee amateur team.

The first game of the season was scheduled against the St. John's Military Academy hockey team January 26 in Delafield, Wisconsin It was postponed due to inclement weather and both teams agreed to reschedule the match for a future date.

On January 29, the Wisconsin hockey team received notice from the Northwestern University Dental School that they wanted to arrange another game March 11 at their home rink in Chicago. Since it was a distinct reality that some of the UW hockey players would be enlisting for the war at the end of the current semester, captain Moran was trying to get the game scheduled earlier than the proposed date.

Part of the regular game schedule this season included a road trip to Culver, Indiana, for the February 2 game against the Culver Military Academy. Moran announced his roster and the men departed Madison Friday February 1 in order to make their way down to the Culver rink.

It was apparent once the game started that this would be a fast game. Although each team worked hard to make offensive attempts, the defense and goaltending succeeded more often than not. The Badgers were playing extremely well together and scored twice. Wisconsin's dynamic captain, E.L. Moran, scored both goals for the Badgers. The boys from the Culver Military Academy responded with two goals of their own. By the end of regulation, the score was tied at 2-2.

A fifteen-minute overtime period was played and failed to break the tie. Despite gallant attempts by both teams, a clear winner could not be declared. The University of Wisconsin left with a 2-2 tie against their opponent.

Wisconsin Lineup: Dohr (Center), Warner (Right Wing), Sturtevant (Left Wing), Pribnow (Cover Point), Fee (Point), captain Moran (Rover) and Baer (Goal). Spares: Stanbury, Teckmeyer and Cusson

In another season matchup, Wisconsin took on the Illinois Athletic Club Tricolorites hockey team in Chicago, Illinois. In the first three minutes of the hockey game, the IAC team demonstrated their superiority over the Badgers and scored their first goal. This opened up the floodgates. The Badgers were badly outplayed and imploded as the game went on. By the end of the twenty-minute first half Wisconsin, was losing 4-0.

Seeing that the Badgers had injured players and others lacking the ability to play at a pace to keep up with IAC, the Illinois captain approached the Wisconsin bench and offered three of his own players to join the UW squad so they could keep playing and keep it interesting. The Badgers truly appreciated the sportsmanship and accepted the offer of Illinois players to join their team for the remainder of this game.

Wisconsin was fortunate they took the IAC up on their kind offer. In fact, the IAC players who were now on the Wisconsin roster scored all five goals for the Badger team! Illinois let up on the gas pedal somewhat so that their offensive attacks were not so overwhelming. But the home team still managed to score six more goals.

When it was all over the Illinois Athletic club hockey team had soundly defeated Wisconsin,   10-5. It would have been twice that for the home team if they hadn't shared players with the Badgers and slowed down their onslaught. It was an invaluable lesson for the Wisconsin team in both sportsmanship and hockey proficiency. The UW team had several improvements to make in how they played hockey.

Wisconsin Lineup: Cusson (Center), Dohr (Right Wing), Baer (Left Wing), Fee (Cover Point), Peterson (Point), captain Moran (Rover) and Teckmeyer (Goal). Referee: G. Weiland. Time Keepers: C.A. Dean and W.M. Thompson. Goal Judges: C. Donnelley and O.A. Barrett.

The anticipated games against Northwestern, St. Johns, and the Milwaukee teams were unable to be played this season due to weather issues, travel challenges and schedule conflicts.

Friday, February 22, was the annual Winter Ice Carnival at the University of Wisconsin. Thousands attended the various ice themed festivities which included a hockey game. Wisconsin originally had secured a return visit from the Northwestern University Dental School hockey team as a feature game at the Winter Carnival. But a few days before the Carnival, Northwestern contacted Wisconsin to let them know they were afraid the ice would be too soft due to another bout of unseasonably warm weather in Madison. The Badgers agreed to postpone their game to a future date.

Since a visiting team was not able to be scheduled as the feature game, the players from the Wisconsin hockey team split into two interfraternity teams, Engineers versus the Commerce. The Engineers were victorious with a 6-2 win over the Commerce team.

Thanks to the countless efforts of the UW players, coaches and students, hockey at the University of Wisconsin was kept alive for another season. As a result, hockey would return next winter on the Badger campus.

1917-18 – Schedule and Results:
Coach Joe Steinauer
0-1-1 Overall

Date	Result	Opponent
February 2	Tie 2-2	@Culver
February 19	Loss 10-5	@Illinois
February 22	6-2	UW Interfraternity*

*Scrimmage Game

Hobey Baker

Over the summer of 1918, famed Princeton University football, baseball and hockey star, Hobey Baker, was a pilot with the American Forces fighting in France during World War I. As an expert aviator and ace he was credited with bringing down more than a dozen enemy planes during his service in the war. He was also promoted to the rank of captain.

In the United States he was glorified as an American hero fighting the enemy. On December 21, 1918, while stationed with the U.S. Army in France, captain Hobey Baker was killed during what was expected to be one last test flight of a recently repaired United States military fighter plane. Later that day he was scheduled to depart for Paris and make his way home since he had received his orders to return to his life in America. Sadly, his return home was in a coffin with full military honors.

Today, the Hobey Baker award is presented annually to the best college hockey player in the nation in honor of our American hero, Hobey Baker. Potential candidates for the college hockey Hobey Baker award are required to demonstrate remarkable traits and accomplishments that include, but are not limited to, the following; exemplary character both on and off the ice, outstanding skills in all parts of the game of hockey, remarkable sportsmanship, impressive scholastic achievement, compliance with all NCAA rules while being a full-time student and directly contributing to the integrity of their team.

Hobey Baker

1918–19 UW Hockey Team

By December 1918, the Spanish Flu pandemic was raging through the United States and had infected over one hundred thousand people in Wisconsin alone. This severe pandemic was caused by the H1N1 virus and was first identified in the spring of 1918 as it spread among US military personnel. The critical challenge facing the University of Wisconsin staff and students was the fact that the mortality rate was exceptionally high among people aged 20-24 years old and 65 years or older. The main demographic of younger people in danger encompassed a majority of college aged individuals.

Control efforts called on everyone to practice good personal hygiene, isolate or quarantine, use adequate disinfectants and to limit public gatherings. Although the Spanish Flu epidemic would be the biggest health crisis encountered by the people of Wisconsin, the state and its citizens responded with one of the most advanced anti-influenza programs in the United States. By February 1919, the Spanish Flu virus was almost entirely eradicated.

In late 1918, Coach Joe Steinauer received his discharge from the

Naval reserve at the Municipal Pier in Chicago where he was a Chief Petty Officer. He returned to Madison in order to assume the head coach position for the Wisconsin hockey team. As World War I was coming to a much-desired end, Coach Steinauer remained a driving force to ensure the club ice hockey team kept the tradition going and that critical momentum was not lost. Practices and inter-team scrimmages were a constant, whenever Mother Nature's frequent outbursts didn't spoil the plans. UW students that were learning and practicing the game of ice hockey welcomed the fun distraction from their studies and the war.

The love of hockey was prospering and growing thanks to the efforts of coach Steinauer and the student athletes who played the game, as well as the many students and townsfolk that enjoyed watching the fastest game on ice.

Wisconsin was fortunate to have three veteran players returning to the squad this year. Warner, McCabe and Maedje were expected to lead the team and help the new players adapt to college hockey.

Wisconsin Ice Hockey Team

Joe Steinauer	Head Coach
C. Maedje	Center
Lester McCabe	Left Wing
Phillip Warner	Right Wing
Mott	Rover
LaDean	Point
Dresen	Cover Point
Adolf Teckmeyer	Goal
Edwin Baer	Utility (Spare)

Scheduling efforts were spent on lining up familiar opponents this season such as the St. John's Military Academy, the Culver Military Academy and the Northwestern University Dental School. Those efforts would never materialize and the only game Wisconsin would play this year would not be against another college. Instead, it was a contest played against a team that went by the name the Milwaukee White Squadron.

Ice boats race and a crowd surrounds the hockey rink to watch the action.

Wisconsin vs. Milwaukee White Squadron on Lake Mendota during the UW Winter Carnival.

At this year's UW Winter Carnival, the 2:30 p.m. hockey game featured the Badger team versus the Milwaukee White Squadron as the special attraction for this event. The White Squadron hockey team belonged to the Upper Milwaukee River Hockey League and was considered to be one of the fastest teams in the country.

Wisconsin vs. Milwaukee White Squadron on Lake Mendota during the UW Winter Carnival

The White Squadron club had already defeated the tough Great Lakes Naval Station hockey team this season. Living up to their reputation, the White Squadron dominated the game from the start. After the first half, Milwaukee had a 4-0 lead. Schinner, who was the Cover Point and manager for the visiting team scored three goals himself. When time expired in the game, the White Squadron team trounced the Wisconsin hockey team by a score of 10-1. Nott, Wisconsin's man playing the Rover position, scored the only goal for the UW. The lone hockey game Wisconsin played this season was one the home team hoped to quickly forget.

Hockey Game

Milwaukee White Squadron, 10; Wisconsin, 1

Wisconsin		White Squadron
Maedje	Center	Robleski
Nott	Rover	Carlson
McCabe	Wing	A. Stoltz
Warner	Cover Point	Schinner
Ladvin	Point	Zottman
Teckemeyer	Goal	Varel

Wisconsin Lineup: Maedje (Center), McCabe (Right Wing), Baer (Left Wing), Warner (Cover Point), Ladvin (Point), Nott (Rover) and Teckmeyer (Goal).

Although the hockey this season was highly anticlimactic, it was still another step forward in building a first-rate hockey program at the University of Wisconsin. Efforts this season ensured that hockey would return when ice formed again next season.

1918-19   Schedule and Results:
Coach Joe Steinauer
0-1-0 Overall

Date	Result	Opponent
February 8	Loss 10-1	Milwaukee

1919-20 UW Hockey Team

Now that World War I was coming to an end, the young men and women on the University of Wisconsin campus could get back to focusing on their studies. And more importantly back to engaging in their extracurricular activities that included athletics, such as ice hockey, when the weather permitted.

Coach Joe Steinauer remained vigilant to ensure plenty of potential skaters were encouraged to make frequent visits to the hockey rink located off the shore of Lake Mendota. Weather permitting, practices were prevalent on the natural skating surface and the players practiced their hockey skills. Steinauer routinely made numerous repairs to the rink boards, ice surface and goalie nets trying to keep up with the wear and tear caused by skaters and Mother Nature alike. When enough hockey players were available and they each had a basic understanding of the rules of the game, the men would play scrimmage games.

Returning players and prospective candidates participated in the first practice of the season on the Lake Mendota rink located behind the Red Gym. Veteran skaters attending this practice included: Fee, Dohr, Dressen, King, Cusson, Grieve, McCabe and Teckmeyer.

Coach Steinauer was again busy attempting to schedule games with formidable opponents such as St. John's Military Academy, Culver Military Academy, the University of Michigan, the University of Minnesota and the Northwestern University Dental School.

Woods   Banks   Teckmeyer   McQuade   Capt. Murdock   McCabe   Reichert
Tuckerman   Shields   Dohr   Grieve   Howard   King   Manager Fee

1919–20 Wisconsin Hockey Club Team

In addition to the hockey rinks on Lake Mendota, there was a rink constructed on the lower campus again this winter. This rink was across the street from the Red Gym. Many were hopeful that conditions would allow for most, if not all, of the games to be played on campus this season. On Saturday, January 10, the Agric (Agricultural) hockey team played a game against the Commerce team on the Lake Mendota rink. It was a popular intramural hockey game that many students enjoyed watching. After three fast-paced periods, the game was tied 5-5. The two sides agreed to play overtime periods until a winner was determined. The two teams battled through three OT periods and neither side was able to break the tie. During the fourth overtime the Agrics were able to score the go-ahead goal and secure the 6-5 win.

Two more intramural hockey games were played Saturday, January 17. Beginning at 2 p.m., the Agrics took on the Letters & Sciences hockey team. Immediately following that game, the Commerce team played the Engineers. The games would be worth points that would again count toward the coveted Nelson trophy, awarded to the fraternity intramural sports champion. The Nelson trophy is awarded to the college that won the highest number of points in a series of intercollegiate contests for both indoor and outdoor sporting events.

The varsity hockey team practices started Monday, January 19 at 4 p.m. on the campus rink. Hockey team personnel put up signs around campus and advertisements in the local papers in an attempt to recruit more potential hockey players:

Attention Hockey Players:
For Information on the Wisconsin Varsity Hockey Team
Please Contact UW Hockey Manager A.H. Fee at B. 193
627 North Lake St. Madison, WI

The annual Winter Ice Carnival at the UW was held January 24. Initially, St. John's Military Academy hockey team was scheduled to play the Wisconsin Badgers hockey team as a featured event during the carnival, however St. John's canceled several days before the big game. An intramural hockey game was played in its place.

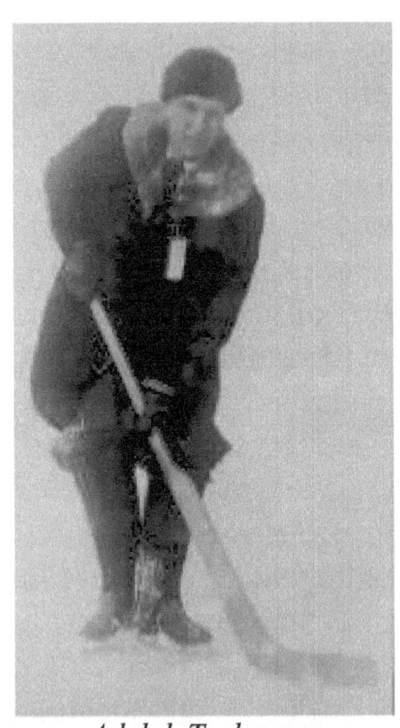

Adolph Teckmeyer

WISCONSIN HOCKEY TEAM

Joe Steinauer, Coach

Player: Position:

John L. Murdock (captain) - Rover
Adolph O. Teckmeyer -   Goal
Gilbert Grieve -   Center
Archibald H. Fee -   Point
M.G. McQuade -   Point
Howard King -   Cover Point
Robert L. Banks -   Cover Point
Donald Dohr -   Right Wing
Lester McCabe -   Left Wing

In a continued attempt at getting hockey to be declared a Minor Sport on the Wisconsin campus, the Wisconsin Ice Hockey Club was formed during the 1919-20 season. Their first important meeting was held Wednesday, January 28 at 7 p.m. in the cabinet room of the YMCA building.

One of their charters was to create and adopt a permanent

constitution that would further their goal of moving hockey to a formally recognized minor sport at the University of Wisconsin. Currently, ice hockey was only designated as an intramural sport at the University.

Athletic Director and UW Track coach Tom E. Jones led discussions with the Wisconsin Ice Hockey Club members on how best to achieve their goal of getting the Athletic Board to recognize hockey as a Minor sport for the first time at the University. Jones also had letters from St. John's Military Academy, Culver Military Academy and the University of Michigan affirming their favor for Wisconsin to have a hockey team so that they can have regular opponents. The club decided to participate in a hockey game Saturday after prom in an attempt to garner even more interest from the student body. The Club was also actively trying to arrange hockey games against Michigan, Minnesota and Northwestern.

During the Badger Hockey Club meeting, John Murdock was elected captain for the 1919-20 University of Wisconsin hockey team. Murdock was also in charge of promoting the interests of the team for the remainder of the season. Tom E. Jones and UW English professor R.W. Babcock were named honorary members of the Badger Hockey Club.

The Badger Hockey Club officers made up of UW hockey team players;

Adolph O. Teckmeyer -	President
Donald Dohr -	Vice President
Gilbert Grieve -	Secretary-Treasurer
A.H. Fee -	Manager

Director of Athletics, Tom Jones, would again formally recommend that ice hockey be added to the list of minor sports at the University of Wisconsin. Once it was deemed a minor sport, ice hockey would receive financial backing from the school and merit awards would be distributed to certain hockey players for team sport-related accomplishments. The proposition to forward ice hockey to the classification of a minor sport was expected to be ratified without objection from anyone.

At this point, the University of Wisconsin Athletic Council took action to deem ice hockey an intercollegiate sport. The team was now authorized to participate in intercollegiate competition. As a disappointment to many, this classification came up well short of the "minor" sport designation that members of the hockey program were lobbying to accomplish.

The Wisconsin Ice Hockey Club scheduled another meeting for March 10 at 7:15 p.m. in the cabinet room of the YMCA. Among the items on the agenda was electing a new team captain and team manager. Captain John Murdock was reelected to serve as captain of the hockey team and Ted McQuaid was elected as team manager for next season. It was expected in 1919-20 that the sport of hockey at the University of Wisconsin would be incorporated in the same manner as other recognized intramural sports on campus.

By the first few weeks of March, Madison was the recipient of a record 31.5 inches of snow. Time and time again UW workers cleared the Lake Mendota rink for the skaters. Due to hardships caused by the inclement weather and planning challenges, the Wisconsin Badgers hockey team was unable to play games against any outside opponents this season. Instead, only intramural hockey games were played on campus this winter.

1919-20   Schedule and Results:
Coach Joe Steinauer

<u>Date</u>   <u>Result</u>   <u>Opponent</u>

No Games Played

Chapter Two
Start of the Roaring Twenties

1920-21 UW Hockey Team

For the first time in the history of the Wisconsin Hockey program, there was a coaching change. UW Director of Athletics, Tom Jones, took over the head coaching responsibilities for the hockey program. Jones, who replaced Joe Steinauer, was fortunate to have five experienced players returning for this season's team. Among the top team leaders were captain Adolf Teckmeyer of Madison, Wisconsin. Archibald H. Fee from Superior, Wisconsin was on last year's hockey squad and expected to return as a leader. Other returning veterans were Gilbert C. Grieve of Madison, Wisconsin and John L. Murdoch, who was a captain on the 1919-20 team, of Sault Ste. Marie, Michigan.

While hockey was now a recognized sport by the Wisconsin Athletic Board, it remained in a classification that was neither a minor or a major sport. Rather, hockey received an intercollegiate sport designation and the University authorized intercollegiate competition for the Badger hockey team. Consequently, letter awards were not allowed to be presented to players until ice hockey was at least formally recognized as a minor sport. Up until this time it was merely designated as an intramural sport.

It was decided this season to build the hockey rink at the lower Madison campus across from the Red Gym instead of on Lake Mendota. The UW Athletic Department determined the campus rink could be kept in better condition with less maintenance hours and costs when compared to the rink on Lake Mendota. The campus rink would also make it easier to accommodate the crowds that came to watch the hockey games.

In addition, it would be easier to reserve the campus rink for sole use by the Wisconsin hockey team. The Lake Mendota rink was often crowded with students participating in general skating or playing pickup hockey games and the skating surface was frequently chewed up from all the skating on the ice. It was a hassle to get the rink vacated and prepared for Wisconsin hockey team practices, scrimmages and games.

As the season progressed, it was decided that the uncooperative weather would not allow for ideal ice-skating conditions at the Lower Campus Rink so the Lake Mendota rinks ultimately needed to be built and maintained. On January 4, the Wisconsin Badgers hockey team began practicing daily.

The 1920-21 season would be a special one in the University of Wisconsin hockey legacy. This is the season that witnessed the creation and start of intercollegiate hockey league matches between the University of Wisconsin, the Michigan Agricultural College and the University of Minnesota. The triangle rivalry would be crucial to the future success of college hockey. Hockey games were also scheduled with the University of Notre Dame, St. Johns Military Academy, Michigan School of Mines and Northwestern University Dental School.

On January 13, the Wisconsin Ice Hockey Club held its third meeting of the year. For the second consecutive time the meeting attendance was record breaking. The course of the hockey program was discussed and new officers were elected for the upcoming season.

Badger Hockey Club Officers:
Gilbert Grieve -   President
Henry Jenswold-   Vice President
Thomas Tredwell-   Secretary-Treasurer
Robert O. Blodgett-   Business manager

An inter-class hockey tournament was scheduled to kick off the 1921 hockey season January 15. These games were supposed to be held on the Lake Mendota rink. Captains of the teams were previously appointed by coach Tom Jones: captain of the senior squad, Teckmeyer; captain of the junior squad, Grieves; captain of the sophomore squad, Murdock and captain of the freshmen squad, Deadman. The tournament schedule had the seniors playing the juniors at 2 p.m. Immediately following at 3 p.m. the sophomores were to battle the freshmen team. Then the winners of the two contests would be scheduled to meet at a later date in order to decide the inter-class hockey championship. Unfortunately, the hockey tournament had to be postponed a week since construction of the hockey rink upon Lake Mendota was not completed in time.

In place of the inter-class hockey tournament games, a hockey game between an All-America team made up of freshman and juniors and another team consisting of sophomores and juniors was played. The All-Americans won this match 4-1.

Mother Nature had other plans as the February games between Wisconsin and Michigan were canceled due to unseasonably warm weather. Temps reached into the low 60s and high 50s a few days before Michigan was scheduled to play the hockey game against Wisconsin. Any momentum the UW hockey program had made was put on hold as the remainder of the season could not be played. Even practices were impossible due to the streak of warm weather. The ice surface simply couldn't be maintained!

Most people are aware that ice forms for decent skating when the temperature gets at or below, 32 degrees. However, consecutive nighttime temps of between 18 degrees and 23 degrees are ideal to ensure ice is frozen solid. Sufficient cold temps at night help to harden the ice and ward off melting when daytime temps get above 32 degrees when the sun comes out. In 1920, the monthly average temperature for February was nearly 34 degrees, and in March it was nearly 46 degrees. The middle of March even saw two days that were 75 and 77 degrees.

Warm, sunny days and mild overnight temps wreak havoc on ideal ice conditions. Resulting in ice chunking up, cracking, becoming slushy and holding puddles on the ice surface. All of which lead to very poor skating conditions. The worst-case scenario being that it is too difficult to skate upon and it's impossible to move the puck along the ice in a game of hockey.

The Badgers hockey squad faced weather-related challenges year after year. It impacted their ability to practice, play games, and travel to and from the sites of rivals for away games. Their refusal to give up and the team's annual effort to schedule another season allowed the program to materialize into a legitimate entity. These early Badger hockey teams would be the crucial foundation for what would evolve into the formally recognized University of Wisconsin's Men's Hockey varsity team and program established later in 1921.

Wisconsin hockey intrasquad scrimmage game on the UW Lower Campus Rink.

Wisconsin hockey intrasquad scrimmage game on the UW Lower Campus Rink.

UW hockey intrasquad scrimmage.

1920-21 Schedule and Results:

Coach Tom Jones

<u>Date</u>   <u>Result</u>   <u>Opponent</u>

No Games Played

Chapter Three
Minor Varsity

1921-22 UW Hockey Team

Finally, this was the magical season when the University of Wisconsin formally recognized hockey as a minor varsity sport! The Wisconsin Athletic Department fully supported this new team and was quick to order the latest state of the art hockey equipment to suit up each varsity player with the best available jerseys, skates, pads and sticks.

As a result of the minor classification, it was also the first time ever at the University that players could be awarded varsity letters in recognition of their participation on the hockey team. Even though hockey had been played at a club level for the past several years, its classification as a varsity sport gave it greater notoriety on campus. Early assessments of this sport were highly favorable among students, faculty and spectators from the Madison area. Around campus popular opinion unanimously concluded that ice hockey would soon match the popularity of other games on campus like football, baseball and basketball, for example.

This change was due in large part to increased interest and independent student action, as achieved last year by the Badger Hockey Club. Previously, the hockey teams were deemed as club teams, intramural or intercollegiate.

The UW Athletic Department approved enhanced construction of the hockey rink on campus. This 100' x 200' ice rink was repeatedly flooded during winter months to make ice as perfect as possible at the time for the team. It was complete with enhanced boards framing up the ice-skating surface and additional bleachers for spectators. It was constructed with standard hockey rink boards that were three and a half feet tall. Campus officials also added canvas sheets in certain sections along the fence that went around the rink to obscure free views and increase the number of spectators that would be persuaded to purchase a ticket to watch the Wisconsin hockey team play. Unlike Lake Mendota, it also provided much needed shelter to minimize the strong winds of winter. Additionally, the ice would be easier to clean and maintain as compared with the ice on Lake Mendota.

The rink was located on the large field across from the Red Gym that is currently adjacent to the Memorial Library building on the UW campus. Often times several hundred curious students would watch the Wisconsin hockey practices. On game days this number would swell as numerous citizens of Madison would join the student fans who were cheering on the cardinal and white skaters.

An original photo postcard from 1911 depicting the Red Gym. Also pictured is the field across the street from the gym where the Lower Campus Rink was constructed each winter primarily for UW ice hockey practices and games. It was also used at times for recreational ice skating.

The first UW minor varsity ice hockey team was coached by Dr. A.K. Viner. Coach Viner, a former Canadian hockey star. He was highly regarded due to his accomplishments both as a varsity player for McGill University in Montreal, Canada and later as a member of a highly competitive and successful amateur team based in Toronto. Aside from his selection to train and lead the varsity team into competitive battles with rival schools, head coach Dr. A. K. Viner was also a member of the university medical staff conducting research work.

On December 21, 1921, the Wisconsin hockey program held a meeting in the Trophy Room of the Red Gym to begin preparations for the varsity squad. Captain Grieve and the other veteran players put out the word in order to recruit potential candidates. It was also decided, weather permitting that instead of practicing and playing on the Lake Mendota rinks, a concentrated effort will be made for all practices and games to occur on the Lower Campus Rink.

Gilbert C. Grieve was unanimously elected January 4 as the first captain of the UW varsity team at a meeting of player candidates. Players that attended this meeting were: Boylan, Campbell, Burns, Kellett, Wood, Blodgett, Tredwell, Baker, Combacker, Maksya and Grieve. Grieve was elected captain of the varsity squad since he had valuable experience on the prior UW teams. His experience proved to be very valuable to coach Viner as they created and trained the team.

At times during the winter months, coach Viner would be absent because of his duties at the Mendota hospital. In those instances, former Coach Steinauer and captain Grieve would be in charge of the hockey players. An ice boat was provided by the UW Athletic Department to enable coach Viner to make daily voyages across Lake Mendota. The ice boat was necessary to take Dr. Viner from the Mendota Hospital to the UW Campus (and back) so that he could supervise daily practices and fulfill the duties as head coach of the hockey program while also taking care of his duties as a medical professional at the hospital.

To kick off the preseason training, coach Viner instructed his 15 Wisconsin players with offensive, defensive and conceptual hockey plays using chalk talk lectures. A call was made campus wide for more potential hockey players to report so that coach Viner could select the very best 12 men for the hockey program. The newly formed UW Badgers hockey team began practicing in preparation for the upcoming season that was fast approaching.

COACH A. K. VINER

CAPTAIN GRIEVE

The start of the program was understandably a rough one. It was reported that only eight students showed up for tryouts and practice. Coach Viner was charged with selecting the top six players since playing "Iron Man," where the starting players play the entire match without substitutions, was the accepted standard at the time. Teams were able to have additional men on the squad that were referred to as "spares." Spares were not routinely substituted in to the hockey games during this period. Instead, they were reserved as replacements for players that were seriously injured or suffering from an illness and unable to play.

1921-22 Wisconsin Hockey Club Team

Since ice hockey was still relatively new, the student athletes at tryouts were especially inexperienced. Realizing that the nearest teams were hours away from the UW Campus, coach Viner created a freshman squad so that the varsity team would have a regular scrimmage opponent. A player by the name of E. E. Johnson transferred to UW Madison from the Michigan School of Mines. As a result, he was deemed ineligible for conference competition as a member of the Wisconsin hockey team. He was tapped to coach the freshman squad.

During the 1921-22 season, teams were required to skate on sides the entire match. This meant that if the puck went back to your end your entire team had to return and skate to a location behind the puck. In order to advance the puck, players were required to pass the puck to a teammate that was equal to them.

Wisconsin and most other colleges in the tri-state area adopted some of the "Canadian Style" hockey rules, but they were not yet consistently playing games with three periods. Instead, the games typically consisted of two 20-minute halves. Teams were allowed to substitute in another player only once every period, which is why teams like the Badgers tried to have "spares" or reserves on their roster. Players that came out of the game were also allowed to return to action with another substitution.

UW Director of Athletics, Tom E. Jones, was working on scheduling other teams to face the Wisconsin hockey squad this season. The revised schedule consisted of eight games against what were considered the best hockey squads from the Midwest region. These teams were the Milwaukee Athletic Club, the University of Minnesota, the University of Michigan and the University of Notre Dame. It was Wisconsin, Michigan and Minnesota that formed the inaugural Western Intercollegiate Hockey League (WIHL). These three teams were also the extent of the Big Ten hockey conference that existed at the time. Eventually, the WIHL added Michigan College and Marquette to the league.

Although the Michigan Wolverines were first on the Wisconsin Badgers hockey schedule, they sent a wire telegraph through Western Union informing the UW hockey program that they would not be making the trip to Madison. This was based upon the soft ice at Ann Arbor that did not allow sufficient practice and the fact that the Wolverines wanted a two-game guarantee if they were to make the long journey, instead of the one game that the Badgers were offering. The game was rescheduled in February on Valentine's Day.

The first game of the inaugural varsity season was scheduled against the Milwaukee Athletic Club (MAC) January 14,1922. With a nationwide reputation as a very strong hockey club, the Milwaukee squad showed up ready to play. MAC was basically a deep semi-pro team with talented hockey players. Face-off was set at 1:30 p.m. and the UW Athletic Department set up a couple extra bleachers for spectators and sold admission tickets at the rink for 35 cents each. Hockey players for both teams would get dressed at the Red Gym and then walk across Langdon Street to the Lower Campus Rink for the hockey game.

It was a close contest initially. MAC jumped out to an early lead but the Wisconsin defense responded and turned away numerous other scoring attempts from the visitors. Coach Viner, who was also operating as the referee, had to send two of the Milwaukee players off the ice to serve penalties for their infractions. Wisconsin players and fans cheered when captain Grieve, a powerful centerman, scored their first goal. It signaled an exciting era for the newly formed hockey program. MAC also scored in the opening period. The thrilling game would remain tied 1-1 through the first and second periods. Every time one team broke into their opponents' zone, the defense or goalie would shut down their offensive attempts.

Baker, the speedy forward, would get the second goal for the UW team. But the Milwaukee club would add three more of their own goals. The Badgers battled hard but ultimately were defeated by their first opponent with a final score of 4-2. Even though the home team didn't win, the enthusiastic crowd thoroughly enjoyed viewing the big-time hockey match between newly arranged intra-Wisconsin rival squads. In fact, the Badgers did incredibly well in this outing when considering the team was formed less than two weeks before the game. In addition, captain Grieve was the only veteran player. Every other player was new to the team.

Wisconsin Lineup: Baker (Center), captain Grieve (Right Wing), Combacker (Left Wing), Blodgett (Right Defense), Hendrickson (Left Defense) and Tredwell (Goalie). Spares: Ledin (Wing), Morius (Wing), Kubosch (Wing), Burns (Defense) and Fiske (Defense). Referee: head coach A.K. Viner from the University of Wisconsin.

Of equal historical importance, the University of Wisconsin Women's Hockey Club team also played their first game at noon on the Lower Campus Rink January 14. Although females from the UW had played the sport of ice hockey over the past decade and a half plus, this season would also mark their formal organization. It would pioneer the Wisconsin women's hockey program which would be national champions on the ice some 80 years later.

Three players that started the season on the UW men's roster had to leave the team due to ineligibility. They were; Wood, Von Sczelski and Johnson. Johnson was deemed ineligible since he was a transfer and had (what was determined to be) an insufficient period of residence at the University of Wisconsin. Von Sczelski and Wood were deemed academically ineligible by the UW.

During the week of January 16, the Wisconsin hockey team began serious preparations for the upcoming two game matchup against the University of Minnesota squad by working on their passing, skating, shooting skills and defense. Four days of hockey practices on the campus rink were ideal to ensure the UW players were in condition. Fortunately, the weather was cooperating so that the Wisconsin rink had suitable ice where they could practice and scrimmage.

Just their second opponent of the season, the Minnesota Gophers visited the UW Madison Campus for two games with the first one scheduled for Friday, January 20 with the face-off slated at 3:30 p.m. Even more seating would be available as bleachers were built around the rink in the days before the Minnesota series. A few dozen students and townspeople would be able to watch this hockey game utilizing the comforts provided by additional seating. Canvas was also used to enclose the rink to cut down on the wind and to ensure spectators paid the price of admission to watch this exciting game.

The Gopher team was well known for their ice hockey proficiency and the Badger players were expected to be on the losing end of this match especially since the UW would be without the participation of Johnson, Von Sczelski and Woods.

This game was moved to 4 p.m., and from the start it was clear that UW was outmatched. The Gophers baffled the Badgers with their team play and strategies. Minnesota's first goal came just a few minutes into the opening period during a scrum in front of the Wisconsin net when the puck got past UW goalie Tommy Tredwell. Just before the end of the first half, the UM captain shot in another goal making the score 2-0 in favor of the visitors.

Early in the second half (last period), Minnesota scored a clean goal off a hard shot on net. At this point the score was 3-0 in favor of Minnesota. In the middle of this final period Wisconsin center Baker punched the puck into the Gophers net but the goal was disallowed due to a penalty. The Badger players were not able to protest the goal too much since the referee was their own head coach, Dr. A.K. Viner. The home crowd had fun howling at the referee as they protested the penalty call that disallowed Wisconsin's lone goal.

The highly regarded Minnesota team beat the Badgers 3-0. A score that was a big disappointment for the skilled Gophers team, however, the Wisconsin skaters found comfort in this close game. Tredwell, the Wisconsin goalie, played a superb game and denied numerous quality scoring chances. As did captain Grieve with his advanced skating, puck handling and shooting that frustrated the Minnesota team.

Wisconsin Lineup: Baker (Center), captain Grieve (Right Wing), Combacker (Left Wing), Blodgett (Right Defense), Hendrickson (Left Defense) and Tredwell (Goalie). Spares: Ledin (Wing), Morius (Wing), Kubosch (Wing), Burns (Defense) and Fiske (Defense) Referee: head coach A.K. Viner from the University of Wisconsin.

In the second game of this series was set for January 21 and the two teams squared off to battle once again at 2 p.m. on the Lower Campus Rink. Unfortunately for both teams, the ice was in terrible condition. The rink had to be flooded early in the morning but a warm winter sun didn't allow the ice to freeze as needed. As a result, players from both sides fell down all game long.

After a scoreless first half, the Gophers scored early in the second half to take a 1-0 lead. Several minutes later Minnesota added their second tally to make the score 2-0. Wisconsin was finally able to score on a nice goal by left winger Bob Baker. He was able to cut the Gopher lead in half with the score at 2-1. Minnesota put the final nail in the UW coffin by scoring a goal with minutes left in the game to take a 3-1 lead.

When the final whistle sounded to signal the end of the game, Minnesota won this match 3-1, making it two straight victories against the host Badger team. The Wisconsin defense continued to excel. Holding Minnesota to only three goals was a victory in itself. In addition, the goaltending of Tommy Tredwell for the Badgers was again equally impressive. He was able to ward off the majority of offensive attacks by the northern visitors. If it wasn't for Tredwell's exceptional play in net, the score would have been a lopsided victory for the visitors.

Wisconsin Lineup: captain Grieve (Center), Fiske (Right Wing), Baker (Left Wing), Burns (Right Defense), Combacker (Left Defense) and Tredwell (Goalie). Spares: Ledin (Wing), Morius (Wing), Kubosch (Wing), Hendrickson (Defense) and Blodgett (Center/Wing). Referee: head coach A.K. Viner from the University of Wisconsin.

The Wisconsin team would get back to practice and preparation for their upcoming trip to the Gophers home rink in a few weeks. Their games against the Milwaukee Athletic Club and Minnesota Gophers this season proved invaluable. By playing such challenging and talented opponents they were beginning to understand what it would take to win. Aside from the need to increase the level of competition, they needed to sharpen all of the skills that made for proficient hockey teams. A warm spell in Madison ruined any chance to skate on ice before the trip to Minnesota.

On February 3, the Wisconsin hockey team took its first road trip. They headed north to St. Paul, Minnesota, to once again play the Gophers. These games were part of the St. Paul Winter Carnival and played at the historic Lexington rink. This indoor facility was able to seat eighteen hundred spectators. The first game was set to begin promptly at 8:15 p.m. The Badgers also didn't have time to get in their customary same day practice on the Lexington rink before the game. The Gopher squad also informed the UW team that this game would be played with three periods to mirror Canadian hockey rules and to also follow the format used by the National Hockey League.

In an outing not nearly as positive as the matches a few weeks earlier in Madison, the Gophers started out hot and scored four goals in the first period. They continued the onslaught, notching five more goals to make it 9-0. Minnesota scored three more times in the third period.

It was impressive that the visitors were able to get on the scoreboard at all. The two Badgers goals were scored in the last period by Howie Combacker and Bob Baker. Three different Gopher players each scored four goals in this lopsided match. The Gophers trounced the Badgers by a score of 12-2. Although the Wisconsin offense was able to score twice, the agony of having 12 goals scored against the Badgers was a painful lesson indeed. It was also the third straight time the Gopher hockey team defeated the Badgers this season.

Wisconsin Lineup: Baker (Center), captain Grieve (Right Wing), Combacker (Left Wing), Burns (Right Defense), Blodgett (Left Defense) and Tredwell (Goalie). Spares: Ledin (Wing), Morius (Wing), Kubosch (Wing) and Hendrickson (Defense). Referee: McPherson from the St. Paul Athletic Club.

The matchup on the following day would be just as unsatisfying. Again, Wisconsin was behind by four after the first period. The Gophers pumped in two more goals in the second period to make the it 6-0. In the third period Minnesota scored another. With a final score of 7-0, it was another win for the Gophers. The bespectacled Minnesota right winger, Bartlett, scored four goals in this game and was so incredibly talented that he ended up being the Gophers leading scorer by season's end. Wisconsin was held to just six total shots on goal. It was also the Gophers fourth straight win over the Badgers.

Wisconsin Lineup: Combacker (Center), Baker (Right Wing), Ledin (Left Wing), Burns (Right Defense), Blodgett (Left Defense) and Tredwell (Goalie). Spares: Ledin (Wing), Morius (Wing), Kubosch (Wing) and Hendrickson (Defense). Referee: McPherson from the St. Paul Athletic Club.

Nearly two weeks of practices back home helped the Badgers distance themselves from the beatings they suffered in Minnesota and they were now focused on their next game against the University of Michigan. The Wolverines would be headed to Madison in mid-February.

Again, due to uncooperative weather, the Wisconsin-Michigan hockey game scheduled for February 10 was postponed. UW Athletic

Director Tom E. Jones sent a wire telegram to the Wolverines hockey personnel to advise of the need for a postponement because of unacceptable ice conditions at the lower UW campus rink. Both teams agreed to reschedule as soon as possible.

On February 13, the rejuvenated Wisconsin hockey team hosted Michigan and was looking for their first win of the season. Sufficient training before this game was impossible since decent ice was nonexistent as a result of a warm weather spell in the 10 days prior. Even though the Wolverines scored first, the Badgers were able to hold them to a 1-0 score when the opening period ended. The UM skaters quickly tallied three more goals after a ferocious attack starting the second period to make the score 4-0. The Badgers were finally able to get their offense going. Thanks to Grieve, Combacker and Ledin, Wisconsin scored three goals against the Wolverines in the third period. But Michigan would be too much to contain with their relentless offensive strikes. The Wolverines would score two more times before the game ended. Although Wisconsin was able to score a season-high three goals, the visiting Wolverines were able to rack up six goals and won this game, 6-3. It was not an easy win and captain Grieve along with his wingers Blodgett and Combacker were observed playing well yet again for the Wisconsin team, as they had also done in the two previous games.

Wisconsin Lineup: captain Grieve (Center), Baker (Right Wing), Ledin (Left Wing), Blodgett (Right Defense), Combacker (Left Defense) and Tredwell (Goaltender). Spares: Morius (Wing), Fiske (Wing), Kubosch (Wing) and Hendrickson (Defense). Wisconsin game substitution: Fiske for Ledin.

In an announcement from the Wisconsin Athletic department, it was revealed that the varsity hockey team would take an extended road trip though Michigan and Indiana for several away hockey games. Scheduled opponents, weather permitting, would include the University of Michigan, the Michigan Aggies and the University of Notre Dame. Players making the trip include starters: Makeys, Tredwell, Baker, Grieve, Combacker and Blodgett. Substitutes also traveling with the team included: Ledin and Fiske.

Pictured above is a 1922 hockey game between Wisconsin and Minnesota at the UW home rink located across the street from the Red Gym on the lower campus.

Next up for the Badgers was a match with the University of Notre Dame hockey team. The Fighting Irish were having a highly successful undefeated season and had their sights set on a league championship. On February 18, the Wisconsin team traveled to South Bend to play Notre Dame on their home rink. The game started promptly at 1:30 p.m. even though rumors were going around on campus incorrectly saying the game was called off due to poor weather.

The playing surface on the Notre Dame rink was especially challenging since the ice had been significantly softened by the unrelenting blend of rain and snow in a messy February storm. Some parts of the ice had more than an inch of standing water. Poor weather conditions were unable to deter the several dozen fans that enjoyed the entertaining hockey game.

In a tremendously competitive hockey match, the Badgers competed in a manner the Notre Dame team was not expecting. Midway through the first period, UND tallied a nifty goal. The Badgers were unable to get much going. Later in the first period the Irish scored again to go up 2-0 over their rivals. In the second period Wisconsin played with much more urgency, but was unable to get into any serious scoring situations. The Badgers made up on defense for what they lacked in offense. Notre Dame took advantage of the Badgers being gassed and were able to net their third goal in the second period to make the score 3-0.

The body checking between these two teams continued to intensify as the game went on. A huge body check from a Badger player knocked an Irish defenseman out of the game in the third period. Although the Badgers battled fiercely, they were unable to better Notre Dame. The final score was 3-0 in favor of the Fighting Irish. Notre Dame would remain undefeated in the league this season.

Wisconsin Lineup: captain Grieve (Center), Baker (Right Wing), Ledin (Left Wing), Blodgett (Right Defense), Combacker (Left Defense) and Tredwell (Goalie). Spares: Morius (Wing), Fiske (Wing), Kubosch (Wing) and Hendrickson (Defense).

The University of Notre Dame Fighting Irish hockey team was supposed to visit Madison for another game scheduled February 25; however, the weather once again was terrible and the contest was forced to be canceled.

The final matchup of the season found the Wisconsin Badgers traveling to Ann Arbor February 21 to face the University of Michigan. The Wolverines dominated the Badgers from the opening faceoff. Michigan recorded five straight goals and Wisconsin only scored once, late in the third period. When time ran out, the final score was 5-1 in favor of Michigan. It was an anticlimactic end to the UW hockey season. A long road trip home to Madison was made even longer after the defeat by the Wolverines.

Wisconsin Lineup: captain Grieve (Center), Baker (Right Wing), Ledin (Left Wing), Combacker (Right Defense), Blodgett (Left Defense) and Tredwell (Goalie). Spares: Morius (Wing), Fiske (Wing), Kubosch (Wing) and Hendrickson (Defense).

MINOR SPORTS 1921-22

Wisconsin hockey action as the Referee monitors the game.

Although the Badgers were unable to record any wins in their eight games this season, the team had a lot of measurable gains. All of the Wisconsin players increased their hockey skill and the men returning next season would help the UW hockey team to be even more competitive. Spectators at the University of Wisconsin-Madison campus truly enjoyed the matches with this new winter sport and the size of the crowds grew with each successive match.

The heightened popularity also helped increase the number of students that would try to make the varsity roster the following year. The first formal University of Wisconsin hockey season was a huge success in many ways regardless of the final record. This inaugural campaign would propel the University forward, both on and off the ice, for many years to come.

1921-22   Schedule and Results:
Coach Dr. A.K. Viner
0-7-0 Third in WIHL   0-8-0 Overall

Date	Result	Opponent
January 14	Loss 4-2	Milwaukee*
January 20	Loss 3-0	Minnesota
January 21	Loss 3-1	Minnesota
February 3	Loss 12-2	@Minnesota
February 4	Loss 7-0	@Minnesota
February 13	Loss 6-3	Michigan
February 18	Loss 3-0	@ Notre Dame
February 21	Loss 5-1	@ Michigan

*Exhibition Game
First year hockey was a varsity sport at the University of Wisconsin.

Chapter Four
Forming the Big Ten

1922-23 UW Hockey Team

With the new season quickly approaching, the program held its first team meeting December 14, 1922 in the Trophy Room at the Red Gym. The gathering put a plan in place for the varsity hockey team, the roster and set in motion the new hockey season.

Hockey continued to grow in popularity on the University of Wisconsin-Madison campus. Students and local citizens frequented the rink to watch the Badger team practice and play games against other schools. Attendance continued to grow with each game. The speed, physical play, and quickness of the players moving around the ice were new to the spectators, and they were eager to see more from this team in its second official year of existence as a team sport at the UW. Ideal weather in December allowed work to begin on the lower campus ice hockey rink. Rules of the game continued to evolve and games would now more consistently follow the Canadian rules as they expanded to three 20-minute periods (from two 20-minute halves). Up to this point, not all teams were consistently following the changes to the number of periods when they historically were used to playing halves, but more and more teams were insisting on the three-period format.

Weather continued to be the one wild card that Wisconsin could not tame. At times the ice surface was far less than desirable so skating was either nearly impossible or the ice simply melted away entirely. It was a constant concerning challenge all hockey clubs reliant on outdoor ice continued to face during these early days of the sport. This season, the team was cursed with a lack of ice over Christmas break and it was detrimental.

The Wisconsin hockey team continued to make vast improvements and worked toward becoming more competitive. Howard R.

Combacker was elected as team captain for this varsity season by head coach Dr. A.K. Viner. Coach Viner also had assistance this season from Rudy Noer who would be acting as team manager for the hockey program.

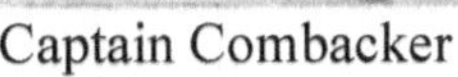

Captain Combacker

Coach Viner

Several experienced players returned this season that included Thomas Tredwell, Robert Blodgett, George Fiske, Haugh, Edwin E. Johnson, John Mokrejs, Martin Moran, Von Sczelski and Willis Wood. Coach Viner was also looking for playing time from Campbell, Kubosch and George Fiske. But those men would have to earn a coveted spot. A transfer from the Michigan School of Mines the year before, Edwin E. Johnson was a highly consistent and competitive hockey player for the Badgers. Tredwell returned as the most experienced goalkeeper and had greatly improved his skills as the UW goal guard.

1922-23 Wisconsin Varsity Hockey Team

Once the ice rink was constructed, the first hockey practice of the season happened January 5. Attendance was light by the UW squad, but that didn't stop the men that showed up from getting in a great practice. In fact, the players skated well into the night after sundown. Coach Viner let the skaters enjoy the pickup game and elected not to make this evening a formal practice working on set plays. Over the next few days, the Wisconsin hockey practices would last several hours each day.

Due to the rising popularity of the sport and the constant need for a scrimmage squad, the Badgers were again able to field a freshman team. The large number of freshmen who reported daily for practices was encouraging. Coach Viner watched practices very closely as he worked on selecting which men would represent the varsity team this season.

Both Minnesota and Michigan participated with Wisconsin in the conference triangular hockey league. These schools agreed that they were to play both home and "foreign" (away) games in scheduled series consisting of two games over a weekend. Teams would ideally play four games against each other during the hockey season. Invitations were sent to other schools in the Midwest that were possibly interested in joining the intercollegiate hockey league. Schools such as: St. Thomas, Notre Dame and the Michigan School of Mines would fit nicely into the conference. Scheduling under this new agreement called for a pair of home and home games between the competing teams. All games would be played following the National Collegiate Hockey Rules in place this year.

The University of Michigan hockey team would be Wisconsin's opponent for the first four games of this sophomore season since getting classified as a minor varsity sport. After outscoring the Badger skaters by a combined two game total of 11-4 during the previous winless season, the UW men were eager to avenge their losses to the Wolverines and get their first official varsity win.

The team was able to schedule some training time during the week of January 8. A practice was held on campus and ran until night fall so that coach Viner was able to select the final two players that would make the trip. The squad received a last-minute announcement that star defenseman John Mokrejs was eligible to play, a huge blessing as they had no suitable spare at his position. On Thursday night, January 11, coach Viner and manager Noer took an eight-man hockey squad to Michigan for a pair of games. Making the trip north was Combacker, Tredwell, Johnson, Fiske, Blodgett, Haugh, Mokrejs and Hilsenhoff.

Coach Viner expressed concern that the Badgers squad would be at a disadvantage since the Wolverines ice rink was indoors and the nighttime game would have the ice surface lit up by artificial lights. The UW skaters were not used to playing games on artificial ice and with arc lighting. This series between the Wisconsin and Michigan hockey teams was the first time that both teams were officially recognized as varsity teams at their respective schools. In fact, it was the first time the Wolverines squad was permitted to wear "Michigan" on their hockey jerseys.

In the opening game, Friday, January 12, Michigan scored first after splitting the defense and putting the puck past UW goalkeeper Tredwell. Wisconsin would counter the pressure and Blodgett would score the only other goal during regulation time with a nice shot that would tie the game at 1-1 in the second period. Each team tried repeatedly to penetrate their opponents' goal, but spectacular defense and goaltending stopped any further scoring.

Ultimately, the game headed to a five-minute overtime period with the Badgers and Wolverines playing equally and still knotted up at 1-1. Neither squad was able to score during the first OT period despite their multiple attempts. The second overtime was close with both teams battling until Michigan snuck the puck into the Wisconsin net for the win in the final minute of the second overtime period. Michigan won 2-1. The Badgers came up short but the popular opinion was that the Wisconsin squad was the superior team in this game.

Wisconsin Lineup: captain Combacker (Center), Fiske (Right Wing), Johnson (Left Wing), Blodgett (Right Defense), Mokrejs (Left Defense) and Tredwell (Goaltender). Spares: Haugh and Hilsenhoff. Penalties: Wisconsin 1, Michigan 10. Referee: Hamilton from Ontario.

These two teams faced off for the second game of their series the following day in another closely contested battle. Michigan came out on top after scoring a flukey goal from a bad angle that found its way into the UW net. That tally secured the 1-0 win for the Wolverines.

Sticky ice made play very difficult for the players on both sides during the game. It was another evenly matched contest and the spectators enjoyed an entertaining game. While Michigan was called for 10 penalties in the first game, this contest was much cleaner and a lot fewer infractions were called on either team. Wisconsin had a long trip home to think about how to improve their play against Michigan. These two teams would meet again the following weekend in Madison at the Lower Campus Rink.

Wisconsin Lineup: captain Combacker (Center), Fiske (Right Wing), Johnson (Left Wing), Blodgett (Right Defense), Mokrejs (Left Defense) and Tredwell (Goaltender). Spares: Haugh and Hilsenhoff. Penalties: Wisconsin 4, Michigan 3. Referee: Hamilton from Ontario.

During a week of practice in Madison, the Badgers skaters had several scrimmage games against each other and practiced for several hours a day. The grueling preparations were to get them ready for the rematch against the Wolverines. In anticipation of even bigger crowds showing up to watch the hockey games, the UW Athletic Department set up a higher number of bleachers than ever before around the rink.

Michigan would have their work cut out for them in this first game in Madison, especially when considering they arrived on campus just a couple of hours before game time. The January 19 game had the Wolverines and Badgers locked up in another close battle. The game remained scoreless after the first period. Both teams made offensive pushes in the second, but no one could break through. There was a scrum in front of the Wisconsin net during the third period and a Michigan player was able to bang in a loose puck to give the Wolverines a 1-0 lead. The Badgers were unable to counter before time expired. Michigan won by squeaking out another 1-0 win against the Badger squad. It was Michigan's third straight victory over the Wisconsin hockey team.

Wisconsin Lineup: captain Combacker (Center), Fiske (Right Wing), Johnson (Left Wing), Blodgett (Right Defense), Mokrejs (Left Defense) and Tredwell (Goaltender). Spares: Haugh and Hilsenhoff.

From the start, the January 20 game was a closely fought battle. Neither the Badgers nor the Wolverines were willing to back down. Wisconsin was able to record their lone goal just over halfway into the first period when Badger left winger Ed Johnson was in the corner and took a shot on net. UW captain Howard "Doc" Combacker raced to the Michigan net to pick up the rebound for the goal!

Wisconsin Badgers versus the Michigan Wolverines at the UW Hockey Rink.

With a 1-0 lead after the first period, Wisconsin battled to fend off the Wolverines in the second. They were successful in that Michigan didn't score at all. The Badgers put on a defensive show that ultimately held the Wolverines scoreless for the rest of the game. Captain Combackers' lone goal would prove to be the game winner! It was essentially a very clean game with only a couple of penalties called on either side.

The Wisconsin Badgers versus the Michigan Wolverines hockey game.

Wisconsin defeated Michigan by a score of 1-0 before an enthusiastic home crowd of a couple of hundred spectators. The Wisconsin hockey team's first win of the season was an important one in the history of this storied program. It cemented what had been in the works for years. Wisconsin was developing into a formidable opponent and was able to compete with the top collegiate hockey schools.

Wisconsin Badgers earn their first official win of the season, 1-0 over Michigan!

The official record would show that it was January 20 when the Wisconsin Badgers earned their first varsity hockey victory!

Wisconsin Lineup: captain Combacker (Center), Fiske (Right Wing), Johnson (Left Wing), Blodgett (Right Defense), Mokrejs (Left Defense) and Tredwell (Goaltender). Spare: Haugh. Referee: Charles A. Smith from the Milwaukee Athletic Club.

On the weekend of February 9, the Minnesota Gophers arrived at the University of Wisconsin-Madison campus. Fortunately, captain Combacker, Fiske, Johnson, Blodgett, Tredwell, Mokrejs and the others all passed their exams at the University of Wisconsin and were able to retain their athletic eligibility.

Friday's faceoff was set for 3:30 p.m. To this point in the season, the Minnesota squad remained undefeated and had not allowed an opponent to score a single goal against them. Primarily made up of players of Scandinavian descent, the Gophers quickly showed off their hockey skills and got the better of Wisconsin. Minnesota was up 2-0 after the first period.

UW captain Howie Combacker was able to score for Wisconsin in the second period. This was a huge goal considering no other opponent had been able to score on Minnesota all season. But the Gophers also scored during this period and at the end of the second Minnesota had a 3-1 lead. They were not done yet as the visitors scored one more goal in the final period. Minnesota outplayed, outhustled and dominated Wisconsin in every aspect of this game. With crowds estimated in the hundreds on hand to watch the hockey match, the Gophers beat the Badgers by a score of 4-1.

Wisconsin Lineup: captain Combacker (Center), Fiske (Right Wing), Johnson (Left Wing), Blodgett (Right Defense), Mokrejs (Left Defense) and Tredwell (Goaltender). Spare: Von Sczelski. Referee: Joe Steinauer from the University of Wisconsin.

A few hundred spectators watch the Wisconsin Badgers versus the Minnesota Gophers hockey action on the Lower Campus Rink. The Red Gym Gymnasium and Armory is visible in the background.

The game scheduled at 2 p.m. February 10 would have an opponent more challenging than either Minnesota or Wisconsin. Mother Nature had plans to make the conditions miserable for all players and spectators alike. For the second game in a row Wisconsin captain "Doc" Combacker scored the lone goal for the cardinal and white.

Minnesota would find a way to tie the game in the second period. A blinding snowstorm made playing the game nearly impossible. The score was tied 1-1 after regulation play. This game went into overtime. After the first five-minute overtime period neither team had scored, so they played a second five-minute overtime period. Once time expired the referee declared the game over since the snowy whiteout was not slowing down and weather conditions continued to worsen. Wisconsin escaped the game with a well-earned tie. To Minnesota, it was an embarrassment. Before this game no team had scored on the Gophers or tied them. Wisconsin had done both this weekend.

Wisconsin Lineup: captain Combacker (Center), Fiske (Right Wing), Johnson (Left Wing), Blodgett (Right Defense), Mokrejs (Left Defense) and Tredwell (Goaltender). Wisconsin Spares: Von Sczelski and Moran. Substitution Von Sczelski for Fiske. Referee: Charles A. Smith from the Milwaukee Athletic Club.

Following the dramatic winter weather that impacted the previous weekend's games against Minnesota, snow removal was necessary during the days before the upcoming weekend visit by Marquette

University in order to clear off the skating surface on the UW hockey rink for practices. Snow storms continued to sweep through Madison. The Lower Campus Rink was covered in snow drifts.

Coach Viner's team was handicapped with the loss of two key team members. Starting goalie Tom Tredwell and star forward Bob Blodgett were unable to play due to serious illness. They remained in the infirmary over the weekend and into the next week getting treatment for a virus they were both fighting. Coach Viner made the necessary adjustments and slated Kubosch to be the replacement goaltender while Johnson slid into the defense position for Blodgett and Moran took Johnson's vacated left-wing post.

With an afternoon home game scheduled, the face off was set for 2:30 p.m. Saturday, February 17 against the Marquette Hilltoppers. This was also the first season that Hilltoppers hockey was recognized as a sport by Marquette University. Both teams had a hard time playing well in the first two periods of this matchup. After being down 1-0 to this point, the Wisconsin squad turned things around in the final period.

The Badger players rallied to score three successive goals against the Hilltoppers. Fiske, the Badger right winger, scored one goal. Johnson, the Wisconsin left winger, followed with two goals for the home team.

The Wisconsin skaters earned a big win when they soundly defeated Marquette, 3-1. This game at Madison, Wisconsin was played in bitterly cold conditions that brutalized the players and spectators alike. A couple dozen brave spectators endured the bitter weather to cheer on their team. It was so frigid that the Marquette team later reported their starting goaltender Garry's feet were clinically frozen. It was a surprise to all that he did not suffer permanent injuries from playing in this hockey game.

Wisconsin Lineup: captain Combacker (Center), Fiske (Right Wing), Moran (Left Wing), Johnson (Right Defense), Mokrejs (Left Defense) and Kubosch (Goaltender). Wisconsin Spare: Woods. Referee: Charles A. Smith from the Milwaukee Athletic Club.

After a decent week of practices, the UW had to prepare for another road trip. The Badger hockey squad left Sunday night to make the trek to Minnesota. On Monday, February 26, the Badgers faced Minnesota for the first of a pair of games during the Minnesota Winter Carnival held in St. Paul. Fortunately for the UW team, Tommy Tredwell would be back as the starting goaltender and Blodgett was back on defense. Minnesota only needed to win one of the two games against Wisconsin in order to claim the Big Ten college ice hockey title. In addition to the enormous pressure, the Badger hockey team had to contend with nearly two thousand five hundred rowdy Minnesota fans and the full University of Minnesota band making noise during this wild game.

The first game was played indoors at the Hippodrome on a much larger sheet of ice than the Badgers were accustomed to. It was a tightly contested match and neither team was able to dominate the other. After three full periods Wisconsin had put forth a herculean defensive effort and was able to keep the game scoreless after regulation, forcing the Gophers into overtime play. The Badgers had previously skated to a 1-1 tie earlier in the season against Minnesota, which was a huge accomplishment for the UW hockey program against the powerful and seasoned opponent from the North.

Minnesota was able to crack the stellar Badger defense as a Minnesota player went end to end and scored first against the UW team in overtime. Wisconsin narrowly lost this game by a final score of 1-0.

Wisconsin Lineup: captain Combacker (Center), Fiske (Right Wing), Johnson (Left Wing), Blodgett (Right Defense), Woods (Left Defense) and Tredwell (Goaltender). Spares: Von Sczelski and Moran. Saves: Wisconsin 29, Minnesota 5. Referee: Garrett from St. Paul Athletic Club.

The next day, February 27, the Minnesota hockey squad was back to its usual form. At just under one minute into the opening period the Gophers were on the board and took a 1-0 lead. Another rowdy home crowd went crazy with the early goal. Several minutes later the home team scored again to go up 2-0. In the second period it was evident that the Gophers were in control of this game.

To the credit of the Badgers, the UW defense blanked the Gophers in the second period. However, Wisconsin was unable score in this period either. After two periods it remained 2-0 in favor of Minnesota. In the third period, the Gophers capitalized on their scoring chances. They scored two more goals and held the Badgers scoreless. The home team handily defeated the cardinal and white skaters from Wisconsin by a score of 4-0. Minnesota won every game against the Wisconsin hockey team, except for the one tie, and went on to win the conference championship.

Wisconsin Lineup: captain Combacker (Center), Fiske (Right Wing), Johnson (Left Wing), Blodgett (Right Defense), Woods (Left Defense) and Tredwell (Goaltender). Spares: Von Sczelski and Moran. Saves: Wisconsin 20, Minnesota 7. Referee: Garrett from St. Paul Athletic Club.

On March 2 and 3, the Badgers returned to Milwaukee to face the Marquette Hilltoppers in a two-game series against their in-state rivals. It would be the last two games on the Wisconsin schedule. The cardinal and white team was significantly hampered since star defenseman John Mokrejs was still hospitalized with a serious illness back home in Madison. Earlier in the season Wisconsin defeated Marquette 3-1 at their home rink on the lower Madison campus.

In the first game at the Arena Ice Gardens in Milwaukee, neither team would back down. Some two thousand plus hockey fans were on hand to watch this game. During the first intermission, the Marquette goalie, Garry, who suffered frozen feet during the game in Madison a month earlier, was again the victim of the grueling demands of his position. He collapsed on the Hilltoppers bench and was rushed to the hospital. Starting Marquette defenseman Montagne was put in to play goalkeeper in place of the ailing Garry.

After a scoreless first period, Marquette netted a goal early in the second period for a 1-0 lead and was on the verge of dominating the Badgers for a win. That is until Wisconsin captain "Doc" Combacker tied the game with less than 30 seconds to play in regulation. Combacker continued to score amazing goals at crucial times this season. He was truly "Captain Clutch!"

Each team only allowed one goal in regulation play. The teams agreed to play two 10-minute overtime periods, after 20 minutes of overtime play neither team was able to score. It ultimately went in the record books as a 1-1 tie after two OT periods.

Wisconsin Lineup: captain Combacker (Center), Fiske (Right Wing), Johnson (Left Wing), Blodgett (Right Defense), Woods (Left Defense) and Tredwell (Goaltender). Spares: Von Sczelski and Moran.

Game No. 2 was eerily similar to the game played the day before. Marquette was able to score first when a fluke goal rebounded off Johnson, the Wisconsin defenseman, and glanced into the Badger goal. Marquette was up 1-0. The game continued at a hectic pace and after two periods the home team had a 2-1 lead.

But the Badgers battled back to get another goal in the Hilltoppers net and knot the score up at 2-2. That was the score when the third period ended. Neither team was able to record a goal during the first or second 10-minute overtime period. After playing to the point of near exhaustion, neither team could better the other on the scoreboard. This game ended as a 2-2 tie and was the last match for Wisconsin's hockey program this season. Three of the final four games were close enough that they were forced into overtime periods.

Wisconsin Lineup: captain Combacker (Center), Fiske (Right Wing), Johnson (Left Wing), Blodgett (Right Defense), Woods (Left Defense) and Tredwell (Goaltender). Spares: Von Sczelski and Moran.

Coach Viner's vision was coming to fruition as his countless hours of instruction and practice were beginning to pay dividends. The UW hockey program was clearly becoming a force to be reckoned with and was no longer going to be a pushover for other hockey opponents around the Midwest. They were clearly able to compete with the region's finest teams.

At the end of this season, Wisconsin captain Howard "Doc" Combacker was honored with a selection to the first team of the Minneapolis Tribune's All Conference Team. Other Wisconsin skaters honored with a selection to the second team were Blodgett, Fiske and Tredwell.

Several players received their "W" varsity letter at the end of this season. They included: Howard Combacker, E.E. Johnson, Robert Blodgett, George Fiske, John Mokrejs and Tom Tredwell.

In April, the Big Ten Conference met and reviewed a recommendation by the University of Minnesota that called for an eight-team hockey conference. Teams would include; the University of Michigan, Michigan Agricultural College, Michigan School of Mines, the University of Manitoba, the University of North Dakota, Notre Dame, the University of Minnesota and the University of Wisconsin. It was expected that the proposed alliance would be approved.

1922-23   Schedule and Results:
Coach Dr. A.K. Viner
2-6-3 Third in WIHL

<u>Date</u>	<u>Result</u>	<u>Opponent</u>
January 12	Loss 2-1 2OT	@ Michigan
January 13	Loss 1-0	@ Michigan
January 19	Loss 1-0	Michigan
January 20	Win 1-0	Michigan
February 9	Loss 4-1	Minnesota
February 10	Tie 1-1 2OT	Minnesota
February 17	Win 3-1	Marquette (WI)
February 26	Loss 1-0 OT	@ Minnesota
February 27	Loss 4-0	@ Minnesota
March 2	Tie 1-1 2OT	@ Marquette (WI)
March 3	Tie 2-2 2OT	@ Marquette (WI)

Chapter Five
New Sweaters

1923-24 UW Hockey Team

The Badger hockey team continued to make significant improvements and had become more competitive. Robert O. Blodgett, a UW hockey player from the prior two seasons at Wisconsin, was now the head coach of the Badger squad after replacing coach A.C. Viner. Coach Blodgett would lead the squad into their third year participating as a formal varsity hockey team representing the University of Wisconsin.

In a meeting held in the Red Gym at noon January 4, coach Blodgett spoke to 25 potential hockey players. The purpose of the gathering was to go over his expectations for the University of Wisconsin hockey program for the 1923-24 season.

Daily hockey practices on the Lower Campus Rink began the first week of January. Although a team was not yet selected at this point, a few skaters stood out. They included Art Saari or Von Rohr in goal, Martin Moran at left wing, Eddie Johnson at right wing, and Mace Harris at the center position. Coach Blodgett was also impressed with the play of Chester Gross and Henry Otterman.

Captain Edwin E. Johnson was a highly skilled player at left defense. W.E. Ritchie was Johnson's defensive partner and played right defense. Ritchie was a solid defenseman and played superbly while teamed up with Johnson on the other defensive point position.

Capt. E. Johnson

Martin Moran was an impressive left winger. Both Moran and Ritchie were players on the Wisconsin roster during the 1922-23 season. The sensational C.A. Gross was a member of the 1923-24 freshman squad. He was known as a competitive right winger with exceptional stick handling skills and an aggressive approach to the way he played the game. George McLean, another phenomenal athlete, would be handling the goaltending duties for the team this season after beating out both heavy favorites for this position, Saari and Von Rohr.

Chester A. Gross – Right Wing

Interest in the University of Wisconsin hockey team continued to soar as a record number of students and others attended practices and games to watch the exciting ice hockey action. A major renovation to the Lower Campus Rink was the installation of lighting. These lights made it possible for the Badger skaters to finally practice into the night and even allowed for evening scrimmages or games as desired. The rink was also enlarged to allow for a bigger playing area. Since the crowds continued to grow each year, more bleachers were installed before the January 12 game against Marquette. University officials charged a nominal admission fee to help offset some of the expenses incurred by the Badger hockey program.

1924 Hockey Squad

Back Row: Manager Noer   Harris   Haugh   Saari
Front Row: captain Johnson   Ritchie   Gross   McLean   Moran   Hilsenhoff
Coach Blodgett

1923 – 24 Varsity Hockey Team:

Martin "Mike" Emmett Moran (Left Wing) Mace Harris (Center)
Chester Gross (Right Wing)
Capt. Ed Johnson (Left Defense) Ritchie (Right Defense)
George McLean (Goalkeeper)
Spares:
Art Saari, Haugh, Fiske, Ray Hilsenhoff, Sarles

Preparations were underway as the club had the Marquette Hilltoppers on the schedule for Saturday, January 12. The Hilltoppers, with weeks of practice completed by this point, would be a strong opponent. Warm weather was a major problem again in Madison since it ruined the ice-skating surface and caused the preseason to be delayed for several weeks. The Marquette game was played when the Badgers had less than two weeks of practice.

Since the on-campus rink was at the mercy of the weather, the UW skaters elected to practice on the Lake Mendota rink in order to not destroy the little ice that was left on the campus rink. Such a reduced amount of sufficient time to prepare and practice the game had a negative impact on the UW squad's ability to compete and perform at the required level. The ideal training period before the season was greatly limited because the ice was virtually non-existent.

Just before the game against Marquette, the Wisconsin team equipment manager, Frank Nickerson, was able to outfit the entire Badger squad with brand-new uniforms that had arrived. The players were ecstatic with the much-needed uniforms that included beautiful red wool crew neck jerseys with "Wisconsin" arched across the chest in white lettering, rectangular tanned white leather reinforcement patches on the inner elbows, white hockey pants with a black belt and red wool socks that matched their jerseys.

The oldest known surviving University of Wisconsin hockey uniform (jersey & pants) is from the 1923-24 season. It is proudly displayed at the U.S. Hockey Hall of Fame in Eveleth, Minnesota.
(Photo Courtesy of Andrew Evans)

On January 12, the Marquette Hilltoppers came to the Wisconsin campus for a hockey game against their in-state rivals. A 3 p.m. face off was scheduled and the general admission rate was set at 25 cents for spectators looking to watch the ice hockey spectacle. Around five hundred people showed up to watch the action.

The Badgers were understandably feeling the effects of little practice time due to the lack of decent ice. Conversely, Marquette was the stronger opponent since they had the benefit of artificial ice at a few of the ice arenas they used in the Milwaukee area.

As soon as the puck dropped, the blue and gold visitors began a very aggressive offensive attack against the cardinal and white. Marquette struck first with a slow dribble shot that got past UW goalie McLean and Marquette had a 1-0 lead. Two minutes later there was a clash of bodies in front of the Marquette net and Mace Harris, the talented Wisconsin centerman, was able to get the puck to the back of the Hilltoppers net to tie up the score at 1-1. That score would last through the end of the first period.

Marquette played a relentless style of hockey and continued to swarm the UW zone. They were able to get two more goals against the Badgers in the second period. Both visitor's goals were flukes as they first hit a Badger player before deflecting into the UW net. Coach Blodgett pulled UW goalie George McLean out of the game and replaced him with Art Saari to see if their luck would change. At the end of the second period Marquette maintained a 3-1 lead.

Coach Blodgett mixed up the rest of the Wisconsin player positions in an attempt to gain an advantage, but it was to no avail as the UW squad would not score any more goals. The Marquette team scored one more time in the third period to win the game 4-1.

Wisconsin Lineup: McLean (Goalie), Moran (Left Wing), Gross (Right Wing), captain Johnson (Left Defense), Ritchie (Right Defense) and Harris (Center). Spares: Saari and Hough. Referee: Carlson from the Milwaukee Athletic Club.

On January 14 the University of Wisconsin Athletic Council voted to send the Wisconsin Badger hockey team and staff to South Bend, Indiana for a pair of games against the Notre Dame Fighting Irish February 22 and 23.

After a week of hockey practices in preparation for their next opponent, Wisconsin made the long trip to Ann Arbor January 18 in order to play a pair of games against the Michigan Wolverines. The host team was also hampered by a lack of ice for practices and scrimmages. This hockey game between the Badgers and Wolverines was part of the University of Michigan's Ice Carnival.

Although the Badgers were simply outplayed, they refused to stop battling. In the first period, the Wolverines jumped out to a 2-0 lead. The Badgers held the Wolverines scoreless in the second period but, the favor was returned and the UW was unable to score in the second. In the final period, Michigan put together some nice scoring opportunities and capitalized on one of them to make the score 3-0. When the game time ran out Wisconsin's chance to get on the scoreboard ended and the UW had to accept the 3-0.

Wisconsin Lineup: McLean (Goalie), Moran (Left Wing), Gross (Right Wing), captain Johnson (Left Defense), Ritchie (Right Defense) and Harris (Center). Spares: Saari and Hough. Penalties: Wisconsin 2, Michigan 3.

On January 19, these two Big Ten teams squared off again. Wisconsin adjusted their game plan and had Michigan bewildered with their swarm offense. In the first period captain Chester Gross ripped a shot from half-ice that scored on the Wolverines goalie. To the shock of their opponents and the home crowd, the Badgers were winning 1-0.

The game was played at a hectic pace during the second period. Due to brilliant goaltending and a smothering defense, neither side was able to score in in the middle period. Heading into the third period, Wisconsin still had the lead, 1-0. The Badgers thwarted multiple offensive attacks from the Wolverines in the third. Michigan kept buzzing the Wisconsin net and got a much-needed goal to tie the game in the final minutes of regulation. This contest was played equally from the start of the game.

The game went into overtime and was still tied after the first 10-minute OT ended. After resting for several minutes, the teams started a second ten-minute overtime. Despite the chunked-up ice that was in terrible condition, the Badgers and Wolverines continued to set up offensive plays that were denied by impressive defensive stands. The second OT was also scoreless. After another ten-minute rest, the two teams hit the ice again to play out the third overtime period! Several minutes into the third extra period Michigan put the puck in the Wisconsin net to take a 2-1 lead. Since the OT period was not sudden death, the game would resume until time ran out. Minutes later the Badgers scored their second goal of the game to tie it at 2-2. The final minutes of the third overtime expired with the game still tied. Neither the Badgers nor the Wolverines were able to secure the go-ahead goal, so the officials decided to end the game. It would go in the record books as a 2-2 tie after three overtime periods.

Wisconsin Lineup: McLean (Goalie), Moran (Left Wing), Gross (Right Wing), captain Johnson (Left Defense), Ritchie (Right Defense) and Harris (Center). Spares: Saari and Hough. Penalties: Wisconsin 3, Michigan 4. Referee: Hamilton from Detroit.

The Minnesota Gophers returned to Madison January 25 for the biggest hockey matchup of the season with a 7:30 p.m. faceoff.

University of Wisconsin Director of Ticket Sales Paul F. Hunter and his staff would be on hand for both games to ensure interested spectators could get their admission tickets for this highly anticipated hockey match. Since electric lights were recently installed at the Lower Campus Rink, this game would be the first time a night hockey game was ever played on the University of Wisconsin campus. The weather was so cold this night that both teams had great difficulty staying comfortable.

Wisconsin started out strong, looking to defend their home ice from the invaders. It was so bitterly cold that the players had a hard time warming up. The Gophers got on the scoreboard first when one of their players scored a goal from just beyond the middle of the rink that took a crazy bounce before finding the back of the Badgers net. Minnesota kept the pressure on the Wisconsin end of the rink, but at the end of the first the visitors were winning 1-0.

The Badgers tried to get the pressure off their goalie during the second period and work the puck out of their zone. Time and time again the Gophers intercepted the puck and buzzed back toward the Wisconsin net. The Minnesota captain took his own long shot from just about half ice and scored to make the score 2-0. That score would stand as the second period expired.

The Minnesota squad stayed with their game plan in the third period and disarmed the Badgers. During the final stanza, the Gophers netted two more goals to push their lead to 4-0. Wisconsin had practiced for better results in the days leading up to this game and had intended to outplay the visitors. It turned out to not be much of a big matchup as the Gophers repeatedly plowed through the Badgers defense and won the first game 4-0. Holding the powerful Minnesota squad to a mere four goals was respectable for the Wisconsin hockey team.

Wisconsin Lineup: Harris (Center), Gross (Right Wing), Moran (Left Wing), captain Johnson (Left Defense), Ritchie (Right Defense) and McLean (Goalie). Spares: Saari and Hough. Referee: Carlson from the Milwaukee Athletic Club.

On January 26, the 2 p.m. game was a little worse for the cardinal and white team as the visiting Minnesota squad continued to demonstrate their hockey dominance. The Gophers had exceptional skating, stellar goaltending and superior puck handling that frustrated the Badgers. A couple Minnesota players routinely knocked the puck off the boards in a pass to themselves and would pick up the puck after getting behind the Badger defenseman. Minnesota had a comfortable two goal lead after the first period.

In the second period, the Badgers were still competing but were unable to get any scoring. The Gophers banged in another goal to extend their lead to 3-0. The third period wasn't much better for the Badgers. Minnesota held them scoreless while netting two more goals before the clock expired. The Gophers won 5-0.

After these two matches it was clearly evident why the Gophers have been the conference champions during the previous two seasons. They were one of the top college hockey teams in the nation. If Wisconsin wanted to be taken seriously as a university hockey team in this league it would have to find a way to consistently compete against Minnesota.

Wisconsin Lineup: Harris (Center), Gross (Right Wing), Moran (Left Wing), Ritchie (Right Defense), captain Johnson (Left Defense) and McLean (Goalie). Spares: Saari and Hough. Referee: Carlson from the Milwaukee Athletic Club.

Tragedy struck the Wisconsin hockey squad this season when Badger hockey player Edwin Carlson fractured his neck in a hockey practice. Carlson, a defenseman, was literally "crashing the net" in an offensive attempt when he lost an edge and hit the goal post with his neck. To the horror of his teammates and the coach, Carlson immediately lost consciousness and was rushed to the hospital. It was there that doctors learned he had two broken vertebrae in his neck.

In the 1920s a broken neck was usually fatal and those that survived such an injury had a grim outlook and a significantly shortened life span. Carlson would be hospitalized for the remainder of the season and well into the next season. Coaches, players, family and friends would visit him at his hospital bedside. Carlson was an unusually tough athlete. In addition to the hockey team, he was also a member the past two years on the UW Football team. His toughness would be an attribute on his road to a complete recovery.

On Saturday February 9 the Badgers played an exhibition against the Janesville Athletic Club. This game was the main attraction of Janesville's third annual Gazette Ice Skating Derby. It would mark the first time the University of Wisconsin team played a game in Janesville. This game only came to fruition after the Director of the Janesville YMCA met with UW Athletic Director Tom Jones to agree in principal and eventually finalize, the Badgers participation as the featured hockey game to be played at the Derby. The Goose Island rink in Janesville located on the Rock River was the site of this matchup.

Repairs to the rink were required since side boards were blown down by high winds a few days before the game. Volunteers also helped shovel snow from the playing surface a day before the game.

Several hundred enthusiastic spectators were on hand for the 2:30 p.m. faceoff. Those in attendance watched Wisconsin play this game against the formidable players from the Janesville Athletic Club hockey squad. Early in the first period, Janesville surprised the Badgers when they scored a nice goal from a pretty pass just outside of the UW net. To the delight of the hometown fans, the home team had a 1-0 lead over the mighty college team. Minutes later the Badgers tied the game.

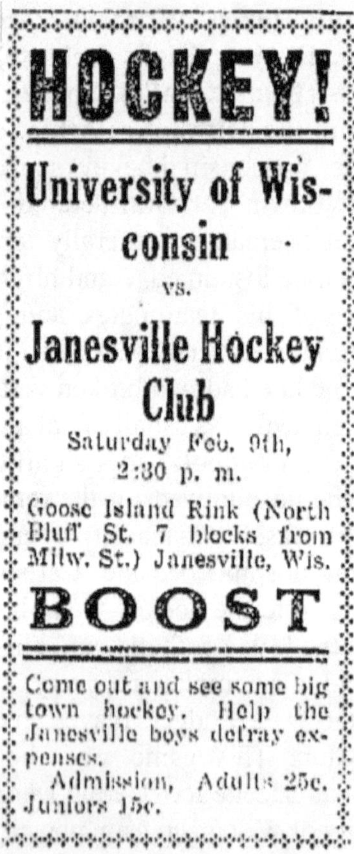

These two teams put on a great display. Even though Wisconsin was the stronger team the Janesville players never backed down. In fact, they held the Badgers scoreless in the second period. Going into the third period the game was tied up at 1-1. In the final period, the

Badgers kept the pressure on the Janesville team and the UW was able to score two more goals. Goal No. 2 came early in to the third period, while the third goal was scored with minutes left in the game. Moran would score twice for the Badgers while Gross netted a single tally. Wisconsin ended up winning this contest, 3-1.

Wisconsin Lineup: Harris (Center), Gross (Right Wing), Moran (Left Wing), Ritchie (Right Defense), captain Johnson (Left Defense) and McLean (Goalie). Spares: Saari and Hough. Referee: V. Klontz. Penalty Time Keeper: Barrett. Goal Official: Luce.

The Janesville Athletic Club hockey team returned to Madison Wednesday, February 13 for a rematch set to begin at 8:15 p.m. It was the Janesville skater's first time playing under the lights for a nighttime hockey game.

The UW players got off to a fast start and were able to score two goals within the first four minutes in the opening period. The Janesville players seemed disoriented on the big ice sheet that had the arc lighting illuminating the playing surface.

Janesville left winger C. Bergmann was able to deke through the Badgers defense late in the third period and scored with a hard, high shot into the top corner of the net. But it was too little too late. The Badgers controlled possession of the puck almost the entire game. The few times Janesville had the puck, it would soon be stripped by an attacking UW skater. Just before the end of the game, Badger left winger Mike Moran dug the puck out from a scrum near the Janesville net and fired the puck in for Wisconsin's third goal. UW won this contest by a score of 3-1 and swept the visitors two games to none this season. Fiske scored twice for the Badgers and Moran got the other goal for Wisconsin this game.

Wisconsin Lineup: Harris (Center), Gross (Right Wing), Moran (Left Wing), Ritchie (Right Defense), captain Johnson (Left Defense) and McLean (Goalie). Spares: Fiske, Saari and Hough. Referee: Bob Blodgett. Timekeeper: Bob Earle.

Coach Barss brought his Michigan Wolverines hockey squad back to Madison for a pair of games scheduled Friday and Saturday, February 15 and 16. Badger right winger Chester Gross was replaced by George Fiske. Coach Blodgett wanted to give Fiske a shot at the starting position since he had been playing so well. In their prior two games, Michigan won a game and tied the other.

The Wolverines had clear control of the first game and toyed with the Badgers. Ice conditions were challenging, but the teams had no choice but to play on.

After a pileup in front of the Wisconsin net, a Michigan defenseman found the loose puck and swatted it in to the Badger net to make the score 1-0. The first period ended with the Wolverines ahead. The Wolverines scored again when one of their players gathered the puck and launched a shot from mid-ice that soared into the Badger net on the fly in the second period. Michigan now had a 2-0 lead. In the third period, it was much the same. The Wolverines scored from right in front of the Badgers net when they won the stick battle and netted their third goal of the game.

The Michigan squad relied heavily on their smothering defense, flawless goaltending and creative offense on their way to a 3-0 victory. The UW had a tough time staying with the fast-skating Wolverines and found themselves unable to get any effective shots near the visitor's goal. Captain Johnson, playing left defense for Wisconsin, took multiple shots from nearly center ice, but the majority of them went wide of the Michigan net.

Wisconsin Lineup: Harris (Center), Fiske (Right Wing), Moran (Left Wing), Ritchie (Right Defense), captain Johnson (Left Defense) and McLean (Goalie). Spares: Saari and Hough. Referee: Barrett.

On February 16, the game was eerily similar for the UW team. A 2:30 p.m. faceoff started the match between the Badgers and visiting Wolverines. Michigan had a nearly impenetrable defense and a powerful offense.

Michigan was the first to score off a short shot toward the UW net in the opening period to take a 1-0 lead. During the second period, Michigan made good off another short shot just in front of the Badgers goal to take a 2-0 lead. The Wolverines scored their final goal in the third period off a long shot that was just beyond the half-ice mark to push their advantage to three goals to none.

The visitors played a solid game scoring in each of the three periods, The Badgers were able to get one goal in the third period when captain Johnson found the puck amongst a pack of battling players in front of the UM net and poked in it for the tally. Michigan immediately protested the goal due to the fact that the goal net itself was moved out of place as players battled for position and control of the puck. Referee Barrett dismissed the pleas from the visitors and the goal stood. But it was not enough as the Wolverines won this game 3-1 and swept the two-game series against the Badgers.

Wisconsin Lineup: Harris (Center), Fiske (Right Wing), Moran (Left Wing), Ritchie (Right Defense), captain Johnson (Left Defense) and McLean (Goalie). Spare: Gross. Referee: Barrett.

During the week of February 18, the UW skaters were going through hard workouts in preparation for the upcoming games against Marquette. On Tuesday and Thursday night the varsity squad scrimmaged the Wisconsin freshman hockey team. Consequently, practices had been hampered the past few weeks by frequent snowfalls and warm weather spells that brought thaws. Fortunately for coach Blodgett, the team did not have any players deemed ineligible.

The weekend series beginning Friday, February 22 required a visit to Milwaukee for a two-game rematch against the Marquette Hilltoppers at the Arena Ice Gardens. The largest crowds ever to watch an indoor hockey game in Milwaukee were on hand for both games. Neither team scored in the first period. Marquette, inspired in part due to the large home crowd scored their first goal against Wisconsin in the second period. The Hilltoppers scored two more goals in the third and ended the night with a 3-0 shutout win over the Badgers. Despite the loss, the spectacular play of captain Johnson and Martin Moran did not go unnoticed on behalf of the Badger squad.

Wisconsin Lineup: Harris (Center), Gross (Right Wing), Moran (Left Wing), Ritchie (Right Defense), captain Johnson (Left Defense) and McLean (Goalie). Spares: Saari and Hough.

On the next night, Wisconsin and Marquette squared off again for the second game of the series. A relatively uneventful and evenly played first period ended without either team scoring. Harris, the crafty UW centerman, was able to crack the Marquette defense and score the first goal of the game eight minutes into the second period. The Hilltopper skaters continued to buzz the Wisconsin net and put together several nice offensive scoring chances during the rest of the second and throughout the third period, but they were turned away by the outstanding play of McLean, the stellar Wisconsin goal guard.

With less than a minute left on the game clock, Marquette jammed a puck into the Badger net and tied the game. Ultimately, overtime was required. After a fast and furious first ten-minute overtime period the game remained knotted at 1-1. A second overtime period was required to determine a winner. Late in the second overtime, Marquette was able to hammer the puck into the Wisconsin net. The Badgers were unable to score before time ran out of the second overtime period. Marquette won, 2-1.

Wisconsin Lineup: Harris (Center), Gross (Right Wing), Moran (Left Wing), Ritchie (Right Defense), captain Johnson (Left Defense) and McLean (Goalie). Spares: Saari and Hough.

The final games of the Wisconsin hockey season required the team to travel to Minnesota for a set of games against Carleton College (Northfield, Minnesota) and the Minnesota Gophers. Badger goalie McLean was unable to make the trip north due to a lingering injury, so Gross was in net for this trip.

The first game at Carleton College was a practice match scheduled for Thursday, February 28 before the two-game series against the University of Minnesota. In this game, the Carleton College skaters were not intimidated by the Badgers and the clash was on from the opening faceoff at Carleton's Lexington rink.

Carleton scored first on a long shot shortly after the game started. Wisconsin tied it after that with their own long shot by Moran to end the first period. Fast skating, stick handling and multiple shots by both teams made for a furious second period. The second period ended with the Badgers on top by a score of 5-4.

Once the third period started, Carleton took control and put in two more quick goals to take back the lead at 6-5. Wisconsin battled on and the cardinal and white skaters were able to tally another goal to tie the game at 6-6 by the end of the third period.

An extra ten-minute overtime period was required to determine a winner. The Badgers were able to score early in OT to take a 7-6 lead. But Carleton College scored twice before time expired. Wisconsin's hard-fought efforts were for naught as the Carleton College hockey team won 8-7.

Wisconsin's scoring came from three players-Moran notched a hat trick and both Johnson and Harris tallied two each in the loss.

Wisconsin Lineup: Harris (Center), Fiske (Right Wing), Moran (Left Wing), captain Johnson (Right Defense), Ritchie (Left Defense) and Gross (Goalie). Spares: Saari and Hough.

On Friday, February 29, the Badgers arrived at the University of Minnesota campus. Warm weather returned and destroyed the outdoor natural ice in the twin cities area. As a result, the games featuring

Minnesota and Wisconsin had to be moved indoors to the old Coliseum rink in St. Paul. Minnesota was sporting an 11-1 record this season and they were looking to clinch the Western Conference championship along with the Big Ten title. Recent weather handicapped the Gophers as they were unable to get in any practice during the week before Wisconsin's visit.

The Gophers were clearly sharper than the visiting Badgers, however Minnesota opened the scoring and had a 2-0 lead at the end of the first. The Gophers had a comfortable 3-0 lead going into the third and added another goal for a 4-0 shutout. It would have been 5-0 had the Gophers not been ruled offside before scoring another goal. Wisconsin simply had no answers.

Wisconsin Lineup: Harris (Center), Gross (Right Wing), Moran (Left Wing), Ritchie (Right Defense), captain Johnson (Left Defense) and McLean (Goalie). Spares: Saari and Hough. Saves: Wisconsin 11, Minnesota 5.

Although the Badgers came out flying in the first period of their game March 1, their efforts were promptly squashed as the Gophers scored quickly. In fact, the Minnesota club would end up scoring three goals in the first period. The Badgers were clearly deflated.

Minnesota continued their offensive attacks into the second period. The Gophers attempts paid off as they scored again. The score was now 4-0 in favor of the home team. Wisconsin took comfort in knowing they held the Gophers scoreless in the third and final period.

Another chapter closed on the Wisconsin hockey program as the season was completed in a highly anticlimactic manner despite the best intentions of the UW coach and his skaters. Blodgett's Badgers were unable to win one game against any conference rivals this season.

Wisconsin Lineup: Harris (Center), Gross (Right Wing), Moran (Left Wing), Ritchie (Right Defense), captain Johnson (Left Defense) and McLean (Goalie). Spares: Saari and Hough.

Coach Bob Blodgett had his players in the Red Gym the following week practicing hockey on the basketball court. He felt that if his team worked out and practiced during the offseason, they would be better prepared to compete when next season rolled around.

The popularity of Wisconsin hockey continued to rise on campus. The winter sport made the cover of the coveted <u>Wisconsin Athletic Review</u> magazine for the first time in February 1924.

The varsity hockey program ended with a 2-11-1 record in their third year, but it was considered a success when compared with the previous two years. Plans were underway to ensure the next season would have an even better record of the Wisconsin Badgers.

At the end of season banquet, coach Blodgett announced Chester A. Gross from Duluth, Minnesota had been elected as captain of the 1924-25 Wisconsin hockey team. Gross was a skilled right winger and one of the team's top players. He made a name for himself on the freshman team as a top competitor last season. Gross was an obvious choice for a varsity roster spot. Like other leaders on the team, coach Blodgett played Gross nearly all game long in each of their matches this season.

Wisconsin hockey staff confirmed their planning for next season would again include rink lighting for nighttime practices and games.

The upcoming team was expected to do very well with returning players and the addition of a few former freshman skaters that became eligible for varsity competition. George McLean, from Duluth, was a gifted goal guard on this season's team and was expected to return.

1923-24   Schedule and Results:
Coach Robert Blodgett
0-10-1 Third in the WIHL   2-11-1 Overall

Date	Result	Opponent
January 12	Loss 4-1	Marquette (WI)
January 18	Loss 3-0	@ Michigan
January 19	Tie 2-2 3OT	@ Michigan
January 25	Loss 4-0	Minnesota
January 26	Loss 5-0	Minnesota
February 9	Win 3-1	@ Janesville*
February 13	Win 3-1	Janesville*
February 15	Loss 3-0	Michigan
February 16	Loss 3-1	Michigan
February 22	Loss 3-0	@ Marquette (WI)
February 23	Loss 2-1 2OT	@ Marquette (WI)
February 28	Loss 8-7 OT	Carleton*
February 29	Loss 4-0	@ Minnesota
March 1	Loss 4-0	@ Minnesota

*Exhibition Games

Chapter Six
No Dates with Girls During the Season

1924-25 UW Hockey Team

With the unexpected resignation of head coach Robert Blodgett, the University of Wisconsin Athletic Department found themselves without a head coach to lead the hockey team. Athletic Director Tom Jones was determined to have a replacement named before January 1. At this point before the season, only a tentative hockey schedule had been determined. Minnesota would obviously be on the schedule. The other regular opponent, the University of Michigan, was a challenge to schedule. A visit to Madison with the UM squad was no problem, but a road trip to Ann Arbor was now complicated by the fact that Michigan's indoor ice rink had burned down over the past summer. The Wolverines hockey staff indicated their contingency plan included quickly building an outdoor rink so that their hockey season would not be interrupted.

Since late December 1924, both the freshman and varsity hockey teams were practicing daily at the Wingra Park lagoon since it was frozen solid. The lagoon at Wingra Park was an ideal skating surface since it would freeze rock hard and was easy to care for when compared with the unpredictable ice surface upon Lake Mendota. Once the cold weather became consistent, the rink on the lower Madison campus would be framed up with boards and flooded for the Wisconsin hockey teams.

The 1924-25 Wisconsin hockey team started the season by welcoming another new Wisconsin hockey head coach. Kay Iverson came from Minnesota to join the UW program. Last season, he was an assistant coach for the Minnesota Gophers hockey team. His brother, Emil Iverson, was the head coach for the Gophers. On Sunday January 4, Iverson arrived on campus and took over the reins. It became apparent from day one that he was dedicated to making this season's hockey squad the best one yet for the Badgers. Coach Iverson was known as a hardworking man that put many long hours into running practices and scrimmages. His energy and enthusiasm encompassed the players and also those students and faculty close to the hockey program. In addition to his dedication to improving the team, he was also focused on improving the skating facilities to ensure it was the best rink possible for both Wisconsin hockey players and recreational skaters. The goal was to have the rink ready to go by January 7 when classes resumed. Practices focused on the importance of solid defense. Upon that belief, coach Iverson would expand the offensive tactics for his club.

Wisconsin Head Coach Kay Iverson

Due in large part to coach Iverson's direction, the Wisconsin Badger hockey team was fortunate to assemble a team that was able to challenge the other schools.

1924–25 Varsity Hockey Team

1924–25 Varsity Hockey Team Roster:
Captain Lidicker (Left Wing)   Gross (Center) Jansky (Right Wing)
Teich (Left Defense)   Moorhead (Right Defense)
McLean (Goalkeeper)
Spares: Emmert, McCarter, Ruf

Only two returning veterans, Chester Gross and George McLean, were available for coach Iverson to build a team around this season. Of the two lettermen, Gross was elected captain. Although initially a player on the freshman squad last year, he made the jump to varsity and played nearly every minute of each game last season. Big things were expected from skater Bill Sarles since he was another player who traveled in order to attend several of the away games last season. Fritz Teich was the captain of last year's freshman hockey team and he was expected to be a key contributor. Phenom Karl Jansky was expected to have a huge sophomore season. Another student known to be more talented as a skater than as a hockey player was Leon Emmert. His fast skating would help to set up many plays and scoring chances.

The defensive pair of Al Moorhead and William Lidicker from last year's freshman team were slated to defend the Badger zone. Experienced goal guard Harold Ruf had the skills to deny many of the scoring opportunities from all opponents. He would challenge McLean to be the starting goalie. Walk-on John McCarter, who entered the University of Wisconsin last semester, would not be eligible for the varsity hockey squad until February. In all, a total of 16 men tried out for the varsity and freshman squads. In comparison, Michigan had 41 men try out for their varsity team while Minnesota had 80 men try out for their squad.

1924–25 Wisconsin Varsity Hockey Team

Wisconsin, Michigan and Minnesota were the only Big Ten schools with a hockey program in 1924-25. Accordingly, the game schedule involved road trips to Ann Arbor to play Michigan and Minneapolis to play Minnesota. Two games would be played at the home rinks of the Wolverines and of the Gophers. Both teams would also travel to Madison for a two-game series on the University of Wisconsin campus. Results of these scheduled games would determine the conference championships.

Four additional games were scheduled by the Badgers with the Marquette Hilltopper (two home and two away). The Badgers hoped to play one game against the Michigan Aggies hockey team during their planned to trip to Ann Arbor for games against the Wolverines. The Badgers also planned to play one game against Carleton College during their trip to Minnesota to face the Gophers. Tentative games were in the works that would have the UW facing Janesville YMCA, the Milwaukee Athletic Club, Notre Dame and St. Thomas.

1924–25 Varsity and freshman Hockey Players & Coaches.

As with the prior seasons, Mother Nature remained in a foul mood and the unseasonably warm winter weather destroyed the ice many times during the season. Air temps ranged from the high 30s to the mid-50-degree mark. Clearly the weather was not cold enough to make and maintain ice for hockey. Opportunities to skate on decent ice were greatly diminished on the campus rink and the Badger skaters worked hard in practice during those few times when the ice was decent enough to skate upon. Practices were held nearly every evening in January when the weather permitted.

Gross

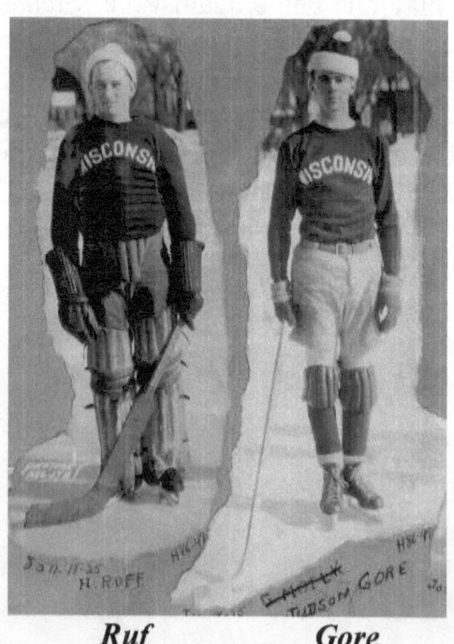

Ruf   **Gore**

Teich

Moelk

Jansky

McCarter

Emmert   *McLean*

Moorhead   *Lidicker*

Knaston   *Munkwitz*

Chamberlain   *Whiteside*

First on the schedule this season was a series versus the Janesville YMCA Hockey Club. These games were a feature match for the Ice Carnival of the Lions Club in Janesville. Prior to the game, Coach Iverson admitted he didn't give his UW team a chance to win after assembling a team just 10 days prior. The first game was scheduled for Thursday night, January 12. Janesville had a great rink to play night games in as there were plenty of lights illuminating the playing surface and high boards lining the hockey rink.

Janesville's coach was very confident. When asked about the games against Wisconsin, which were part of Janesville's Ice Carnival, he said if the home team doesn't win then then he wouldn't consider the event a success.

Upon hearing the Janesville coach's remarks, Wisconsin coach Kay Iverson made it clear that although he was unable to work miracles with 10 days of preparation for his team, he was headed to Janesville intent on earning the first win of the season for the Badgers and ruining the carnival for Janesville.

To the delight of coach Iverson, Wisconsin was in total control of the first game from the opening faceoff. Captain Gross scored on a beautiful shot early in the first period to give the Badgers a 1-0 lead. Star left defenseman Fritz Teich was credited with the second goal of the game in the middle period to push the score 2-0 in favor of the visitors. Right defenseman Bill Lidicker scored the final goal in the third on a nifty shot from afar for a commanding 3-0 lead. The redesigned Badger team earned a 3-0 shutout.

The Janesville side and home crowd were clearly not happy that the college boys from Madison came down and gave their club a loss during their own carnival. It was a relatively clean game with only one infraction called against either squad. Officiating the game was Mr. Parrett, a former hockey star from Madison, Wisconsin.

Wisconsin Lineup: Harris (Center), captain Gross (Right Wing), Moran (Left Wing), Lidicker (Right Defense), Teich (Left Defense) and McLean (Goalie). Penalties: Wisconsin 1, Janesville 1. Referee: Parrett of Madison.

Wisconsin faced a more determined Janesville club the next day. The teams battled back and forth without any scoring in the first period. The second period was similar to the first as both teams were big on defense and denied any offensive attempts. After two periods it was still scoreless. The teams lined up in the dark, cold Wisconsin winter night to hopefully determine a clear winner in the final period. No matter what they tried they could not score any goals in this match. When regulation time expired the second game ended in a 0-0 tie against the more experienced Janesville squad.

An overtime period was not played since the game started so late. Janesville was motivated to play this game and tried to erase the embarrassment caused in the prior game from the young UW players visiting from Madison, but clearly coach Iverson's defensive structure had already started to take shape.

Wisconsin Lineup: Harris (Center), captain Gross (Right Wing), Moran (Left Wing), Lidicker (Right Defense), Teich (Left Defense) and McLean (Goalie).

Wisconsin players scrimmage during hockey practice on the Lower Campus Rink, Sunday, January 18, 1925.

Wisconsin players scrimmage during hockey practice on the Lower Campus Rink, Sunday, January 18, 1925.

The next two games against Janesville in Madison were ultimately canceled due to weather. Warm temperatures eroded what little ice was left in the days prior. On January 31, there was enough decent ice on the Lower Campus Rink that coach Iverson scheduled a 5 p.m. scrimmage between his first and second teams.

In between semesters on the UW campus, the Badger hockey team suffered a significant setback. A total of 12 skaters became scholastically ineligible and were forced to part ways with the program. One of the key players, starting goalie George McLean, was a victim of the scholastic consequences. But it seemed he would be able to return soon. Harold Ruf would take over the goaltending duties.

Coach Iverson was known as a strict disciplinarian. He had one rule, an edict that was very unpopular among his players: **<u>No Dates with Girls During the Hockey Season</u>**. It was reported that the players were compliant with this challenging demand, at least as far as the coach knew. Iverson had other strict rules that applied to his players and he was a firm believer in long, grueling practice sessions in preparation for upcoming opponents.

The first conference games of the season were against the Michigan Wolverines. So, the Badgers traveled to Ann Arbor for the two-game series scheduled to begin February 7. Upon their arrival, the UW contingent was notified that the games had to be canceled due to the terrible ice condition and inclement weather.

A game with the Notre Dame Fighting Irish was scheduled in Madison February 11. Rather than play the Badgers, the Irish ended up taking an extended trip through Minnesota to play a few teams up there instead.

As luck would have it, the reconstructed Badger hockey team would face the mighty Minnesota Gophers next on the schedule. The February 13 and 14 games would be a huge challenge for Wisconsin. It was the first time in college hockey that two brothers coached opposing teams as coach Kay Iverson led the Badgers and his brother, Emil Iverson, coached the Gophers.

Brothers and rival coaches Emil Iverson (Left – Minnesota) and Kay Iverson (Right- Wisconsin) pictured on the University of Wisconsin-Madison campus.

The first game was slated for Friday, February 13 at 7:30 p.m. The

Gopher skaters had little resistance from their cardinal and white opponents. Minnesota scored a few minutes after the game began. They scored another just before the end of the first period to make it 2-0. Several minutes into the second period, Wisconsin left winger Bill Lidicker scored for the Badgers to cut the lead in half, but that would be as close as the UW would get.

Unfortunately, coach Kay Iverson's strategic gamble did not pay dividends. He elected for an unorthodox player formation and went with four players in a defensive position protecting the Badger net. This left one player in charge of advancing the puck on offense and attempting to score as the opportunity arose. Clearly that strategy did not work against the Gophers.

The Minnesota team put in three more goals before the game ended. Last year's conference champs were pleased as they handed the UW a 5-1 loss. Without a doubt the lone goal was a much-needed confidence booster for the Wisconsin players.

Wisconsin Lineup: captain Gross (Center), Jansky (Right Wing), Lidicker (Left Wing), McCarter (Right Defense), Gore (Left Defense) and Manierre (Goalie). Spares: McLean, Sarles, Yahn and Moelk. Substitutions: Sarles for Gross and McLean for Manierre. Referee: Thompson from the Milwaukee Athletic Club.

The next day, game two of the series began at 4 p.m. Saturday afternoon. Wisconsin was better prepared by coach Iverson for this game and their incredible effort made them more competitive. The Badgers surprised the Gophers with stellar team work and spectacular individual play.

Manierre, the newly placed Wisconsin goaltender, was sensational as he turned away multiple offensive attacks from the Gophers. Wisconsin even had more shots on goal in the first period than did Minnesota, a rare feat indeed. By the end of regulation, the score was locked up at 0-0. The Iverson brothers agreed their teams would play two overtime periods.

Minnesota struck first during the initial overtime period. It was the only score of the first OT. UW also failed to counter with a goal in the second overtime period and lost, 1-0. However, they held Minnesota scoreless through three periods as well as the final overtime frame, an impressive feat for a program under new leadership.

Wisconsin Lineup: captain Gross (Center), Jansky (Right Wing), Lidicker (Left Wing), McCarter (Right Defense), Gore (Left Defense) and Manierre (Goalie). Spares: McLean, Sarles, Yahn and Moelk. Referee: Thompson from the Milwaukee Athletic Club.

Next on the schedule was Carleton College, a small private school located in Northfield Minnesota. Last season they handed the UW an overtime loss. They routinely assembled teams that were highly talented and tough to play. Before their game against the Badgers, one of the star defensemen for Carleton College was seriously injured in a scrimmage game against St. Thomas when he was cut by a skate blade that sliced through his skate and caused a significant laceration on his foot. Due to the severity of the injury, he was expected to miss the rest of the season. The Carleton College hockey team had won nine straight games before playing Wisconsin.

On February 20, the game scheduled for 7:30 p.m. between Wisconsin and Carleton was delayed until 8:30 p.m. Wisconsin hockey staff determined the rink would need to be reflooded and that it needed an hour to freeze. Some thought the game would not happen since another recent bout of warm weather wreaked havoc on the Lower Campus Rink skating surface. Reports claim that this game was played with at least an inch of standing water upon the ice surface. Several hundred folks were in attendance to watch the hockey contest.

Carleton battled through the adversity and their star centerman was able to notch two goals in the opening period. It was mainly because Wisconsin let him skate around their positions instead of playing the body. Down two goals, coach Iverson made some adjustments to his team's style of play in an attempt to stop Carleton College's explosive offense. Suddenly, his players made sure they body checked any invading Carleton players and it was enough to offset their offensive attacks toward the UW zone. After two periods, it was still 2-0 in favor of Carleton.

Wisconsin left defenseman Gore recorded the lone score for the Badger squad in the third period, but it would not be enough. Even though the Badgers halted any further scoring by Carleton College after the first period, the visitors were able to hold off the UW with a 2-1 victory. Carleton's decision to go into a defensive formation held off any solid scoring chances by the Badgers.

Wisconsin Lineup: captain Gross (Center), Jansky (Right Wing), Lidicker (Left Wing), McCarter (Right Defense), Gore (Left Defense) and Manierre (Goalie). Spares: McLean, Sarles, Yahn and Moelk. Referee: Thompson from the Milwaukee Athletic Club.

A second game scheduled between these two teams was canceled due to soft and unplayable ice conditions on the UW campus rink.

The following week, February 27, the always powerful Michigan Wolverines returned to Madison for a two-game series. During the first game, the Wolverines notched goals at practically the end of regulation time in both the first and second periods for a 2-0 advantage. The Badgers were unable to respond. Wisconsin kept the pressure on the Michigan net for most of the third period, but were unable to capitalize on their scoring threats. A Michigan player was ejected from the match for excessive roughness toward the end of the third period.

Wisconsin lost 2-0, but the story of this game was the physical play. Michigan brought an extraordinary brand of rough hockey to Madison and the Badgers were not pleased. The Wolverines played so incredibly dirty that following the game coach Iverson proclaimed, "I am sorry that I taught my team to play clean after tonight's game." (1) Four Wisconsin players were placed on the injured list after receiving significant injuries in this game.

Among the battered Badger players: captain Gross required stitches after the game to close a nasty cut on his eyebrow, Jansky suffered a jaw injury, McCarter had a suspected broken nose and Sarles received an injury to his knee. One Michigan player was also added to the injured list with a cut over his eye that required stitches.

At the conclusion of this game, coach Iverson and coach Barss participated in a lengthy shouting match with each other sharing their displeasure with how each other's team played the sport. The Michigan coach also took issue with how referee Jake Thompson, from the Milwaukee Athletic Club, officiated the game. Iverson yelled back at Barss repeatedly to express his anger with the thuggery observed from the Wolverines during this contest.

Wisconsin Lineup: captain Gross (Center), Jansky (Right Wing), Lidicker (Left Wing), McCarter (Right Defense), Gore (Left Defense) and Manierre (Goalie). Spares: McLean, Sarles, Yahn and Moelk. Referee: Jake Thompson from the Milwaukee Athletic Club.

Game Photos from the Wisconsin versus Michigan Game in 1925.

The Saturday, February 28 game was slated for a 4 p.m. start. Both teams played a penalty-free game as this match was played with a lot more restraint. The playing surface was very slushy. In the end, the Wolverines edged the Badgers by a score of 1-0. Michigan netted their goal in the first period and kept the pressure on the UW net for most of the game.

Wisconsin fought back and dominated the second period, but was unable to score. The third period was a back-and-forth battle. The biggest thrill for the spectators was the handful of players that fell on the sloppy ice and caused noticeable splashes.

Michigan demonstrated their on-ice proficiency and left the UW campus with a pair of shutout wins by margins of 2-0 and 1-0. Despite the creative skating and strong team work demonstrated by the Badger skaters, the Wolverines were able to return to Ann Arbor with the victories. Even with the losses, there was still plenty for Wisconsin to be positive about considering Michigan won the conference championship last season.

Wisconsin Lineup: captain Gross (Center), Jansky (Right Wing), Lidicker (Left Wing), McCarter (Right Defense), Gore (Left Defense) and Manierre (Goalie). Spares: Sarles and Johnson. Referee: Jake Thompson from the Milwaukee Athletic Club.

Coach Iverson was gaining tons of praise for the coaching talent he demonstrated, especially considering the level of competition he had constructed from a highly inexperienced base of available men on campus. He also received accolades for facing the challenges presented by the uncooperative weather this season.

Appreciation for the sport of hockey at the University of Wisconsin was at an all-time high. Spectators and fans alike were falling in love with the fastest game in the world. Several hundred to nearly a thousand people continued to attend practices and games to watch ice hockey at the UW. The passion for the game demonstrated by coach Iverson, along with a heightened interest shown by spectators, was directly responsible for the surge in popularity of the Wisconsin hockey program.

Hockey's monstrous jump in popularity this season had impacts all over the University of Wisconsin campus. The Wisconsin Athletic Department had historically constructed a hockey rink on Lake Mendota. In addition, they also constructed the hockey and skating rink on the lower campus that is primarily for the varsity hockey team's practices and games. However, any open ice time on the Lower Campus Rink was used for recreational skaters. Due in large part to the heightened popularity of ice hockey and ice skating at the UW, the Wisconsin Athletic Department built a rink on the Camp Randall football field. To handle the mix of hockey players and leisure skaters, a larger rink at Camp Randall was made to accommodate two recreational hockey games at once. In addition, an area of ice comparable to a quarter mile track was made available. At night, the Camp Randall Stadium floodlights were turned on so skaters and hockey players could skate. On a typical winter evening it was estimated that as many as four hundred skaters were enjoying the Camp Randall skating areas at one time.

Wisconsin hockey coach Kay Iverson, formerly an assistant coach at Minnesota, had previously created and maintained many large hockey rinks and recreational skating areas at the University of Minnesota. Iverson provided significant input and expertise in the design and maintenance of all the rinks located around the University of Wisconsin campus in Madison.

On March 4, Iverson took his team to Portage, Wisconsin for a demonstration hockey match in an attempt to grow the game around the state. Iverson's first and second team would be on display scrimmaging against each other as "Team Wisconsin" and "Team Portage." The Wisconsin coach would also double as the referee for this exhibition. The game was played at the Portage Curling Club. Team Wisconsin demonstrated their scoring skills, recording three goals in a short span of time in the opening frame. At the end of the first period, it was Team Wisconsin 3 and Team Portage 0.

During the second period, Team Portage started playing good hockey scored their own goal. The score was 3-1 in favor of "Team Wisconsin" at the end of the second period. In between the second and third periods, coach/referee Iverson took time to explain the concepts and rules of the game of ice hockey to the local spectators.

Wisconsin captain Chester Gross was one of the Badger players that coach Iverson put on the "Team Portage" squad for this exhibition. "Team Portage" scored two more goals to tie the game at 3-3 by the end of regulation. It was agreed that the two sides would play five-minute overtime periods until a winner was crowned. After the first OT period the score remained 3-3 so the two sides battled on in OT No. 2. At the end of the second OT the score was still tied. A third overtime period was the one when a winner was determined. "Team Portage" scored goal No. 4 to win the match 4-3 over "Team Wisconsin."

This game was not without the usual injuries that occur during a typical competitive varsity hockey game. Wisconsin Left Defenseman John McCarter sustained a serious cut on his mouth and Wisconsin Right Wing Karl Jansky received a black eye.

Exhibition Game at Portage Lineups:
Team Portage:
Captain Gross (Center), Jansky (Right Wing), Kneebone (Left Wing), Moorhead (Right Defense), Jahn (Left Defense) and Ruf (Goalie).

Team Wisconsin:
Whiteside (Center), Moelk (Right Wing), Lidicker (Left Wing), Gore (Right Defense), McCarter (Left Defense) and Manierre (Goalie).

Referee: Kay Iverson (Wisconsin head coach).

After the game the Wisconsin players and staff joined their hosts for a luncheon in the lobby of the Portage Curling Club rink clubhouse. As they were leaving after lunch, the Badger skaters showed their appreciation to the attendees and their hosts by shouting out an enthusiastic' "Rah-'Rah for Portage and the Curling Club!" (2)

The Badger hockey team had two weeks to prepare for the final series of the season at rival Minnesota's newly constructed indoor home rink, the Minneapolis Arena. Having an indoor rink, which was not at the mercy of unsuitable weather, was a huge advantage for all of the Minnesota teams that took advantage of this new state of the art facility. Again, the Wisconsin skaters were as prepared as they could be for the games under the leadership of coach Iverson.

The spring-like weather melted away the ice in Madison for the week prior to this series. As a result, coach Iverson had his men completing daily five-mile runs. There were also gymnastics and flexibility drills at the Red Gym for the Badger skaters. Iverson was hoping this regimen would keep his men in peak condition since skating was not an option.

The Badgers were able to get in a much-needed pregame practice at the Minneapolis Arena, but their luck remained on the same path it had been on all year. After battling the Gophers to a scoreless first period it would be the second period that featured the game-winning goal. Six minutes into the middle period, a Gopher forward took a long shot toward the Wisconsin net. On the way it bounced, skipped, slid and hopped awkwardly before finding the back of the UW net to give the home team a 1-0 lead. The period ended without any further scoring. The third period was a back-and-forth affair that was heavy on skillful goaltending, stingy defense and mediocre offense. When time expired, Minnesota won 1-0.

Wisconsin Lineup: captain Gross (Center), Jansky (Right Wing), Lidicker (Left Wing), McCarter (Right Defense), Gore (Left Defense) and Manierre (Goalie). Spares: Sarles, Johnson, Moelk, Elstran, Weideman and Jahn. Saves: Wisconsin 21, Minnesota 2. Penalties: Wisconsin 0, Minnesota 3. Referee: Nick Kahler from Minneapolis.

Game two was much the same. Wisconsin came to play and Minnesota edged them out. They also outlasted the Badgers and again won by a score of 1-0. Although the losses stung, Wisconsin was able to take great comfort in holding the talented Minnesota club to only one score in each game. It was a tough way to end the season for the UW hockey team, though.

Wisconsin Lineup: captain Gross (Center), Jansky (Right Wing), Lidicker (Left Wing), McCarter (Right Defense), Gore

(Left Defense) and Manierre (Goalie). Spares: Sarles, Johnson, Moelk, Elstran, Weideman and Jahn

Hockey as a varsity sport at Wisconsin was still in its infancy when compared with the other schools that were on the Badger schedule this season. Popularity among students, staff and spectators across the state signified that this sport would continue its pursuit of excellence and success. It was only a matter of time before Wisconsin would become a championship hockey program.

The Hotel Loraine, Site of the 1924-25 Wisconsin Hockey Team Banquet.

Coach Iverson knew the importance of rewarding his players for their efforts this season so he arranged for a hockey banquet at the famed Hotel Loraine in downtown Madison Monday, March 16. The venue was a new ten-story tall building in downtown Madison that was completed in 1924. During the banquet, coach Iverson presented the team with medals as a token of his appreciation for all of their work. The players also showed their appreciation for coach Iverson by giving him a plaque with his name and the names of every player on the team this year. Captain Chester Gross was reelected as captain for next season. Players on the team who received their "W" varsity letters were Gross, Jansky, Lidicker, McCarter, Gore, Sarles and Manierre.

Ice hockey was also just beginning to gain national recognition at the amateur and professional levels. The 1924-25 season was the first time that the Boston Bruins, a professional hockey team, competed for the coveted Stanley Cup trophy.

Wisconsin was only able to tally one victory and one tie during this season and lost six games by one goal. Big expectations surrounded the team for the coming year. Only Manierre, the Badger goalie, was lost to graduation. Almost all of the team would be returning for the cardinal and white. This included captain Gross, who was clearly one of the best centers in the Midwest. Top defensemen Gore and McCarter would also return and play a vital role. Highly talented wingers Jansky and Lidicker would be back. Both men had a highly successful season and were expected to contribute even bigger things during the upcoming campaign.

Hockey at the University of Wisconsin had exploded in popularity and finally made it to the same level as football, basketball and baseball on campus. Coach Iverson would be busy during the offseason executing a variety of strategies to ensure the hockey program would be more competitive and successful than seasons past.

1924-25   Schedule and Results:
Coach Kay Iverson
0-6-0 Third in WIHL   1-7-1 Overall

Date	Result		Opponent
January 15	Win 3-0		@ Janesville*
January 16	Tie 0-0		@ Janesville*
February 13	Loss 5-1		Minnesota
February 14	Loss 1-0	2OT	Minnesota
February 20	Loss 2-1		Carleton*
February 27	Loss 2-0		Michigan
February 28	Loss 1-0		Michigan
March 4	4-3	3OT	Portage**
March 13	Loss 1-0		@ Minnesota
March 14	Loss 1-0		@ Minnesota

*Exhibition Games

**Intrasquad Scrimmage Game

Chapter Seven
Tied for First in WIHL

1925-26 UW Hockey Team

Head coach Kay Iverson returned for his second and last, season leading the cardinal and white skaters as they competed with teams across the Midwest. While hockey was still a relatively young sport at Wisconsin, the school was all in and coach Iverson was largely credited with its skyrocketing popularity on campus.

The University constructed a monster-sized hockey rink for its era and it was purported to be the largest outdoor ice hockey rink in the country. The sheet of ice measured 110 feet by 250 feet on the lower campus. Last season's hockey rink was barely two-thirds of the one built for this season. Bleachers were erected to accommodate two hundred spectators and there was even room for a couple of thousand more to stand around the rink or on the library stairs. Coach Iverson also had two small rinks built near the varsity rink. One would be used by the freshman team and the other was allocated for a UW women's hockey club.

Kay Iverson is one of the most successful coaches of hockey in the country. "Ivvy" Iverson has won a place in the hearts of all Wisconsin students by his enthusiastic encouragement of all winter sports, making them take a prominent place in the athletic program here.

Wisconsin Hockey Head Coach Kay Iverson

Cold weather brought ice to the Madison lakes in early December. Coach Iverson took the weather as an indicator it was time to review players that would make up his varsity and freshman hockey squads. The returning veterans were Gross, Jansky, Lidicker, McCarter and McLean. Other top prospects for the team included Whiteside, Murphy, Carlson and Chamberlin. At the preseason meeting, coach Iverson reminded the men to pay more attention to their books and less attention to extracurricular social activities. This was especially important as their ultimate goal was to win the Western Intercollegiate Hockey League championship.

A record number of student skaters turned out in hopes of making the wildly popular Badger hockey team during tryouts for the 1925-26 squad. The men talented enough to make the cut for the varsity and freshman hockey teams soon found themselves training for battle under the leadership of coach Iverson. The players frequently worked out at the gymnasium annex running an average of 5 miles a day and participating in various grueling calisthenics in preparation for the upcoming season.

Most students returned to their home towns during the Christmas break to enjoy home cooked meals and the relaxation of being away from the pressures of their studies. However, it was not easy for the Badgers hockey team who had been faithfully training. They were required to leave on Christmas Day to tour the Iron Range of northern Minnesota and play a handful of exhibition games before the regular season commenced.

The preseason schedule was designed to challenge the team and the first stop in Duluth was an eye opener. The home team was stacked with highly skilled players and they played in the Duluth Intermediate League. Gross, the captain and center for the Wisconsin Badgers, hailed from this city.

The game was held at the Duluth Curling and Skating Club. Built in 1913, it was a palace in size and amenities. The lower level had 12 sheets of ice and enough seating to accommodate three thousand people. The second level hosted ice hockey games in the winter and it was used for roller skating in the summertime. This second level could seat two thousand spectators alone. One of the most interesting features of the main hockey playing area was that the dasher boards were incredibly low. They were only waist-high and without the comforts of protective chicken wire or other barriers. Fans oftentimes found themselves accidentally in the action feeling the effects of an errant stick, puck, shove from a player's glove or the impact of hockey players spilling out of the playing area and into the stands while a game was in progress.

Duluth Curling and Skating Club

In their first exhibition game, the UW players were recognized for their proficient stick handling and for being all-around good skaters. But the lack of practice time on suitable ice was evident throughout the game. Duluth had far better skaters during this matchup. Since the Wisconsin game against Duluth was technically an exhibition game, it was agreed that they would play three fifteen-minute periods.

Wisconsin didn't back down from their talented opponents. Duluth scored with three minutes left in the first period. Midway through the second period, the Curling Club team notched their second goal on a nice solo effort from their defenseman as he went from his end all the way into the Wisconsin zone before getting the puck past Badger goaltender McLean. At the end of two periods, Duluth had a comfortable 2-0 lead.

The Badgers tightened up their defense in the final period but couldn't get any pucks past the talented Duluth goalie, Mitchell. Wisconsin kept Duluth scoreless in the third period, but it wasn't enough. The young Badger squad was shut out by the Duluth Curling Club in the first exhibition game of the Christmas trip, 2-0. Duluth goalie Don Mitchell was clearly the game's most valuable player as he turned away many quality shots from the visitors and kept them completely off the scoreboard.

Unbeknownst to any players or participants at the time, future Badgers were directly involved with the host side of this matchup. Duluth goaltender Don Mitchell would become the starting goalie for the Wisconsin Badgers the following year in 1926-27 season. The referee for this exhibition game, Willis "Rube" Brandow would replace Kay Iverson as the head coach at Wisconsin the next season.

Wisconsin Lineup: captain Gross (Center), Kneebone (Right Wing), Whiteside (Left Wing), Ruf (Right Defenseman), Murphy (Left Defenseman) and McLean (Goalie). Substitutes: Chamberlain and Jansky. Penalties: Wisconsin 0, Duluth 4. Referee: Willis R. Brandow from Duluth.

The Badgers traveled another hour north in Minnesota to take on two opponents in as many days in Eveleth. UW played the Eveleth Cubs December 31 and the Eveleth Junior College Norseman January 1. They were soundly defeated by scores of 7-0 and 2-0 against the highly skilled Eveleth skaters.

The final exhibition game of the tour was against a team from Virginia, Minnesota. The closely contested match found the Badgers on top earning a 3-2 victory.

Every day since Christmas of this school year, the Badgers practiced with the teams from Duluth, Eveleth and Virginia, Minnesota. The Minnesota skaters enjoyed the on-ice workouts and friendly pickup games with the college guys from the UW.

The proposed Northern Intercollegiate Hockey association was formed in January 1926. In total, 16 Midwestern schools organized to make up the new hockey conference. After the January meeting, it was announced that the following schools would participate in the NIHA: Wisconsin, Notre Dame, Marquette, Michigan, Michigan State, Michigan College of Mines, North Dakota University, North Dakota Agricultural College, Carleton, St. Thomas, St. Olaf, Macalester, Minnesota and the junior colleges of Eveleth and Hibbing. The new hockey association was set to tentatively begin in 1927. It proved to be too lofty of a plan since grouping so many schools into one mega hockey conference was not practical at the time.

Gross

Lidicker

Ted Gross from Duluth was the captain for the 1925-26 Wisconsin hockey team. He was a highly competitive and athletic skater. Captain Gross was a superb student athlete that was well qualified to lead the Badger in both practices and games. He was known for his aggressive style of play and played through several injuries that would have sidelined most men. He was a star center for the UW team and made countless contributions to the success of this year's team. Gross was joined by his close friend and gifted linemate Bill Lidicker. Lidicker was a naturally talented offensive skater and was adept as a two-way player. His brand of offense was also balanced with defensive play and helped keep opponents frustrated.

1925-26 Wisconsin Hockey Team

On January 6, a group of Midwest college hockey head coaches met to revise some of the standard rules of the game of hockey. Specifically, the major and minor penalties were addressed so that the integrity of the game would remain intact while also protecting the players.

It was agreed that the following would define Major penalties: (a) deliberately disabling an opponent by hitting, (b) hooking or cross checking with the stick, (c) deliberately kicking an opponent with one's skate, (d) throwing a stick which might prevent a goal, (e) offensive or profane language aimed at an official, opponent or spectator, or any other conduct unbecoming to good sportsmanship. Any player deemed to have committed a Major penalty would either be ejected from the game or required to sit out a five-minute penalty in the penalty box.

This committee also defined what would constitute a Minor penalty: (a) deliberately cross- checking an opponent, (b) deliberately tripping an opponent, (c) deliberately charging an opponent, (d) deliberately delaying the game, (e) deliberately loafing offside, (f) deliberately holding an opponent by the uniform, body or stick, (g) offside interference, (h) deliberately charging the goaltender to score or otherwise and (i) ragging or stalling the puck. A player who commits a Minor penalty will be required to sit in the penalty box for either one minute or two minutes, as determined by the referee.

The first home series of the 1925-26 season for Wisconsin featured the Marquette Hilltoppers visiting the Madison campus. Before these games, coach Iverson exclaimed to the sports reporters, "We play Marquette Friday and Saturday. Both games will be hard fought thrillers. Madison students and townspeople are in for a treat if they have never seen this game of speed, thrills, and sheer nerve played as it should be played." (3)

On January 8, the daily training the UW skaters received during their tour of northern Minnesota in preparation for the season paid off as the Badgers crushed the Marquette team 11-0 in a blowout. A crowd in excess of three thousand people watched the Wisconsin skaters make the Hilltoppers look foolish in this one-sided game. It was the largest crowd to ever observe a UW hockey game in Madison, Wisconsin.

An unlikely star of this event was not even on the ice. It was the former head coach of the hockey team and current UW Swimming coach Joe Steinauer. The coach put on his own show as he led the crowd in various cheers and demonstrated how students could keep warm with his dancing antics. He was so popular interacting with the crowd that officials from the Wisconsin hockey program urged him to return often in his role as head cheerleader during the home games on the lower campus. In addition, university officials added more bleachers to accommodate the overflowing crowds.

Star captain Ted Gross started the scoring onslaught with a quick goal that got the rowdy crowd into the game early. Gross found the rebound after teammate Lidicker shot the puck on net. Coach Iverson was trying some radical new hockey game strategies at the time by making frequent player substitutions. This allowed the Badgers to keep the pressure on with continually rested players that overwhelmed the visiting team. One of those subs, Jim Whiteside, rose to the occasion and took advantage of nearly every opportunity he had on the ice. Even as a sub, Whiteside was able to demonstrate his skills and racked up an impressive five goals against Marquette. Captain Gross notched two goals. Over three thousand fans were in attendance for contest. One of the biggest crowds ever recorded for a home Wisconsin Badgers hockey game to date.

It was a cold night in Madison and coach Iverson wanted to ensure that a large crowd would return with similar numbers for their future games. In between periods he announced to the home crowd that the university would be installing several outdoor heaters so that spectators would have some of the comforts offered by an indoor rink while watching the hockey action.

Wisconsin Lineup: captain Gross (Center), Chamberlain (Right Wing), Lidicker (Left Wing), McCarter (Right Defense), Moorhead (Left Defense) and McLean (Goalie). Substitutes: Jansky (Right Wing), Sarles (Left Wing), Whiteside (Center) and Murphy (Goalie). Scoring: Whiteside 5, Gross 2, Jansky 1, Moorhead 1, Sarles 1 and McCarter 1. Referee: Jake Thompson from the Milwaukee Athletic Club.

The following day, January 9, the Marquette team was able to regroup and play a more respectable game. In a change of tactical strategy, the Marquette players intentionally stacked up players in front of their own net to thwart the numerous attacks by Wisconsin. In fact, they were three and four players deep in front of their own goalie. This radical defensive posturing frustrated the Badger offense and greatly diminished their scoring chances. The first period was fairly even except for the Hilltopper player that was sent to serve a penalty for wielding his stick as a weapon, rather than using it as an integral piece of hockey equipment.

It was rising star Jimmy Whiteside that scored first for the Badgers toward the end of the second period. The number of penalties called in the second period were plentiful as players from both teams served time for their various rule infractions. The timekeeper was especially busy since he was also in charge of the penalty boxes.

In the third period, captain Gross was finally able to score his first goal of the game to give the Badgers a 2-0 lead. A short while later Lidicker scored again for Wisconsin. In the end, Marquette lost by a score of 3-0. Another huge crowd showed up to watch this game. It was nearly as cold as the night before so the spectators stomped their feet, clapped their hands and participated in several cheers in attempts to keep warm as they kept themselves and the others entertained. When the timekeeper fired his starters pistol to signal the end of the game the crowd stayed for quite a while to keep the party going.

Wisconsin Lineup: captain Gross (Center), Chamberlain (Right Wing), Lidicker (Left Wing), McCarter (Right Defense), Moorhead (Left Defense) and McLean (Goalie). Substitutes: Whiteside (Center), Jansky (Right Wing), Sarles (Left Wing) and Murphy (Goalie).

Thanks to the continued enthusiasm expressed by coach Steinauer, the crowd again had a wonderful time cheering and dancing during the game to show appreciation for their team and to thwart the lingering effects of the bitterly cold weather. It was estimated that more than six thousand plus spectators were on hand to watch both of these games against Marquette at the UW campus.

The Wisconsin hockey team had a few days to try to get in more practice before the University of Minnesota series. Coming off a pair of wins, the Badgers were highly confident they would perform well against the Gophers.

A week after the Marquette series, the traditionally strong Minnesota Gophers returned to the Badger rink to face the UW skaters for the latest matchup in this growing rivalry. Adding to the intensity of this clash was the fact that it would be another battle between the Iverson brothers, Kay for the Badgers and Emil for the Gophers.

The opening game January 15 was set for 7:30 p.m. Right away, the combatants for both teams took turns going back and forth in a defensive lockup. Each goaltender put on a classic display blanking all shooters. Unseasonably warm weather again wreaked havoc with the playing surface causing the ice to be slushy and slow. The two teams had no choice but to accept the demise of the ice. Players had trouble moving the puck and several fluky shots entertained the crowd.

It was a remarkable defensive chess match as the first, second and third periods were all played without any goals scored. Wisconsin and Minnesota would need overtime to determine a clear winner. After the 10-minute overtime, the game remained scoreless and the teams were forced to accept a 0-0 tie. The coaches for both teams agreed only one extra period would be played this night. It would go in the record books as a scoreless tie.

UW goalie McLean impressed the players and spectators alike with his performance. He singlehandedly stopped multiple scoring chances from the northern invaders. McLean made a total of 14 quality saves in this match. The Badgers were more proficient in the big body checking part of this game. The Wisconsin players sent several Gophers sprawling during this game to the delight of the home crowd. Lidicker sat out a one-minute penalty for offside interference, an infraction that both coaches agreed before the game would not be allowed and referee Thompson was watching for it. Chamberlain was also called for charging. Holding Minnesota to a scoreless game was a huge victory as far as the Wisconsin side was concerned. The Badger players were looking forward to the next game on the following day.

Wisconsin Lineup: captain Gross (Center), Lidicker (Right Wing), Jansky (Left Wing), McCarter (Right Defense), Moorhead (Left Defense) and McLean (Goalie). Substitutes: Whiteside, Chamberlain, Sarles, Murphy, Carrier and Carlson. Saves: Wisconsin 14, Minnesota 11. Referee: Jake Thompson from the Milwaukee Athletic Club. Timekeeper: Fry from Wisconsin.

"Spike" Carlson had worked tirelessly to get back into the lineup by mid-January. He had beaten the odds recovering from a major injury. During his freshman season in 1923, he broke his neck after hitting the goal net on the during practice on the Lower Campus Rink. Game No. 2 took place on the following day at 3:30 p.m. The January 16 match was also subject to poor ice as a result of the mild weather. Another large and rowdy crowd showed up to voice their excitement during every play. The two powerhouse teams battled back and forth in a very close matchup.

There was a considerable delay after one of the Minnesota skaters crashed violently into the Wisconsin goal post and was severely injured. It was unclear whether a Wisconsin skater helped him to find the post in a creative defensive play. The Badgers were very focused on keeping the crease clear at all times, especially during attacks from the opposition.

Wisconsin players continued their heavy hitting and put several big body checks on the guest players in the opening period. Minnesota opened the scoring in the second period when their captain shot the puck over Badger goalie McLean to take a short-lived lead. A few moments later Teddy Gross picked up the puck in his own end and charged up the middle of the ice. He ripped a shot that breached the Gopher crease for a Wisconsin goal. Although there were multiple attempts by both teams the third period was scoreless. At the end of regulation, the Gophers were again embarrassed to be locked up in a 1-1 tie with the Badger team.

McLean

Yet another 10-minute overtime failed to distinguish a clear winner and it was officially recorded as a 1-1 tie. Upward of thirty-five hundred spectators watched the tightly contested matches between the Badger and Gopher skaters this weekend and were wildly delighted with the level of play.

McLean, the starting Wisconsin goaltender, was a sure bet for MVP of the weekend series as he repeatedly shut down the Gopher attacks and consistently made saves on what should have been goals. He was credited with 11 saves in the second game versus the Minnesota Gophers. In addition, it was discovered after the game that McLean was playing with a painful cracked rib. It was not known how long "Mac" would be out of the Wisconsin lineup with the upper body injury.

Wisconsin head coach Kay Iverson was thrilled that his Badger hockey team was able to hold the mighty Minnesota Gopher hockey squad to a pair of ties over the weekend. The only thing that would have made the weekend more spectacular would have been a couple of wins for the club.

Wisconsin Lineup: captain Gross (Center), Lidicker (Right Wing), Jansky (Left Wing), McCarter (Right Defense), Moorhead (Left Defense) and McLean (Goalie). Substitutes: Whiteside, Chamberlain and Sarles. Saves: Wisconsin 11, Minnesota 6. Referee: Jake Thompson from the Milwaukee Athletic Club. Time Keeper: Fry from Wisconsin.

The Badger players had a recover and train following the prior series. McLean got some much-needed rest and was expected to be in the lineup for the upcoming series against Janesville. The Lower Campus Rink was outfitted with arc lighting so hockey workouts could occur at night. The Badgers hockey team took full advantage and trained several hours a day. Many of those practices went well into the night. Due to the continued surge in popularity, the sport of hockey continued to pique the curiosity of UW students and townspeople passing by the rink. More and more people were stopping to watch practices this year than ever before.

During the weekend of January 22 and January 23, the Janesville (Wisconsin) YMCA Athletic Club made a return visit to Madison. The weather was ideal for ice in the first game but was not welcoming to any potential spectators. The 7:30 p.m. faceoff was a challenge for players and spectators alike. The temperatures were bitterly cold and caused attendance among hockey fans to drop to just a few hundred, down several thousand fans in comparison to the prior weekend. And fans steadily trickled away from the game as the night went on. In what was not entirely uncommon at the time, coach Bergman, the leader of the Janesville Hockey Club, laced up the skates to play center and help his team to keep the game close. Bergman was also the director of the Janesville YMCA.

Coach Iverson switched up his lineup to get his second team some experience in starting a game and rendered his usual starters to the role of substitute players. Eight minutes into the opening period, Wisconsin's Lidicker scored an unassisted goal. One minute later, captain Teddy Gross scored on a beautiful pass from his teammate Jansky. Badger spare Mike Murphy scored on an unassisted goal when he pushed the puck past the Janesville goalie from a tricky angle. Murphy would score again in the third period, but Referee Thompson waived it off declaring the puck was kicked in during an offside violation. Bergman played a strong game for the visitors, but he was unable to get any worthwhile offense going for Janesville. The game was clearly dominated by Wisconsin and Janesville was shut out in the eventual 3-0 loss.

Interesting to note, the Janesville team was made up of veteran working-class men that played for the love of the game. In the three years this team had been around, they most enjoyed playing against the college boys at Madison. Both teams shared exceptional sportsmanship and kept the games friendly, even during the most heated competitions.

Wisconsin Lineup: Chamberlain (Center), Kneebone (Right Wing), Whiteside (Left Wing), McCarter (Right Defense), Murphy (Left Defense) and McLean (Goalie). Substitutes: Ruf, captain Gross, Jansky, Lidicker, Carlson, Carrier and Moorhead. Referee: Jake Thompson from the Milwaukee Athletic Club. Time Keeper: Fry from Wisconsin.

The second game started on the following day at 3:30 p.m. The weather remained bitterly cold for this contest as well and kept the spectators well below a couple of hundred sitting in the bleachers or standing on the perimeter to watch. Captain Ted Gross put on another display of superior hockey abilities in this game. He scored in the opening period and so did Lidicker for the UW. Gross scored again for the cardinal and white in the second period.

The men from the YMCA team tried to remain competitive but were outmatched by the college players from Wisconsin. Gross and Lidicker both scored again in the third period as they recorded a 5-0 victory over Janesville. It was an impressive hat trick for captain Gross in this match. To no surprise, Gross was the finest hockey player this weekend. Wisconsin won both games against Janesville and kept their opponents scoreless.

Wisconsin Lineup: Chamberlain (Center), Lidicker (Right Wing), Jansky (Left Wing), McCarter (Right Defense), Moorhead (Left Defense) and McLean (Goalie). Substitutes: Whiteside, Jansky, Kneebone, Carrier and Murphy.

After the Janesville games, coach Iverson would let his players have the week off from practices and workouts so they could focus on their exams. Afterward they would reconvene to prepare for Notre Dame and then a pair of games at Michigan.

The rigors of final exams did not go well for some Wisconsin hockey players. Star goalie George McLean, winger Ross Chamberlain and defensemen Al Moorhead were deemed academically ineligible to participate on the UW team. They didn't pass their exams as required to maintain athletic eligibility. Coach Kay Iverson had to rely on other players to make up for the huge loss.

At this point in the season the Wisconsin Badgers were still undefeated and held the top spot in the standings. This was a result of the Badgers sweeping Marquette and playing to a tie in both games against Minnesota. The only conference goal scored against Wisconsin in conference play was the lone goal scored by the Gophers. However, there were a lot of games left and the team was compromised with the loss of players due to eligibility challenges. Iverson would only be able to squeeze in about three decent practices before his men took on the Fighting Irish hockey team.

Jansky

Lidicker

Whiteside

McCarter

Carlson   **Carrier**

A February 6 game had the Badgers hosting the University of Notre Dame hockey team. The Fighting Irish skaters were a serious opponent and had accomplished great results over the past few years including a championship. The Wisconsin hockey team was as prepared as they could be for this 2:30 p.m. Saturday matchup. The Badgers played smart and aggressively as they challenged the Irish in every aspect of this game. Soft ice made play difficult for both squads. At the end of the first, the game remained scoreless.

The Fighting Irish scored a few minutes in to the second period and took a 1-0 lead. Wisconsin continued to battle and got their break when Badger star defenseman McCarter rushed up the ice with the puck and drove toward the net where he snapped a hard shot that beat the Notre Dame goalie and tied up the game at 1-1. The two teams fought to the end of the third, but the score remained tied.

Since coach Tom Lieb and his Notre Dame Fighting Irish players had a train connection to make in order to return to Indiana, it was not possible to play any overtime periods to determine a clear winner. Begrudgingly, both teams accepted a 1-1 tie as the final score. The Badgers were fortunate to get out with a tie since the Irish kept the puck in the Wisconsin zone most of this game. Coach Iverson was very happy with the play of rising star Harold Ruf in goal.

An estimated crowd of over one thousand spectators showed up for this match. This included several hundred students, along with a large number of curious citizens who were in attendance to watch this well-fought game on the UW-Madison campus.

Wisconsin Lineup: Whiteside (Center), Lidicker (Right Wing), Jansky (Left Wing), Murphy (Right Defense), McCarter (Left Defense) and Ruf (Goalie). Substitute: captain Gross. Referee: Jake Thomsen from the Milwaukee Athletic Club. Time Keepers: Steinauer and Fry from Wisconsin.

The Goal Judge keeps a watchful eye on the goal during the Wisconsin varsity hockey game

Coach Iverson ran his boys through a week of hard drills in order to be sufficiently prepared for the upcoming series against Michigan. Focus was on filling the holes that UW goalie McLean and right defenseman Moorhead left on the Badger hockey team roster since they were not permitted to play due to academic ineligibility after failing to pass their exams. Michigan also had the advantage of a rink with artificial ice, not dependent upon cooperative weather.

On Thursday, February 11, the Badger hockey team left Madison at noon. They had to make the journey to Ann Arbor, Michigan to face the always dangerous Michigan Wolverines. Wisconsin would be without three key players who were academically ineligible so coach Iverson had to get creative with his roster. Harold Ruf from Green Bay, Wisconsin would replace McLean and Mike Murphy from Manitowoc, Wisconsin would take over for Moorhead. The UW hockey squad making this trip consisted of 10 players: Ruf, Murphy, McCarter, Jansky, Lidicker, captain Gross, Kneebone, Carrier,

Carlson and Whiteside. Along with coach Iverson was team manager Buetihe.

These two teams matched up pretty evenly. Through the first and second periods the game remained scoreless. Karl Jansky of Wisconsin was able to score the first goal of the match early in the third period. With a last-ditch effort, Michigan forced the puck past the UW goalkeeper with only seven seconds left on the clock in the third period to tie the game at one all.

A 10-minute overtime of additional play was unable to determine a definite winner. Wisconsin reluctantly left the rink with a 1-1 tie. The Michigan Wolverines were especially thankful to get that score, especially considering they were outplayed offensively for most of the game until the lucky goal was scored with a few seconds to go in regulation play.

Wisconsin Lineup: captain Gross (Center), Jansky (Right Wing), Lidicker (Left Wing), Murphy (Right Defense), McCarter (Left Defense) and Ruf (Goalie). Substitutes: Kneebone, Carrier, Carlson and Whiteside. Referee: Bradfield from Windsor.

During the second game of the series the following afternoon, both teams got off to a fast start right after the opening faceoff. Each team was able to score a goal in the first few minutes of the game. Michigan opened the scoring with a goal on a difficult angle and Karl Jansky tied the game at 1-1 moments later with a long shot that fooled the Michigan netminder.

It was end to end action after that as the Badgers and Wolverines made spectacular plays to stop goals and get the puck out of their own ends. Each goaltender made skillful saves and turned away many scoring attempts. Michigan's captain netted their second goal of the game to give the home team a 2-1 lead. Despite the best attempts from the Badger squad the third period was scoreless when the game clock expired.

The Wisconsin hockey team left town with a 2-1 loss. However, this was a great showing by the Badgers considering the Wolverines won the Northwest Intercollegiate Hockey League championship last season. Captain Gross was looking forward to a few days of rest in order to heal several injuries he received during the Michigan hockey series.

Wisconsin Lineup: captain Gross (Center), Jansky (Right Wing), Lidicker (Left Wing), Murphy (Right Defense), McCarter (Left Defense) and Ruf (Goalie). Substitutes: Kneebone and Whiteside. Referee: Bradfield from Windsor.

Kneebohm **Moorhead** **Murphy**

Carleton College, located in Northfield, Minnesota, sent their hockey team to the UW campus to compete against the Badgers February 19 and 20. Historically, Carleton made easy work of the Wisconsin team and was used to handing them losses. In the first game, Wisconsin went right after their guests as soon as the puck dropped and kept the pressure on with new plays from coach Iverson and his experienced UW skaters.

Team captain Ted Gross, who was still recovering from injuries sustained the week prior during the Michigan series, was suited up and saw enough ice time to tally a goal for the Badgers. The goal judge standing directly behind the Carleton net raised his arm to signal the goal was good! Gross was only able to play the last few minutes of the first period exiting the game after he scored as his injuries prevented him from participating further.

In the third period, Whiteside, one of the better Badger skaters, made an incredible play by stickhandling through the entire Carleton squad and scored. It was said to be one of the finest goals ever scored on the Madison rink to date.

Late in the third period frustrations were heightened for Carleton after they assumed they scored. Referee Thompson waved the goal off since he witnessed the Carleton player smack the puck into the Wisconsin net using his glove while sprawled on the ice.

The Wisconsin skaters defeated Carleton College, 2-0. Spectators described this game as one highlighted by excessive roughness and impressive speed from both teams. Badger goalie Ruf was credited with the shutout, allowing no goals after many fine attempts by the visitors.

Wisconsin Lineup: Whiteside (Center), Jansky (Right Wing), Lidicker (Left Wing), McCarter (Right Defense), Murphy (Left Defense) and Ruf (Goalie). Substitutes: captain Gross, Boyer and Carrier. Penalties: Wisconsin - Gross two-minutes for rushing goalminder, McCarter two-minutes for tripping, Murphy two (2) two-minute penalties for checking in mid-ice. Carleton - one checking at mid-ice infraction and three tripping violations. Referee: Jake Thompson from the Milwaukee Athletic Club.

The following day, Carleton College didn't take long to find the back of the net. The visitors scored three minutes into the game and again with three minutes left in the opening period. The visitors had a 2-0 lead at the end of the first period. Coach Iverson gave his players a stern talk that hit home before the start of the second.

Wisconsin clearly turned up the pressure and put the heat on the Carleton netminder. One minute into the middle period, captain Todd Gross scored for Wisconsin even though he was still visibly dealing with injuries obtained during the Michigan series. Just 10 seconds later, Lidicker tied the game at 2-2. With eight minutes left in the second period, Lidicker scored again to give the Badgers a 3-2 lead.

The third period started with the Badgers leading 3-2. Bill Lidicker was still hot and put a shot on goal that appeared covered and in control of the Carleton goaltender. But Wisconsin's wingers charged the net as the save was made and the visiting netminder had the puck slip into his goal. The UW squad now had a 4-2 advantage. Lidicker had notched a hat trick with his three goals in this game. No other goals were scored for either side. Wisconsin won the game, 4-2.

Wisconsin Lineup: captain Gross (Center), Jansky (Right Wing), Lidicker (Left Wing), McCarter (Right Defense), Murphy (Left Defense) and Ruf (Goalie). Substitutes: Carrier, Kneebone and Whiteside. Penalties: Wisconsin - McCarter twice for tripping two minutes each time, Murphy twice for tripping and once for slashing - two minutes each time, Jansky tripping two-

minute penalty and Gross tripping two-minute penalty. Carleton - three tripping penalties and one charging the netminder penalty. Referee: Jake Thompson from the Milwaukee Athletic Club. Time Keepers: Fry, Messare, Larson, Schwarz and Weathers.

During construction of the new Field House next to the Camp Randall Football Stadium, coach Kay Iverson made it known he would be strongly lobbying for an indoor hockey rink. Iverson's vision had the current gymnasium set up in the Red Gym getting converted to a hockey rink with artificial ice. A new gymnasium could easily be moved into the new Field House and the vacant space in the Red Gym would be an ideal space to convert into Wisconsin's new indoor hockey rink. His vision for the Badgers to have an indoor rink on the University of Wisconsin campus that would accommodate thousands of spectators would not come to fruition for another 73 years.

Michigan was scheduled to return to Madison February 26 and 27 but Mother Nature had other plans. After spring-like rains that came down a couple of days before the weekend, incredibly heavy snow storms followed that destroyed the Lower Campus Rink playing surface. The series against the Wolverines would have to be delayed at least a week before the games could be played in Madison. Michigan was going to swing up to Minnesota for an early pair of games against the Gophers before coming back down to face off against the Badgers. Since the Wisconsin hockey team did not have any decent ice for skating, they were back at the Red Gym every afternoon and evening participating in rigorous gymnastics workouts. Coach Iverson was expertly trained in the Swedish system of gymnastics when he attended school in Copenhagen, Denmark. The hope was that the extraordinary conditioning and workouts would give them a better chance to be prepared since on-ice workouts were not an option.

Due to weather issues, the Michigan Wolverines were rescheduled for Thursday, March 4 and Friday, March 5 in Madison. The prior meeting between these two teams had games that were filled with all sorts of hockey violence. Michigan elected not to follow the collegiate rules of ice hockey that Midwestern schools were expected to follow. Rather, the Wolverines chose to instead follow the Canadian professional rules of hockey which allowed for more physical play without consequence. Several Wisconsin players were injured during the last series between these programs. Coach Iverson was hoping for more civility and sportsmanship during the next series. The Badger players were more than ready to go with a rough style of hockey when they played Michigan again.

The Badgers and the Gophers remained tied for first place in the WIHL and the only undefeated teams in conference play at this point in the season. Wisconsin had scored 33 goals against their opponents while only allowing six to be scored against them.

During the first game against Michigan Thursday night, the Badgers came out flying and played an aggressive offensive game with some great passing plays as they defended their own net and attacked the visitor's goal. In a game dominated by physical play, the UW men were able to get the best of their Wolverine counterparts. Excessively rough play by Michigan would lead to their demise. Wisconsin's Karl Jansky scored the first goal while three Wolverines were in the penalty box. His shot at the net was inadvertently aided by a misplaced Michigan player's stick as the puck ricocheted past the Michigan goaltender.

McCarter scored on a beautiful play that put the Badgers up 2-0. It was a rebound shot from Whiteside during the second period. In the third period Michigan's strategy was to use a five-man offense, but Wisconsin was able to fend off all but one of their attempts to score. With less than three minutes to play, the Wolverines scored their lone goal. The Badgers won with a 2-1 score. Although it was reported that the Michigan players outweighed the slenderer Wisconsin players by an average of 45 pounds, they did not possess the speed, strength and determination exhibited by the victorious UW squad. This victory put Wisconsin in contention for a Big Ten championship series against Minnesota. It was an especially impressive showing when taking into consideration that the Badgers only had two days of decent weather for hockey practice on their home rink. Harold Ruf put on a stellar goaltending show stopping nearly every shot fired in his direction. Ruf was credited with 26 saves in this contest.

Wisconsin Lineup: captain Gross (Center), Jansky (Right Wing), Lidicker (Left Wing), McCarter (Right Defense), Murphy (Left Defense) and Ruf (Goalie). Substitutes: Carrier, Kneebone and Whiteside. Saves: Wisconsin 26, Michigan 14. Penalties: Wisconsin - Lidicker one minute for holding, McCarter 2 - two minutes for body checking and two minutes for holding, Murphy

two minutes for tripping and two minutes for holding, Gross two minutes for tripping and Whiteside two minutes for tripping. Michigan - 14 minutes in penalties for violations that included tripping, loafing, body checking and throwing the puck. Referee: Jake Thomsen from M.A.C. Timekeeper: Fry from Wisconsin.

Action during the Wisconsin versus Michigan hockey game

The second game started at 4:30 p.m. Friday, Coach Iverson had his team ready to execute another intelligent and aggressive game plan as they outhustled and outscored the Wolverines again. This was another particularly rough game and there was no love lost between these two rivals. After a scoreless first period, McCarter got the scoring started for Wisconsin 16 minutes into the second period. He skated the puck down the rink, weaving in and out of the Michigan opponents, and drove a powerful shot at the Wolverine net that bounced off the defenseman's chest and dropped in front of the net allowing McCarter to slam home the rebound for a goal. In the third period, Lidicker picked up the puck in the Michigan zone and, with a hard shot that deflected off a Wolverines defender, scored the second goal for the cardinal and white squad.

The rough play continued throughout this game and exploded in the final period. The Wolverines were clearly the main aggressor in this contest and were called for nine penalties. The Badgers were only charged with three penalties. Wisconsin recorded the win with a 2-0 score. Badger forward Karl Jansky continued to make a name for himself this weekend and his superior skating speed did not go unnoticed. Wisconsin goalie Harold Ruf was again the star of the game and was credited with 13 saves and a shutout after not allowing any goals. It was the first time a Wisconsin team had recorded a pair of wins over the University of Michigan team. Many spectators, estimated to be around three thousand or more, came out to watch this exciting hockey match.

Wisconsin Lineup: captain Gross (Center), Jansky (Right Wing), Lidicker (Left Wing), Whiteside (Right Defense), Murphy (Left Defense) and Ruf (Goalie). Substitutes: Carrier, Kneebone and McCarter. Saves: Wisconsin 13, Michigan 27. Penalties: Wisconsin - Gross one minute for holding and two minutes for tripping, Whiteside two minutes for roughing. Michigan - 16 minutes in penalties for violations that included tripping, roughing and charging. Referee: Jake Thompson from the Milwaukee Athletic Club.

Coach Iverson was in communication with Portage City officials that wanted the University of Wisconsin hockey team to return for another exhibition hockey match Saturday, March 6. Last season, coach Iverson mixed up his two lines to make two teams, Team Portage and Team Wisconsin that demonstrated the game of hockey to the enjoyment of all that were around to watch the game. The event was a huge success and thoroughly enjoyed by the locals. If the weather cooperated, the Badger team would return to the Portage Curling Club. The scrimmage game was scheduled to begin at 8 p.m. and spectators would be charged 50 cents for adults and 25 cents for children.

After a few weeks of planning and preparation the Wisconsin Badgers exhibition game in Portage was unexpectedly canceled a few hours before it was set to begin. University of Wisconsin Athletic Director, George Little, would not allow the game to go on as planned. Little cited the fact that he was not made aware of the plans for the scrimmage game and, after the physically grueling session against Michigan, the Badger hockey team was not cleared to play a fun game.

Harold Ruf, the Wisconsin Varsity Goalkeeper

Last on the season schedule was a mid-week return trip to face the perennially tough Minnesota Gophers hockey team at the Minneapolis Arena. Bringing an 8-1-4 record with them into the Twin Cities, the Wisconsin club was having the best season in the history of the program. The Wednesday, March 10 game had a lot on the line before the referee even dropped the puck since these two teams were fighting for the Big Ten and Western Intercollegiate Hockey League (WIHL) championship.

The Badgers had never previously won a conference championship and this season they were as close as they had ever been. An unusually large crowd was on hand and witnessed an extremely fast and hard-fought game between the border rivals.

The Badger skaters were virtually shorthanded as a good number of their men were slowed or missing due to injuries. Mike Murphy, a Wisconsin player, had his glasses broken during practice before the first game even though he was wearing protective metal wire eyewear designed to allow spectacles to be used during hockey action. His broken glasses left Murphy unable to adequately see and would likely keep him out of both games against Minnesota. Edwin Carlson was slated to fill the lineup void left by Murphy. Coach Iverson made the difficult decision to play Murphy anyway. Even with his vision compromised since he was without his eye glasses, he was the most talented defenseman they had. Murphy would play both games in their entirety.

Michigan jumped out to a two-goal lead. UW captain Ted Gross, who was still banged up from the prior series against Michigan, played this game against the Gophers. Gross scored in the second period for Wisconsin to cut the Minnesota led to 2-1. Then in the third period, Lidicker scored for the Badgers to tie it at 2-2. The Gophers scored twice more in the final period to snag a 4-2 win over the visiting UW team. The win clinched the Big Ten title for Minnesota in front of two thousand hockey fans.

Wisconsin Lineup: captain Gross (Center), Jansky (Right Wing), Lidicker (Left Wing), McCarter (Right Defense), Murphy (Left Defense) and Ruf (Goalie). Substitutes: Whiteside, Carlson and Kneebone. Penalties: Wisconsin 2, Minnesota 0. Referee: Nick Kahler from Minneapolis. Umpire: Jack Thomson from M.A.C.

Thursday, March 11 was another key matchup for the Badgers and the Gophers. The start time was 8:15 p.m. at the Minneapolis Arena. Action was relatively even at the beginning with both teams trying to mount offensive attacks that were shut down. Minnesota scored with two minutes left in the first period to take a 1-0 lead. Both teams played an extremely fast and hard-fought game with a heightened level of intensity. The spectators saw another exhilarating game as the two teams went end-to-end and displayed their skating and playmaking time and time again. A scoreless second period set up an exciting finish in the third.

Wisconsin outplayed Minnesota in the final two periods, evidenced by the Badgers 32 shots on goal versus the Gophers 27. Minnesota lucked out with a goal 15 minutes into the final period to put them up 2-0. Refusing to quit, the Badgers battled on and Lidicker scored on the Gophers with under four minutes left to make it 2-1. But it was not enough. When time expired the Gophers had a 2-1 win over the respected cardinal and white visitors. It was the last game of the season for both teams.

Wisconsin Lineup: captain Gross (Center), Jansky (Right Wing), Lidicker (Left Wing), McCarter (Right Defense), Murphy (Left Defense) and Ruf (Goalie). Substitutes: Whiteside, Carlson and Kneebone. Penalties: Wisconsin: 7, Minnesota 3. Referee: Nick Kahler from Minneapolis. Umpire: Jake Thomsen from M.A.C.

The Badgers had completed one of their most impressive seasons to date. Ultimately, Wisconsin's final regular season record of 8-3-4 earned them a tie for first place. They won the Western Intercollegiate Hockey Association championship, a championship they begrudgingly shared with their northern neighbors, the Gophers. However, it was the best finish in the history of the Wisconsin hockey program. They also finished second in the Big Ten. The hometown fans, students, faculty and UW Athletic Department savored the championship season and the growing tradition of winning hockey at the University of Wisconsin.

The majority of games this season were played in front of standing room only crowds. The popularity of hockey and ice skating continued to grow as the University of Wisconsin had five skating rinks on campus and one on Lake Mendota this year. The crowds for both practice and games continued to increase this season from past seasons and the UW skaters were able to get a considerable advantage over visiting teams due in large part to their rowdy fans cheering them on.

After the Wisconsin hockey team achieved their best finish in the history of the program, Head coach Kay Iverson vacated his position without warning in late March 1926. He had decided to take the head coaching post with Marquette University, one of Wisconsin's biggest rivals. While at the UW, Iverson was only a part-time employee and he wanted a full-time position with a university. Shortly before departing campus Iverson remarked, "Wherever I go I will always have a warm spot in my heart for Wisconsin and I will always be a well-wisher for the athletic success of this institution." (4)

Iverson recommended 10 members of the hockey team to receive their "W' varsity letter for their meritorious work this season on the ice. Up for the award were: Ted Gross, captain; William Lidicker, captain elect; John McCarter, Mike Murphy, Edwin Carlson, Tom Kneebone, James Whiteside, Harold Ruff, Karl Jansky and Earl Carrier. Justifying his nominations, Iverson said, "these men have worked hard for the success of their team and are all equally deserving of their varsity letter. The loss of Gross, Carlson and Whiteside (to graduation) while a hard blow, is not irreparable as the freshman squad has a number of star men, and next year Wisconsin should win the championship." (4) In May, the Wisconsin Athletic Board passed the motion to issue awards including Iverson's recommendation awarding varsity letters to the Badger hockey players.

Years later when reflecting upon the 1925-26 season, senior UW player, William "Bill" Sarles recalled his toughest decision made as a varsity hockey team member. "I was on the hockey team and a trip to northern Wisconsin was scheduled over the Christmas vacation. Also scheduled was a meeting of the Society of American Bacteriologists. I had to decide then and there whether to be a BMOC (Big Man on Campus) or a bacteriologist. I went to the meeting." (5) Sarles would earn his Bachelor of Science from the University of Wisconsin in 1926, his Master of Science in 1927, his doctorate in 1931 and eventually became a distinguished professor of Agricultural Bacteriology at the University of Wisconsin.

1925-26   Schedule and Results:
Coach Kay Iverson
4-3-3 Tied for first in WIHL and second in Big Ten   9-6-4 Overall

Date	Result	Opponent
December 26	Loss 2-0	@Duluth*
December 31	Loss 7-0	@ Eveleth (MN) Cubs*
January 1	Loss 2-0	@ Eveleth (MN) Junior College*

January 2	Win 3-2	@ Virginia*
January 8	Win 11-0	Marquette
January 9	Win 3-0	Marquette
January 15	Tie 0-0 OT	Minnesota
January 16	Tie 1-1 OT	Minnesota
January 22	Win 3-0	Janesville*.
January 23	Win 5-0	Janesville*
February 6	Tie 1-1	Notre Dame*
February 12	Tie 1-1 OT	@ Michigan
February 13	Loss 2-1	@ Michigan
February 19	Win 2-0	Carleton*
February 20	Win 4-2	Carleton*
March 4	Win 2-1	Michigan
March 5	Win 2-0	Michigan
March 10	Loss 4-2	@Minnesota
March 11	Loss 2-1	@Minnesota

*Exhibition Games

Chapter Eight
Karl Jansky

1926-27 UW Hockey Team

The Director of Athletics, George Little, and the captain of the UW hockey team, Bill Lidicker, worked on trying to find a new coach. The Badger hockey players reported for tryouts and conditioning in early December, as was normal at the start of every season.

Tom Lieb, the head coach of the Wisconsin Track squad, was directed to take on the role of acting interim head coach until Iverson's replacement was finalized. Coach Lieb was from Faribault, MN and was most recently an assistant to Knute Rockne with the football program at the University of Notre Dame, as well as assistant track coach and head hockey coach. Both Little and Lidicker's attempts to identify and secure a new head coach before the Christmas break proved unsuccessful.

Consequently, the Wisconsin hockey team was not allowed to travel and participate in their customary exhibition hockey games against other college teams around the Midwest during the month of December. This meant the Badger skaters were without valuable scrimmage games and conditioning that was necessary at this level of collegiate hockey competition. Instead, they had to rely on high tempo daily practices that began in early December.

Immediately after the disappointing Christmas break, W.R. Brandow arrived on campus and was named the new Wisconsin Badgers head hockey coach. "Rube" Brandow was a former professional hockey player. He was well known in both the amateur and professional hockey circles and had a reputation as a highly intelligent, successful and competitive hockey player. During the 1916-17 season, Brandow was playing as an amateur for the team in Selkirk, Manitoba. That year Selkirk won the Manitoba Intermediate Championship. At the end of the 1917-18 season, Brandow's team won the Manitoba Junior title. After the 1918-19 season, Brandow's Selkirk team were the champions of Western Canada. His team lost the national Canadian championship to Hamilton, Ontario in overtime. In December 1926, Brandow was playing for the Detroit Greyhounds and would report to the UW January 1. Brandow's role as the head coach of the Wisconsin hockey program would prove to be his most challenging endeavor to date.

Wisconsin Head Coach "Rube" Brandow

Coach Brandow only had two weeks to get his players into peak physical condition and ready for competition. The upcoming weeks would also be used to get his skaters familiar with the plays and hockey strategies he wanted them to execute. His immediate focus was teaching the importance of fast passing and shot selection with an emphasis on accuracy. After reviewing the list of players, Coach Brandow quickly realized he had another challenge on his hands. There was a concerning lack of eligible players from which to mold a strong team. He had no choice other than to make the best team with the skaters at his disposal. Captain Lidicker and Jansky were expected to lead the team in scoring this season as the most experienced and talented players on the UW squad. The spare players, Cahoon, Rahr and Ruf, would obviously be seeing a lot of playing time this season due to a thin core line up.

Ice hockey continued to be a popular winter sport on the Wisconsin campus. Much of the attraction was due to the league formed between Wisconsin, Michigan and Minnesota. Each team was a member of the Big Ten and hockey matches had seen attendance increase at amazing proportions each season. Significant credit in the surging popularity among students was due to the efforts of interim coach Tom Lieb. Under his direction a few skating rinks had been constructed on the field of Camp Randall during the winter. Some were designated hockey rinks, one was a general skating rink, and a track for skate races was also built. A few of these rinks were designated for students only while others were available for the general public. The varsity rink at the lower Madison campus had been constructed along with bleachers to accommodate the spectators. Rinks were also constructed in this area for the freshman squad and the women's hockey club.

Captain Bill Lidicker

Don Mitchell

1926–27 Wisconsin Varsity Hockey Team

Front Row Left to Right: Silverthorne, Jansky, Rahr, Mitchell, captain Lidicker, Boyer, Kynaston and Drummond

Back Row Left to Right: Coach Brandow, Ruf, Murphy, Mason, Morris, Cahoon, Moelk, Moorhead and Manager Soulin

UW Hockey Roster:

Captain Bill Lidicker –   Left Wing
Karl Jansky -   Right Wing
John Silverthorne –   Center
Mike Murphy –   Left Defense
James Mason –   Right Defense
Don Mitchell –   Goal Guard

Substitutes: Cahoon, Rahr and Ruf.

The first hockey game of the season featured the Janesville Hockey Club returning to the UW campus for a single practice match January 7 with a 4 p.m. start time. A recent cold spell had the ice in near perfect condition. Just over two thousand people showed for the contest. Three returning veterans were back this season: wingers Bill Lidicker and Karl Jansky, along with defenseman Mike Murphy. Coach Brandon started James Drummond, a strong and smart skater, at center. However, Drummond was one of the players marked as academically ineligible and was restricted from playing in any of the upcoming conference games. The players for Janesville were experienced veterans, working men that played hockey for fun but were extremely proficient at all aspects of the game.

Wisconsin did not disappoint in this first game and played Janesville with great effort and skill, winning 4-1. Scoring for the Badgers were captain Lidicker, Jansky, Drummond and Rahr. Much of the credit was given to the defensemen, Murphy and Mason, both of whom played an outstanding game and easily frustrated their opponents. One of the key spares, Rahr, also played an impressive game and scored one of the four goals for Wisconsin. He was expected to earn accolades as the outstanding spare of the year once the season was completed. Little did coach Brandow know that soon his team would be hit with several players being ruled ineligible. As a result, Rahr would become a starting player on the UW varsity team.

Wisconsin Lineup: Drummond (Center), Jansky (Right Wing), captain Lidicker (Left Wing), Mason (Right Defense), Murphy (Left Defense) and Mitchell (Goalie). Substitutes: Boyer, Silverthorne, Kynneston, Rahr, Cahoon, Moelk, Moorhead and Ruf. Saves: Wisconsin 14, Janesville 22.

Cahoon

Silverthorne

The conference began with a doubleheader scheduled against the University of Minnesota on January 14 and 15. The highly competitive Gophers returned to Madison to add another chapter to the growing rivalry. In the first game several hundred fans showed up despite the below zero temperatures putting the deep freeze on Madison. All game long the spectators had to endure numerous wintery gusts of wind that made viewing the game downright painful at times.

Coach Brandow's eligible squad was uncomfortably low in numbers. In fact, the UW team did not have the ideal number of players to rotate in an adequate number of substitutes. The Wisconsin starting sextet would need to carry most of the load in these games. Crafty Wisconsin veterans captain Bill Lidicker and Karl Jansky played with all the skills, tricks and determination they possessed in order to keep the Badgers in the game so the Gophers would not embarrass them on their home rink. After a scoreless first period, the Gophers got on the scoreboard first with a goal in the second period.

It ended up being the game-winning goal. The third period was scoreless and the Badgers lost their first outing 1-0.

Wisconsin Lineup: Silverthorne (Center), Jansky (Right Wing), captain Lidicker (Left Wing), Mason (Right Defense), Murphy (Left Defense) and Mitchell (Goalie). Substitutes: Rahr, Cahoon and Ruf. Saves: Wisconsin 24, Minnesota 28.

The second game was scheduled for 4 p.m. at the Madison campus ice rink and the Wisconsin skaters were ready for another battle against Minnesota. Newcomers to the Wisconsin team, John Silverthorne and William Rahr, skated to the best of their abilities in this game, as did the rest of their crew. But the hockey Gods were not with Wisconsin on this night. The first Gopher goal was the result of a Badger player attempting to clear the puck and it was inadvertently hit into his own Wisconsin net in the first period. Again, in the first period another Gopher goal was a fluke deflection off a Badger players skate blade that changed the direction of the puck into the back of the UW net without resistance.

In addition, Minnesota coach Emil Iverson, a great hockey strategist, quickly realized that frequent substitutions of fresh skaters would exhaust the formidable Wisconsin players. Both Jansky and Lidicker were required to play both games against the Gophers without taking any breaks other than the time allowed in between periods. It was Silverthorne who finally scored the lone goal for the Badgers in the first five minutes of the third period. Coach Iverson's strategies, along with the counter efforts of the Minnesota squad were enough to defeat the best efforts of the Badger skaters. The Gophers were victorious in this second game by a score of 3-1.

Wisconsin Lineup: Silverthorne (Center), Jansky (Right Wing), captain Lidicker (Left Wing), Mason (Right Defense), Murphy (Left Defense) and Mitchell (Goalie). Substitutes: Rahr, Cahoon and Ruf.

January 21, 1927 proved to be a very special and significant date in Wisconsin college hockey history. The Badgers welcomed the legendary University of Manitoba hockey team from Winnipeg, Canada to their Madison campus. They would face off in the first international hockey game ever played at the University of Wisconsin. Famous Canadian goalie Johnnie Farquhar was the coach of the visiting squad. The Manitoba hockey team was known as the most elite and skilled squad in all of college hockey at the time. Prior to their arrival in Madison, they had beaten the University of Minnesota in a pair of games by scores of 2-0 and 4-0. Manitoba also crushed St. Thomas (Minnesota) 16-0.

A capacity crowd estimated to be a few thousand spectators braved the subzero elements to watch this game that began at 8 p.m. The hockey proficiency, strength and synergy of the Manitoba team was immediately on display after the opening faceoff. Not even a minute into the match, the giant center for the visiting team scored their first goal. They would soon add four more tallies. Manitoba scored five straight goals in the first period of the game! Wisconsin was not playing well. Before the start of the second period, UW coach Rube Brandow lit up his men with a stern lecture at a volume that many fans were able to hear. Wisconsin also switched to a six-man defensive strategy in an attempt to slow the scoring onslaught. The "pep talk" and strategic player alignment worked well as the Badgers got back to business in the second period. In fact, Manitoba was kept off the scoreboard during the third period. Keeping Manitoba scoreless in a single period was an amazing feat at the time. Although the Badgers also did not score.

Even though captain Lidicker and Jansky played to the best of their abilities and never backed down, it was to no avail against the mighty Manitoba hockey team. Despite their repeated attempts, they were unable to score a single goal against their Canadian opponents. Although the score would seem to indicate otherwise, UW goaltender Don Mitchell played a brilliant game between the pipes. Time after time he turned back the University of Manitoba players to prevent the game from being a blowout. To add to his challenges, Mitchell received a painful head injury mid-game. Keep in mind goalies were without any head or face protection while playing hockey in these days. Mitchell stared down a hard shot and the puck deflected off his skull. He received a severe laceration that delayed the game for a considerable amount of time. Without a backup goalie, Mitchell elected to remain in the game and demonstrated heroic courage that earned him enormous respect. He recorded a total of 44 saves in the game.

The visiting team scored twice more in the final period. To make matters worse, star defenseman James Mason was the recipient of a deliberate charge from a Canadian opponent. He was so badly injured that he was required to go to the hospital. The Badgers were held scoreless and lost this game 7-0 against the Canadians. The players for the University of Manitoba hockey team easily beat the schools they played in Minnesota and Wisconsin. In fact, Manitoba was so dominant that they finished the rest of their season without a single goal being scored against them.

Wisconsin Lineup: Drummond (Center), captain Lidicker (Right Wing), Jansky (Left Wing), Moorhead (Right Defense), Mason (Left Defense) and Mitchell (Goalie). Substitutes: Silverthorne, Rahr and Murphy. Saves: Wisconsin 44, Manitoba 12. Penalties: None. Referee: Corbett from the Milwaukee Athletic Club.

Mother Nature was again uncooperative to the Wisconsin hockey team this season with their efforts to practice, scrimmage and host games on decent ice. Bouts of warm weather during the winter months took a toll on the ice surfaces at the campus rink and on the Lake Mendota rink, delaying the Badger team's ability to skate. The unseasonably mild weather caused the cancellation of the game scheduled against the Milwaukee Town Club hockey team in Milwaukee as well as a rematch against the veteran Janesville YMCA Hockey Club.

In addition, the academic ineligibility of more Wisconsin hockey players further challenged the UW club. Coach Brandow was informed that Drummond, Mason, Moorhead and Silverthorne were to be removed from the team for future varsity hockey competition after exam scores were posted. Coach Brandow continued to do his best by playing the cards he was dealt and to make the remaining men into a competitive team.

A bit of good news for the Badgers arrived with the announcement that Ross Chamberlain of Hibbing, Minnesota had returned to the University of Wisconsin for the second semester. Chamberlain was not in school for the first semester. Chamberlain was a fine skating and hard shooting forward that was a welcome addition to the team. Coach Brandow was now able to take a decent number of skaters to Minneapolis for their games against the Gophers. The following players made the trip north: Boyer, Mathews, Murphy, Moelk, Cahoon, Mitchell, Ruf, Moorhead, Rahr, Lidicker and Jansky.

| *Moorhead* | *Rahr* | *Moelk* |

The lack of suitable ice for skating combined with the players deemed ineligible proved to be a huge obstacle as the team headed to Minneapolis Sunday, February 13. Wisconsin had a two-game series with the Gophers scheduled for Monday, February 14 and Tuesday, February 15. The UW used Monday afternoon to practice on the Minnesota Arena rink so that they could become acclimated with the artificial.

Again, Minnesota head coach Iverson utilized his deep bench and robust bag of tricks to fully exhaust the Badger skaters. Wisconsin was able to hold Minnesota from scoring until just over 15 minutes into the first period. It was 1-0 going into the second period. The Badgers fought admirably, but the Gophers scored again at the twelve-minute mark and went up 2-0. Four minutes later Minnesota scored and increased their lead to 3-0. After four minutes elapsed in the final period, the home team pushed their lead to a commanding 4-0, which was how it ended. Wisconsin was blanked. Badger goalie Mitchell made 28 saves to prevent the score from being much worse.

Wisconsin Lineup: Rahr (Center), captain Lidicker (Right Wing), Jansky (Left Wing), Ruf (Right Defense), Murphy (Left Defense) and Mitchell (Goalie). Substitutes: Moelk, Mathews and Cahoon. Penalties: Wisconsin: 4, Minnesota: 2. Saves: Wisconsin 28, Minnesota 18. Referee: John Farquhar from Manitoba.

On Tuesday February 15, the Badgers faced off again with the top-rated Gophers in game two. Wisconsin came out fighting and gave Minnesota a heck of a battle but Minnesota was up for the fight and regained control by scoring four minutes into the opening period. The first period ended with a 1-0 score. Nearly eight minutes through the second period the Gophers scored again to take a 2-0 lead. During the third period the Badgers continued to bring the fight. Their persistency paid off as Wisconsin was able to score with five minutes left in the game and ruin the Gopher shut out. Badger forward Bill Rahr intercepted a Minnesota pass and skated down ice with the puck before pulling up mid-ice to rip a long shot that found the back of the Gopher net. But it was not enough as the Badgers lost 2-1.

Badger goalie Mitchell racked up an impressive 30 saves in this match. Multiple player substitutions and a customized game plan proved to be too much for the Wisconsin squad. Ironically, future University of Wisconsin head coach, John Farquhar from Manitoba, was the referee for both of these hockey games.

Wisconsin Lineup: Rahr (Center), captain Lidicker (Right Wing), Jansky (Left Wing), Moelk (Right Defense), Murphy (Left Defense) and Mitchell (Goalie). Substitutes: Boyer, Mathews, Ruf and Cahoon. Penalties: Wisconsin 2, Minnesota 1. Saves: Wisconsin 30, Minnesota 18. Referee: John Farquhar from Manitoba.

Michigan was the next opponent on the schedule for Wisconsin. The Wolverines traveled to Madison February 19 for a two-game series. Badger forward, William Rahr, continued to shine as one of the top Wisconsin skaters. He was the starting center against the Wolverines. Spectators estimated to be well over two thousand watched a tightly contested affair. After a scoreless first period, Michigan scored on an odd goal after 13 minutes into the second period. Wisconsin's Mike Murphy had been sent off to serve a two-minute penalty when the visitors scored.

Wisconsin switched to a five-man offense in the third period in an attempt to create some scoring chances. The Wolverines goalie and defense proved to be enough and were able to hold off the cardinal and white attackers, notching a 1-0 win. Wisconsin goalie Don Mitchell made 13 saves while the Michigan goaltender had 22 stops.

Wisconsin Lineup: Rahr (Center), captain Lidicker (Right Wing), Jansky (Left Wing), Moelk (Right Defense), Ruf (Left Defense) and Mitchell (Goalie). Substitute: Murphy.   Saves: Wisconsin 20, Michigan 22. Penalties: Wisconsin 5, Michigan 6.

The second Wisconsin versus Michigan game, set for Monday February 21' was postponed due to warm weather. The unseasonably, high temperatures continued for the next several weeks and postponed this game twice. It would now be played as part of a three-game set against the Wolverines in Ontario.

Without any suitable ice to practice on, the UW players were once again forced to find creative ways to stay in peak physical condition. The Badgers were actually creating one of the first dryland hockey programs in the country out of necessity. Their conditioning routines consisted of playing basketball, basic calisthenics and running at the Red Gym Annex to remain fit.

On March 4 1927, the University of Wisconsin hockey team departed from the Madison campus by train to Windsor, Ontario for a very special game the following day. The Badgers were set to face off against the Michigan Wolverines in the <u>first</u> American intercollegiate hockey game ever played outside of the United States of America. Over five thousand spectators packed the bleachers and filled up the standing room spots to watch this special match up featuring two of the top American college hockey teams from the Midwest.

Wisconsin conducted practices at the game rink on both Saturday and Sunday so that they could become accustomed to the indoor ice. Along with the starting players, coach Brandow brought along four spares. Kynaston was recently declared eligible and would be a substitute for wingers. Rahr was the sub for the center position. Cahoon was the spare for defense and Boyer was on the trip in case he was needed to cover the goal position.

Both teams were in awe of the size of the rowdy crowd. Trying to capitalize on the hoopla of this international hockey game, the University of Michigan band attended the game. All 75 band students played a wide variety of songs before the contest, in between periods and after the game to the delight of the crowd.

Wisconsin and Michigan battled from the moment the game started. After nearly 15 minutes of play in the first period, the Wolverines were able to score. The first period ended with the Badgers down 1-0. Several minutes into the second period Michigan responded with their second goal of the game. Midway through the middle period, captain Lidicker got Wisconsin on the scoreboard with a pretty goal to make the score 2-1. The third period, like the other two periods, was highlighted with fast skating, fancy passing and several offensive opportunities. The third period was scoreless for the Badgers. Despite their best efforts, the UW skaters were defeated 2-1 by Michigan in the first game.

Wisconsin Lineup: Moelk (Center), Jansky (Right Wing), captain Lidicker (Left Wing), Ruf (Right Defense), Murphy (Left Defense) and Mitchell (Goalie). Substitutes: Rahr, Cahoon and Kynaston. Penalties: Wisconsin 3, Michigan 2. Saves: Wisconsin 28, Michigan 19. Referee: E. Lowry from Windsor.

In the next game March 7, both teams locked up in a true offensive and defensive struggle. The Badgers and Wolverines played each other so tightly that neither team was able to score a goal in regulation. Late in the third period, an errant Michigan stick caught Wisconsin defenseman Mike Murphy right in the face and shattered his eyeglasses. Murphy had numerous lacerations from the broken metal and glass. Fortunately, his eyes were not damaged by the high stick he took to the head.

Michigan had several extra spares in this game and used them regularly to keep fresh players in the game. After 60 minutes of regulation, overtime was needed to determine a winner. The game remained tight after the first 20 some minutes of play. It was 28 minutes into the overtime period that the scoreless tie was broken, on a Michigan goal. The Badgers had another loss on their hands. This one was a 1-0 defeat after 30 minutes of extra play.

Wisconsin Lineup: Moelk (Center), Jansky (Right Wing), captain Lidicker (Left Wing), Ruf (Right Defense), Murphy (Left Defense) and Mitchell (Goalie). Substitutes: Rahr, Cahoon and Kynaston. Referee: E. Lowry from Windsor.

Before the final game against the Wolverines, Badger players were entertained by a group of University of Wisconsin Alumni residing in the Detroit area. The entire team was provided a sightseeing tour around Detroit. Afterward, they were surprised with a banquet at the Book-Cadillac Hotel, located at the corner of State Street and Detroit's Washington Boulevard. It opened in 1924 and, at the time, was the tallest hotel in the world with 33 floors and 1,136 rooms for guests. Understandably, it was a real treat for the representatives of the Badger hockey team to experience such a high-end hotel. Madison was without any buildings remotely close to the magnitude and opulence of this hotel.

The third game of this historic hockey series in Ontario was played March 8. It was a makeup for the game canceled in Madison. After scoreless first and second periods, Michigan scored with just six minutes left in the third period to go up 1-0. It would be the game winner as Wisconsin could not find the back of the net.

Wisconsin Lineup: Moelk (Center), Jansky (Right Wing), captain Lidicker (Left Wing), Ruf (Right Defense), Murphy (Left Defense) and Mitchell (Goalie). Substitutes: Rahr, Cahoon and Kynaston. Penalties: Wisconsin 1, Michigan 2. Referee: E. Lowry from Windsor.

Although Wisconsin lost all three games, they had reasons to hold their heads high. The Badgers held the Wolverines to only four goals in 210 minutes of game action that included 3 overtime periods. Michigan also had deep reserves of spare players while Wisconsin's starting players typically played the entire game.

Immediately after the final game against Michigan, the Wisconsin squad was surprised with a dinner banquet honoring the team that was provided by recent University of Wisconsin graduates residing in the Canadian province. The gathering was at the Prince Edward hotel in Windsor, Ontario just across the Detroit River from Detroit. During the festivities, standout goalkeeper Don Mitchell was elected as captain of the Wisconsin hockey team for the upcoming 1927-28 season. Captain Bill Lidicker would be lost to graduation.

At the end of this season, in what would become an ongoing problem, the University of Notre Dame Fighting Irish decided to drop its varsity ice hockey program. It was because of poor ice due to unpredictable weather conditions that forced the cancellation of games and led to inconsistent practice schedules.

Karl Jansky wearing his UW letterman "W" sweater that he was awarded for being a Varsity player on the Wisconsin Ice Hockey Team

Karl Jansky, an integral member of the 1925-26 and 1926-27 UW hockey teams, completed his playing days and graduated in 1927 with a degree in physics. He was also elected into Phi Beta Kappu, the prestigious national honorary scholastic fraternity. Jansky would go on to have a legendary career as an American physicist and radio engineer. In 1931, he was the first to discover radio waves emitted from the Milky Way and he's considered one of the Founding Fathers of radio astronomy. During the second World War, Jansky worked on the development of direction finders that were used to locate enemy submarines from Germany. After the war, Dr. Jansky dedicated his work to developing frequency amplifiers that had numerous applications.

1926-27   Schedule and Results:
Coach "Rube" Brandow
0-8-0 Third in WIHL   1-9-0 Overall

Date	Result	Opponent
January 7	Win 4-1	Janesville*
January 14	Loss 1-0	Minnesota
January 15	Loss 3-1	Minnesota
January 21	Loss 7-0	Manitoba*#
February 14	Loss 4-0	@ Minnesota
February 15	Loss 2-1	@ Minnesota
February 19	Loss 1-0	Michigan
March 5	Loss 2-1	Michigan**
March 7	Loss 1-0 OT	Michigan**
March 9	Loss 1-0	Michigan**

*Exhibition Game

#First ice hockey game against international opponent played at the University of Wisconsin (Exhibition Game).

**First American intercollegiate ice hockey games held outside of the U.S.A. and were played in Windsor, Ontario.

Chapter Nine
Down Goes Minnesota

1927-28 UW Hockey Team

In mid-November, the now annual call for potential varsity hockey prospects was sent out campus-wide. Nearly 50 students responded and attended the informational meeting in order to show their interest and abilities. Each of them was assigned a locker and began training regiments to get them into the necessary physical conditioning. The extracurricular training was conducted in the Red Gym. Overall, the prospective players for this squad were very promising. Several veterans returned to the team and many of the players were known for their fast skating and advanced conceptual grasp of the game of hockey.

Two of the veteran players from last year's hockey team, John McCarter from Madison, Wisconsin, and Earl Carrier from Essex Falls, New Jersey, returned to this year's team and would replace the positions vacated by captain Bill Lidicker and Karl Jansky, both of whom graduated. John McCarter was known as a tall and crafty player who was a solid defenseman that had the ability to combine his speed and hockey intelligence to make him a feared Badger hockey player. He played for the Badgers the previous two seasons and brought invaluable experience to the team. Earl Carrier was an experienced winger that had previously played with McCarter and would make great contributions to this team.

Fortunately, around 10 veteran players from last year's squad returned to play for the team this season. The following students formally declared themselves as candidates for the varsity hockey team: Ed Swiderski, Dahlman, Schroeder, Jacobson, Allan, Don Meiklejohn, Harold Ruf, Reinke, Pautch, Heilback, Robert Goetz, Gil Krueger, Kustof, Bolton, Ted Poquette, Maynard Brown, Matthews, Roger Cahoon, Earl Carrier, Spoeni, John McCarter, James Mason, Boyer, Max Murphy and Don Mitchell.

Among the most valuable was Don Mitchell from Duluth, Minnesota. Mitchell had an outstanding performance last season as the UW goalie. In fact, he turned down an offer to play professional hockey so that he could finish out his eligibility with the University of Wisconsin hockey team. His skill set and experience earned him the role of team captain for 1927-28.

James Mason, from Winnipeg Canada, was another veteran that returned to this year's team. He was a fan favorite because of his incredibly fast skating while handling the puck and earned a spot on the team at the defense position. At goalie, Sam Boyer from Duluth, Minnesota, would be content in his role as a backup to Don Mitchell, also from Duluth. Boyer played in a few games last season and was expected to shore up the reserve goaltending needs of the team.

Harold Ruf from Green Bay, Wisconsin, had previously played the position of goalie on the 1924-25 and 1925-26 teams, but was transitioning to the position of defense. He was a talented defensive player and was a regular defenseman on last year's team. He showed up for this season in excellent condition with the intent of securing a spot on the roster at defense again this year.

New faces on this season's varsity team include center Don Meiklejohn. He was a center on last year's freshman team and quickly became the frontrunner for the varsity center position. He was the son of professor Alexander Meiklejohn, Chairman of the Experimental College. Another standout from last year's freshman team was Gilbert Kreuger from Neenah, Wisconsin. He earned a reputation as an exceptionally fast winger and demonstrated a high level of hockey skill and ability on the freshman team last season.

Before the start of the regular season, the team had to adjust to some new rule changes that were introduced into the game this year which were made in an effort to speed up the game. The puck would now be allowed to be shot from one blue line to the other as long as another teammate received the long pass. In addition, players could intentionally kick the puck as they desired during the course of the game. Lastly, teams would be allowed to change players (substitute in spares) without the referee stopping the game.

Ice hockey rules at this time continued to evolve, but most clubs followed basic rules and a shared understanding of how the game was to be played. Some teams modified the rules slightly, but the game was rather similar. A typical hockey rink was 190 feet long and 90 feet wide. The skating surface was divided into three sections or zones that were marked with blue lines. Between the blue lines was the middle of the ice, also known as center ice. Goals were located in areas referred to as end zones. Goals were to be 6 feet by 4 feet in size and enclosed by a net. Typically, the goals were placed 6 feet away from the boards at the ends of the rink. Each team had six players on the ice: a center, right wing, left wing, right defenseman, left defenseman and goalie. Some teams preferred to put three men back and only two men up on offense, or some other miscellaneous offensive or defensive positioning of players during this era. There was a 10-minute rest between periods.

After the dismal one-win record compiled under the leadership of head coach W.R. "Rube" Brandow last season, the UW hockey program was again faced with finding a new head coach for the 1927-28 season. George Little, the Director of Badger Athletics, had the responsibility to identify and secure a quality hockey coach to lead the University of Wisconsin team.

A Badger hockey game on the cover of *The Wisconsin Athletic Review*

While on-ice practices began in early December, the first nighttime practice was held December 14. This was possible since the UW had finished installing lights at the campus rink earlier in the day. The Badger team was again granted the opportunity to participate in preseason exhibition games and their December holiday tour took them into Michigan and northern Wisconsin. The club departed from Madison for the trek without the guidance of a formal head coach.

John Farquhar was subsequently hired as coach and joined the team during the tour which correlated with the Christmas vacation semester break. Coach Farquhar came to the UW with worldly hockey experience. Before coming to Wisconsin, he had been residing in Winnipeg, Canada, and had been both a player (goalie) and coach at the legendary University of Manitoba. The Manitoba team was known as one of the most dominant and feared college hockey teams in existence during the 1920s. Farquhar was very familiar with the University of Wisconsin hockey program and had witnessed a couple of Badgers versus Gophers hockey games in Minneapolis. He also brought his University of Manitoba team to Madison for a game during the 1926-27 season.

Coach John Farquhar in a University of Wisconsin hockey uniform.

Preseason hockey games, were vital to the training and preparation of the team as they were needed in order for the team to be competitive for the upcoming regular season that was quickly approaching. These games, scheduled primarily in December, allowed the players to bond and grow together as a cohesive unit. Facing multiple opponents in various ice rinks also provided the UW skaters with much needed experience before regular season play commenced.

A total of 11 Badger hockey players made the weeklong exhibition trip. The team was comprised of: captain Don Mitchell, John McCarter, James Mason, Ted Poquette, Gil Krueger, Don Meiklejohn, Bob Goetz, Maynard Brown, Roger Cahoon, Max Murphy and Earl Carrier. They left their dorms and apartments on Christmas Day to head to Michigan. The five game "vacation" schedule lasted just over a week and took the team to northern Wisconsin and Michigan. Joining them on this trip would be assistant coach and team trainer Bill Fry.

Their first exhibition game was in Marquette, Michigan, December 27 against a challenging foe in the Marquette Owls Hockey Club. Despite their efforts and physical play, the Badgers lost a close game by a score of 3-2.

The 1927–28 University of Wisconsin Varsity Ice Hockey Team

Assistant Coach Fry & Team Manager Pearce

Wisconsin arrived in Houghton, Michigan Thursday, December 29, to face the Michigan Mining School or Houghton School of Mines. Formally known as the Michigan College of Mining and Technology. No matter what they were called, they always fielded a tough hockey squad.

Michigan Mining School ice hockey team was a formidable opponent and they were highly skilled. Clearly the boys from the School of Mines got the better of the Badgers as the game was a blowout loss with a final score of 6-0. The Wisconsin skaters were unable to get one past the Houghton goalie while the skaters from the School of Mines ran up the score.

A rematch was scheduled for the following day Friday, December 30. Both teams played an epic defensive battle and were unable to score during most of the game. But the Badgers came to play, wanting to avenge the bad loss from the previous day. After an epic back and forth battle, the score was knotted at 0-0. Neither side was able to tally a goal. Overall, it was a very clean game with each side getting called for only one penalty. Wisconsin goaltender Don Mitchell was recognized for his outstanding play as he made a total of 38 saves compared with just seven stops by the Michigan goalie. It was the first time in three years that Michigan College was held scoreless.

Wisconsin Lineup: Meiklejohn (Center), Goetz (Right Wing), Krueger (Left Wing), McCarter (Right Defense), Poquette (Left Defense) and captain Mitchell (goalie). Substitutes: Mason, Cahoon and Murphy.

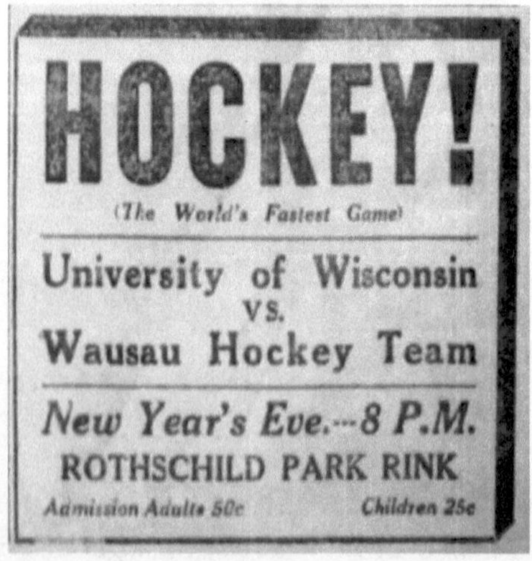

The UW players were back in Wisconsin on New Years Eve for a game against the Wausau Cardinals Hockey Club. It was an 8 p.m. start at the Rothschild Park Rink. Wisconsin winger Ted Poquette was from Medford, Wisconsin, and several folks from Medford showed up in Wausau to watch Poquette play. The Badgers were not able to dominate the veteran hockey club from Wausau. Although the Badgers scored first, the Cardinals were able to tie up the game. Both teams had to accept a 1-1 draw once the game concluded.

Wisconsin Lineup: Carrier (Center), McCarter (Right Wing), Poquette (Left Wing), Brown (Right Defense), Murphy (Left Defense) and captain Mitchell (Goalie). Substitutes: Mason, Krueger, Meiklejohn, Cahoon and Goetz.

The final game of their exhibition tour was in Oshkosh, Wisconsin, January 2 and the cardinal and white players were set to play the members of the Oshkosh Hockey Club with a 2:30 p.m. face off at the Menominee Park rink. The spectators had to brave incredibly cold weather. Many locals showed up to watch this game and catch a glimpse of hometown hero (and UW Varsity star) Gilbert Krueger. Only a sophomore, Krueger was already looking like a top performer on the Badger team.

Coach Farquhar had the Badger team ready to play with a heightened focus and some additional plays from the Manitoba playbook. Oshkosh dominated possession and had the puck in the Wisconsin zone over 70% of the time. Don Meiklejohn opened the scoring with a nice top corner shot five minutes into the first period. A few minutes later Meiklejohn got a nice pass from Billy Goetz and buried the second goal of the period, which gave the Badgers a 2-0 lead. In the second period neither team scored.

The Badgers were able to score two more goals during the third period. One was a nice individual effort by Maynard Brown for the third goal of the game. In the final minutes, some fancy passing between Goetz, Meiklejohn and Krueger resulted in the fourth goal for the Badgers. This game was physical and hard-fought but the Badgers were able to find the back of the net four times. Captain Mitchell was able to orchestrate a shutout in the 4-0 win over Oshkosh.

Wisconsin Lineup: Meiklejohn (Center), Krueger (Right Wing), Goetz (Left Wing), Mason (Right Defense), McCarter (Left Defense) and captain Mitchell (Goalie). Substitutes: Cahoon, Murphy and Brown.

The exhibition tour ended with a 1-2-2 record in preparation for the upcoming season. They did very well considering several of the teams they faced had a level of talent higher than typical college clubs. Some of those teams were considered semi-pro caliber teams. In addition, the UW men were able to gel as a group and forged great relationships in the early part of their hockey season.

Coach Farquhar quickly realized the team he took over was a group of skaters that had a strong core from which he could field a strong team. The skaters were mostly sophomores with the exception of returning veterans; captain Don Mitchell (Goalie), Jim Mason (Defense), John McCarter (Defense) and Earl "Red" Carrier (Defense). However, the core group of second year skaters had some serious talent and coach Farquhar quickly figured out his best combination of players. Don Meiklejohn, son of UW professor Alexander Meiklejohn, was one of the standout skaters at the sophomore level. He was assigned the center position where he excelled. Meiklejohn was credited with either saving or winning numerous games during the season. Gil Krueger was a smaller athlete, but his speed on skates had the coach convinced to put him at the position of wing.

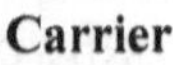

| Carrier | Drummond | Meiklejohn | Mason |

Coach Farquhar also understood that the success of the game of hockey on the Madison campus would take some creative marketing efforts. **"Hockey, the Fastest Game on Earth"** was more than a statement often repeated by coach Farquhar. It was the slogan on numerous signs posted around campus and the UW gym. It was much more than a catchy motto. Farquhar knew he could prove his assertion that hockey was, in fact, the fastest game on earth. The signs invited students, faculty and the citizens of Madison and surrounding communities to journey down to the lower campus watch a practice. Better yet, folks were invited down to catch a game and witness firsthand the skating, speed, puck movement, physical play and action provided by the game of ice hockey.

The regular season began as Kay Iverson, the former University of Wisconsin hockey coach, and his new Marquette University (WI) team visited the Madison campus for a game January 6, 1928. This contest was a marquee feature of the Winter Sports Frolic. Several hundred fans filled the bleachers and overflowed the standing room only areas to watch this game. The Marquette skaters were a familiar opponent that always brought Wisconsin a physically and mentally challenging hockey game. The Hilltoppers finished with the conference title last season.

Wisconsin and Marquette each played a slightly different style of hockey positioning. The Badgers played what was considered normal player positioning with three forwards and two defensemen. Marquette chose to play only two forwards with three men back on defense. These two teams played an amazingly close game and Marquette scored first in the second period and added a second goal later in the period. Rough play took over and numerous penalties were called on both teams. In fact, Badger right winger John McCarter was ejected from the game for aggressive play, fighting and for what the referee deemed was a general disregard for hockey etiquette. Star center Don Meiklejohn scored both of the UW goals in the third period with impressive individual efforts that penetrated the Marquette defense. But the UW skaters had two players in the penalty box in the closing minutes of the game which allowed a Marquette player to score the go-ahead goal. The Badgers suffered the loss in this home opener by a score of 3-2. UW goalie Mitchell had 38 saves while the Marquette goalie stopped 27 shots.

Wisconsin Lineup: Meiklejohn (Center), McCarter (Right Wing) and Krueger (Left Wing), Brown (Right Defense), Mason (Left Defense) and captain Mitchell (Goalie). Substitutes: Murphy, Carrier, Cahoon, Goetz and Poquette.

The final feature game of the Winter Carnival had Wisconsin scheduled to play the Wausau Hockey Club Saturday, January 7. These two teams previously met during the Christmas break exhibition tour so they were not unfamiliar foes. It was a scoreless game once the first period completed. Halfway through the second period, crafty Badger forward Gil Krueger scored on a close shot near the net. A few minutes later Wausau tied the game at 1-1. "Red" Carrier, the spare center and a tall player known for his red head of hair, was able to take a shot from the middle of the rink and score on the Wausau goalie to put the Badgers up 2-1.

With minutes left in the third period, a Wausau player shot a puck on the Wisconsin net that was gloved by Don Mitchell. As he was holding the puck, two Wausau players attempted to shove Mitchell into his own net in order to get the goal to count. Understandably, a heated argument ensued as both sides debated whether such a move should count as a goal. Several fist fights almost flared up, but the on-ice officials were quick to declare that bull rushing a goalie holding the puck into his own net was in itself a penalty. Since Badger goalie Mitchell had possession of the puck it was ruled no-goal. Wisconsin won the game 2-1.

Wisconsin Lineup: Meiklejohn (Center), Goetz (Right Wing) and Krueger (Left Wing), McCarter (Right Defense), Mason (Left Defense) and captain Mitchell (Goalie). Substitutes: Murphy, Carrier, Cahoon and Poquette.

James McCarter   *Don Mitchell*   *James Mason*

One of the major recurring challenges that faced the Wisconsin puck chasers each season was the threat of unseasonably warm weather. Since the UW squad only had outdoor ice, they were held hostage by poor or nonexistent, ice frequently during each season. Practices, scrimmages and games were postponed or canceled altogether. This season was no different and the poor ice challenges remained a constant issue. It soon became apparent to coach Farquhar that his starting lineup would be Meiklejohn (Center), Krueger (Winger), Goetz (Winger), Mason (Defense) and McCarter (Defense). Many hockey enthusiasts would proclaim this starting line would be arguably the fastest forward line Wisconsin had ever put on the ice this decade.

Thomsen

Without any other games to be played in January, the Wisconsin ice hockey team had to wait and prepare for the first weekend in February when the Minnesota Gophers would return to Madison to continue their legendary rivalry. The Minnesota team was practically the same group that tied for first in the Big Ten conference with Michigan during the previous season. They were an exceptionally strong team.

As he stepped off the train in Madison, Minnesota head coach Emil Iverson confidently proclaimed, "I have the greatest college hockey team I have ever coached!" (6) The majority of his team was made up of veteran players and he was quick to point out that the new skaters were nearly equal to his older skaters. Many across the nation felt this Gopher bench was the strongest collegiate hockey team in the land. Minnesota was again favored as the team to clinch the Big Ten hockey title. In fact, they were originally invited to represent the United States at the upcoming Winter Olympics in St. Moritz, Switzerland. However, the University of Minnesota athletic director declined the Olympic invitation.

It is interesting to note the national attention turned to the sport of amateur ice hockey as there was controversy surrounding which ice hockey team was slated to represent the United States of America at the 1928 Winter Olympics to be held in St. Moritz, Switzerland. In fact, Major General Douglas MacArthur was asked to intercede in the hockey dispute because he was Chairman of the American Olympic committee. At the center of the controversy, was the fact that the Augsburg College hockey team from Minnesota was initially selected to be the USA hockey team at the upcoming Olympics.

However, many objections surfaced as the University Club of Boston hockey team was highly regarded as probably the finest amateur team in America at the time. Opponents were quick to point out that a "tryout game" between these two clubs would determine a clear winner to represent the USA in ice hockey. But Major General MacArthur dismissed any potential playoff type game between the two hockey clubs. The U.S. Olympic committee, in a highly controversial decision, canceled the appointment that Augsburg College hockey team would be representing the United States, just days before the team was to leave for Europe. Ultimately, the United States did not send a hockey team to represent our country at the 1928 Winter Olympic games.

Wisconsin coach Farquhar was relieved to find out that all of his players had passed their exams and would be eligible to complete the remainder of the season. Furthermore, Max Murphy, also known as "the Little Green Bay Blonde," returned to school and brought his hockey experience back to the active roster for the UW. Murphy's return made him the fourth Badger skater that played the game of ice hockey with the assistance of prescription glasses. Along with Murphy, Don Meiklejohn, Gil Krueger and John McCarter all wore protective eye-gear with steel cages that were worn over the glasses. Hockey players that wore glasses while playing the sport at the college level were extremely rare at this time.

Although warm temperatures and mushy ice would threaten the first game, it went on as scheduled. February 3, 1928 would be a largely memorable day in the history of the University of Wisconsin hockey program. Fortunately, the UW installed extra bleachers for the overflowing crowds that would be on hand to watch the hockey battle. Former hockey coach Joe Steinauer would be broadcasting play-by-play of the hockey match on the air waves provided by WHA broadcasting.

Start of Minnesota Game

The Gophers were introduced to a new era of Wisconsin hockey at 3:30 p.m. on this Friday. The Badgers surprised them by outhustling their northern rivals with a heightened level of effort and unveiled a handful of new plays provided by head coach Farquhar. Star winger Gil Kreuger was far too light to be effective against the tall and muscular Gopher squad so he was quickly replaced by Murphy and did not see much ice time in either game.

Wisconsin got on the scoreboard first when left defenseman John McCarter took a long shot from the blue line. It bounced just in front of the Gopher netminder and ended up in the back of the net. The desperate Gophers were finally able to score late in the third period on a nice rebound. With no love lost between these two teams it was an especially rough game. Referee Thomsen was frequently challenged in his constant attempts to separate heated players. After calling several penalties, both teams realized they were not going to get away with any extra stuff and decided to play hockey. Even though Wisconsin dominated Minnesota for most for the game, the score was knotted at 1-1 after the end of regulation play.

The poor ice was quickly deteriorating throughout the game which prevented Minnesota from playing their brand of hockey. Netminder and captain Don Mitchell played a superb game and only allowed the Gophers to get one goal past him. Don Meiklejohn and Gil Kreuger played outstanding as well. Neither team was able to score in the first overtime. During the second overtime, both teams battled back and forth. With less than two minutes remaining Meiklejohn received a pass from Carrier and ripped a shot from nearly the center of the rink that smoked past the Minnesota goaltender for the victory! Wisconsin won 2-1, and had earned a monumental triumph over Minnesota.

This was the <u>FIRST</u> time **Wisconsin defeated Minnesota** since the two programs began playing ice hockey. It also put Wisconsin in first place in the Big Ten hockey standings. Badger goalie Don Mitchell was clearly one of the stars of the game, recording 31 saves. The Gopher goalie had 25 saves.

Wisconsin Lineup: Meiklejohn (Center), Goetz (Right Wing), Kreuger (Left Wing), Mason (Right Defense), McCarter (Left Defense) and captain Mitchell (Goalie). Substitutes: Murphy and Poquette. Saves: Wisconsin 31, Minnesota 25. Referee: Jake Thompson from the Milwaukee Athletic Club.

On February 4, in front of another large and excited crowd, the Badgers played a fierce brand of hockey that had the Gophers on their heels from the start. What was supposed to be a morning game was delayed until 9 p.m. due to poor ice. This was the big story as both teams sloshed around, unable to accomplish any decent skating. So bad was the ice that it was described as ankle deep water. The two teams played a tightly contested match. Wisconsin attacked the Minnesota zone repeatedly and expertly defended the Badger end of the ice. The Gophers struggled to get any offensive threats going. Both the first and second periods were scoreless.

A fluke moment occurred mid-game when the puck sailed into the crowd and injured Wisconsin varsity basketball player Lycan Miller. He was watching the game with some of his teammates and was struck in the face, which caused a significant laceration just above his eye. Miller was rushed to the infirmary for treatment and received multiple stitches to close the gash.

Nearly three minutes into the third period, the Gophers scored after a scrum in front of the Badgers net. The Wisconsin squad tied the game with six minutes left when two Gopher players were serving their roughing penalties. Max Murphy, in on a substitution, skated through the Minnesota defense and shot the puck into the net. Both teams were locked in a 1-1 tie at the end of regulation and provided with a much-needed ten-minute rest.

The first overtime period did not produce a game-winning goal. Neither did the second or third overtime period. After the fourth overtime period, the officials ruled the game would go into the record books as a tie. Both teams had battled to the point of exhaustion with fierce skating, slashing, passing and body checking. A grueling sequence of four five-minute overtime periods was unable to determine a winner. The Gophers were denied any chance to avenge the loss they were handed on the previous day by the Badgers. Wisconsin was able to maintain their grip on first place in the conference.

Three days later, Tuesday, February 7, the Wisconsin basketball team was scheduled to play Notre Dame. Lycan Miller would not be cleared to participate in the UW basketball game due to the extent of the injury he suffered above his eye at the UW hockey game.

Wisconsin Lineup: Meiklejohn (Center), Murphy (Right Wing), Kreuger (Left Wing), Mason (Right Defense), McCarter (Left Defense) and captain Mitchell (Goalie). Substitutes: Swiderski, Carrier, Peterson and Brown. Saves: Wisconsin 29, Minnesota 17. Referee: Jake Thompson from the Milwaukee Athletic Club.

Due to the continual challenges of warm temperatures and the ill effects it had on the ice surface at the rink, coach Farquhar changed the varsity practice times to 6 a.m. for the Badgers hockey team. This would offer the best ice surface to practice upon and it would minimize the destruction of the skating surface that typically happens once the ice gets warm and begins to chunk up. In order to conserve the ice, Coach Farquhar also worked tirelessly to cover the ice at the Lower Campus Rink with black building paper and canvas so that it could be shielded from the sun following each practice.

The Wisconsin team remained undefeated after their big weekend against Minnesota. Now coach Farquhar's skaters had to prepare for the upcoming games against the Michigan Wolverines. At this time, the Wolverines were in first place in the Western Conference. Last season, Michigan tied Minnesota for first place.

Coach Farquhar learned the disappointing news that he had lost four-star players due to ineligibility rules. The players were Bill Goetz, Ted Poquette, Bill Reinke and Bill Rahr. The Wisconsin coach did not publicly elaborate on which rules were broken. Even though the four players passed their exams and were academically eligible, they were lost for the season and would never return to the University of Wisconsin hockey program.

On February 10, the Michigan Wolverines were scheduled to face the Badgers at their home rink on the University of Wisconsin-Madison campus and record crowds were expected. Both home games would be broadcast over the AM airwaves of WHA and feature the play-by-play of Joe Steinauer. Friday's game was slated to start at 7:30 p.m. The contest February 11, would not begin until approximately 8:45 p.m. since the UW Athletic Department wanted the hockey game to start after the Wisconsin versus Minnesota basketball game.

However, Wisconsin officials were forced to cancel the games this weekend due to the poor condition of ice on the rink. The spell of warm weather in the Madison area had turned the rink's ice soft and left pools of water on the surface.

Coach Farquhar made a point to get the word out to fans who noticed that the bleachers at the Lower Campus Rink were being torn down should not assume the hockey season is over. In fact, the bleachers were quickly being rebuilt in order to handle the increasingly large crowds who were clamoring to watch the fastest game on ice. The news seating would be finished in time for the faceoff between the Badgers and Wolverines.

The Wisconsin hockey varsity team on the night they played Michigan.

The Wisconsin hockey team had been nicknamed the "stick candy" team (also known as the candy canes) due to their striped white and cardinal colored hockey sweaters and socks.

Wisconsin had Michigan scheduled for games February 16 and 17. These would be the last home games of the season. By Thursday night, the UW ice was sufficient to play the rematch games. Both were scheduled to begin at 8 p.m. All of the prior preparations could not help the Wolverines contain "The Don" — star center Don Meiklejohn and impenetrable goalkeeper captain Don Mitchell. The Badger skaters dominated their opponents with adept stick handling, passing and skating.

They also attacked the Wolverines whenever they had the puck. As usual, this classic matchup was a highly physical affair that entertained the crowds, as did the finesse play by the cardinal and white skaters.

Wisconsin got on the scoreboard first in the opening period after Swiderski was able to pound the puck into the goal after his teammates helped set up in the Wolverine's zone. The rest of the period was scoreless, but both teams racked up penalties due to rough play. During the second period, two UW players were removed due to penalties and Michigan scored during the power play. Later in the second period, Max Murphy scored after anticipating the Michigan goalie's attempted pass to a teammate. Murphy intercepted it and slammed home the creative goal. In the final period, Don Meiklejohn initiated a breakaway play and topped it off by dekeing the Wolverines goalie, who came way out of the net one way and bit on the fake, while Meiklejohn went the other way, and escorted the puck unchallenged into the net for the final tally. The Badgers won this first game 3-1.

Wisconsin Lineup: Meiklejohn (Center), Murphy (Right Wing), Kreuger (Left Wing), Mason (Right Defense), McCarter (Left Defense) and captain Mitchell (Goalie). Substitutes: Swiderski, Carrier and Drummond. Saves: Wisconsin 19, Michigan 25. Referee: Jake Thompson from the Milwaukee Athletic Club.

Wisconsin had their hands full with Michigan during the following game Friday, February 17. The Wolverines had clearly modified their playbook. Meiklejohn displayed his extraordinary talents and opened the scoring by shooting in a rebound to put the UW up 1-0. Michigan tied the score in the second period. The third period had plenty of fireworks.

The Wolverines were playing what was considered a pro-style of ice hockey that included big hits and lots of checking. Wisconsin was playing what was deemed a collegiate style of hockey that was built on fast skating, finesse plays and elaborate passing. The Badgers would not be intimidated by the physical game from their opponents and gave it right back to them each time with every opportunity. Numerous times during the contest it appeared an all-out brawl would erupt. Referee Thompson penalized the visiting Wolverines players so many times that they vehemently protested the infractions. The last half of the final period was very hard fought and Michigan went with a four-man offense to keep constant pressure in the UW zone and on the Wisconsin net.

At the end of regulation, the score was tied 1-1. Neither team scored during the first overtime, but Wisconsin buzzed the Michigan zone and pounded the Wolverines net for the majority of the extra period. During the second overtime period, Meiklejohn scored a beautiful goal on perfect pass from Murphy to give the Badgers the victory! A big part of the credit for this win was given to star goaltender Don Mitchell along with the ferocious Badger defensive duo of Mason and McCarter, who denied multiple attacks from the Michigan skaters. Wisconsin won the second game 2-1, capping off a three-game winning streak. An estimated one thousand plus spectators witnessed this game and thoroughly enjoyed the hockey action on the Madison campus. The UW team was still on top in the conference.

Wisconsin Lineup: Meiklejohn (Center), Murphy (Right Wing), Krueger (Left Wing), McCarter (Right Defense), Mason (Left Defense) and captain Mitchell (Goalie). Substitutes: Carrier, Drummond and Swiderski. Saves: Wisconsin 40, Michigan 42. Referee: Jake Thompson from the Milwaukee Athletic Club.

The UW hockey team had to travel to Minnesota to face the Gophers next February 20 and 21. Minnesota had a distinct advantage by practicing and playing on artificial ice, a luxury the Wisconsin skaters were forced to do without every season. Clearly, Minnesota had not forgotten the beating Wisconsin handed them earlier in the season and had revenge in mind.

After a scoreless first and second period, the Gophers scored two minutes into the third period. The first game at the Minneapolis Arena ended in a 1-0 loss for the Badgers.

Wisconsin Lineup: Meiklejohn (Center), Murphy (Right Wing), Krueger (Left Wing), McCarter (Right Defense), Mason (Left Defense), and captain Mitchell (Goalie). Substitutes: Carrier, Drummond and Swiderski. Saves: Wisconsin 38, Minnesota 15. Penalties: First Period - None. Second Period - (W) Krueger – slashing, (M) Brown – tripping, (W) Swiderski – clubbing, (M) Galob – holding. Third Period: (M) Conway –slashing, (M) Gustafson – slashing.

The UW skaters were unable to get much going this weekend. Minnesota opened the scoring around six minutes into the opening period of the second game. Five minutes later they added a second goal to take a 2-0 lead. After a scoreless second period, Wisconsin's Don Meiklejohn scored on a beautiful pass from Max Murphy to tally the first goal for the Badgers just over a minute into the third period. The score was 2-1. Around 15 minutes later, Minnesota scored again to stretch their lead to 3-1. To add insult to injury, the Gophers scored with less than a minute and a half left in the game to make it 4-1.

Throughout the game, the intensity and rivalry caused numerous scraps. Only one nearly evolved into a full-blown brawl when Badger defenseman "Red" Carrier and the Minnesota captain locked up and exchanged pleasantries. Fortunately, the referee was able to separate the men and the game continued.

The Gophers handed the Badgers a 4-1 loss to end the weekend series. Around seven thousand five hundred people were in attendance to cheer on the Minnesota team as they again clinched the Big Ten title.

Wisconsin Lineup: Meiklejohn (Center), Murphy (Right Wing), Krueger (Left Wing), McCarter (Right Defense) Mason (Left Defense), and captain Mitchell (Goalie). Substitutes: Carrier, Drummond and Swiderski. Saves: Wisconsin 40, Minnesota 9. Penalties: First Period – None. Second Period - (M) Brown – slashing, (M) Galob – slashing. Third Period- (W) Krueger – tripping (W) Murphy –tripping. Referee: Bill Haman from St. Paul.

Kreuger   Meiklejohn   Goetz

Max Murphy

John McCarter

A makeup game forced the Badgers back to Milwaukee Friday, February 24 to play the Marquette Hilltoppers. Marquette had won the previous game, 3-2. Marquette also assumed first place in the Western Conference Hockey League once Minnesota swept Wisconsin the week before. As expected, the Hilltoppers played brilliantly and smoked the Badgers by a score of 6-2. Both Meiklejohn and Swiderski had the only goals for Wisconsin. This was the Hilltoppers 12th straight victory this season.

Wisconsin Lineup: Meiklejohn (Center), Kreuger (Right Wing), Murphy (Left Wing), Carrier (Right Defense), Mason (Left Defense) and captain Mitchell (Goalie). Saves: Wisconsin 35, Marquette 11.

The Badgers returned to Detroit to face the Michigan Wolverines in the final two games of the season. Wisconsin's hockey squad was guaranteed to take second place in the Big Ten conference regardless of whether they won or lost these last two games. The first game February 27 at the Olympia Stadium rink was a defensive battle as the two teams had to settle for a 0-0 tie even after an extra overtime period was exhausted. The hockey game lasted for a total of 70 minutes.

Wisconsin Lineup: Meiklejohn (Center), Kreuger (Right Wing), Murphy (Left Wing), Carrier (Right Defense), Mason (Left Defense) and captain Mitchell (Goalie). Saves: Wisconsin 41, Michigan 31. Referee: Sid Rankin from Windsor.

On February 28, Michigan came out flying and scored their first goal one minute into the game. Late in the first period the Wolverines scored a second goal. With less than one minute left in the first period, the Michigan skaters shot a third goal past the distracted UW goalie from 15 feet away. The Wolverines had a 3-0 lead after one period. Badger forward Jimmy Mason scored the lone goal for Wisconsin in the second period. Michigan easily came out on top and handed the Badgers an unsettling 3-1 defeat. The anti-climactic end to the season was a bitter pill to swallow, especially for those UW skaters that had ended their collegiate hockey careers in Michigan.

Wisconsin Lineup: Meiklejohn (Center), Kreuger (Right Wing), Murphy (Left Wing), Carrier (Right Defense), Mason (Left Defense) and captain Mitchell (Goalie). Saves: Wisconsin 27, Michigan 25. Referee: Sid Ranking from Windsor.

Farquhar, who quickly became a popular and well-liked coach at the UW, made it well known before he departed for his home in Winnipeg over the summer break that he wished hockey would be designated a major (varsity) sport, at the University of Wisconsin. He knew hockey deserved the same respect and funding as that of the other major sports on campus. The throngs of people attending hockey games and the surge in popularity surrounding the sport backed up his assertion. 1927-28 was also the first season the Badger women held a hockey tournament. Their efforts would continue to pave the way for the NCAA to one day recognize women's hockey.

Players from the University of Wisconsin hockey team that were awarded their "W" varsity letters this season included captain Don Mitchell (Duluth, Minnesota), James Mason (Winnipeg, Ontario), John McCarter (Madison, Wisconsin), Don Meiklejohn (Madison, Wisconsin), Earl Carrier (Essex Fells, New Jersey) Max Murphy (Green Bay, Wisconsin), Gilbert Krueger (Neenah, Wisconsin), Ed Swiderksi (Duluth, Minnesota), James Drummond (Cleveland, Ohio), and manager Edward Konkol (Ashland, Wisconsin). Captain Don Mitchell, John McCarter and Max Murphy would be lost to graduation.

Goal keeper Don Mitchell, was honored to be selected as the team captain. He was the first goalie selected to be team captain in the history of the University of Wisconsin ice hockey program. His toughness, exemplary play and competitive spirit made him a logical choice for this vital role. In fact, he went on to have a superb season as both the captain and goaltender.

Mitchell

In a letter to the *Wisconsin Athletic Review*, published in May 1928, head coach Johnny Farquhar would nominate captain Mitchell as the most valuable player in the conference. The selection letter from coach Farquhar explained why Mitchell received the accolades, "He has been selected solely on his wonderful performance this past season, and the reason that Wisconsin made such a remarkable showing this year was due to his canny work between the posts. Don has probably had more experience than any other conference player, coming from the hockey town of Duluth, where he had an opportunity of practicing with senior and professional clubs for many seasons before entering the university." (7)

1927-28   Schedule and Results:
Coach John Farquhar
3-5-2 Second in WIHL/Big Ten   5-7-4 Overall

Date	Result	Opponent
December 27	Loss 3-2	@ Marquette (MI)*
December 29	Loss 6-0	@ Michigan College*
December 30	Tie 0-0	@ Michigan College*
December 31	Tie 1-1	@ Wausau*
January 2	Win 4-0	@ Oshkosh*
January 6	Loss 3-2	Marquette (WI)

January 7	Win 2-1	Wausau*
February 3	Win 2-1 2OT	Minnesota
February 4	Tie 1-1 4OT	Minnesota
February 16	Win 3-1	Michigan
February 17	Win 2-1 2OT	Michigan
February 20	Loss 1-0	@ Minnesota
February 21	Loss 4-1	@ Minnesota
February 24	Loss 6-2	@ Marquette (WI)
February 27	Tie 0-0 OT	@ Michigan#
February 28	Loss 3-1	@ Michigan#

*Exhibition Games

#Played at Olympia Stadium.

Chapter Ten
Sweeping Away the Gophers

1928-29 UW Hockey Team

As the weather grew cooler, the sounds of hockey returned. Hockey blades cut into the ice, sticks smacked pucks and skaters shouted to one another. Those hopeful to make the Badgers hockey team spent the fall working on their conditioning so they would be ready for this annual tradition.

Coach Farquhar reported to Madison December 15 and agreed to lead the Badgers for another season. The Wisconsin Athletic Department formally confirmed Johnny Farquhar and contracted him to coach the UW hockey team for a second season. He had a strong prediction about ice hockey as one of many sports at the University of Wisconsin, "We'll be king soon." Even though hockey was in its infancy when compared with football, basketball, baseball and other sports, it had all of the necessary traits to become a top varsity sport among spectators, students and athletes at the UW. Farquhar is credited with growing the Wisconsin hockey fan base and the loyalty of his skaters with his dynamic personality and enthusiasm for improving the hockey program. Coach Farquhar also committed to making additional improvements to the current hockey rink on the Madison campus.

Discussions and negotiations were underway during the start of this season that would see Illinois and Northwestern join the hockey league along with Wisconsin, Michigan and Minnesota. Minnesota, Michigan, Illinois and Northwestern also had the luxury of indoor ice rinks with artificial ice. Wisconsin was the only school forced to rely on outdoor, natural ice.

Coach Farquhar had only two players returning from last year's varsity team to build this year's team around. They were captain Don Meiklejohn, a center that was last year's leading scorer and Gil Kreuger, a small winger affectionately known by the fans as "the baby cyclone."

Playing with Krueger at the other wing was Art Thomsen from Milwaukee. Gordon Meiklejohn, the younger brother of Don, would alternate for playing time with Thomsen. At the urging of coach Farquhar, Harold Rebholz, a veteran fullback on the UW football team, showed up at hockey practice. Even though Rebholz had never played hockey before, he was a natural athlete that was taught how to be an effective defenseman for the Wisconsin hockey team. Art Frisch and Milo Lubratovich, both sophomores on the football squad, were the leading hockey players trying out for the backup goalie position behind starting goalie and captain, Don Mitchell. Mitchell had turned down several offers to sign contracts with professional hockey teams at this point in his life and instead elected to finish his collegiate career.

Five students were competing for the two open defensemen positions. A couple of players that had a distinct advantage in hockey skills included Harold Rebholz, a fullback on the football team and Jim Gallagher, who was a star on the freshman hockey team two years ago. Others vying for the defensive positions included Bardes, Schroeder and Siegel.

Skaters from last year's freshman team would fill out the remaining roster spots for this year's varsity Wisconsin hockey team if needed. Unfortunately, Swiderski was deemed academically ineligible for this season and would not return until the 1929-30 campaign.

Don Mitchell, the star goalie and captain for the Wisconsin hockey team was in the net to begin the year. Mitchell was considered to be one of the most talented goalies to play the varsity sport in America. Consequently, he was forced to unexpectedly vacate the position and depart from the Badger hockey team due to an undisclosed illness. He was ultimately deemed ineligible as a result of leaving the University. His lengthy recuperation back home in Saranac Lake, New York and poor health prevented him from returning to compete for a third year as a Badger goaltender at Wisconsin. Goalie Arthur Frisch, who was also a guard on the UW football team, was selected to replace Mitchell and fill this critical vacancy on the hockey team.

After a brief preseason training regimen both on and off the ice, the 1928-29 team was ready for some games. The club started their training competition with an exhibition schedule consisting of four games. While Christmas break was a relaxing time for the majority of students at Wisconsin, the hockey squad prepared for the upcoming regular season with a road trip. Preparations involved twice-a-day hockey practices in order to get in the best possible shape and to work on set plays.

This year their travels took them to the Upper Peninsula of Michigan for a pair of late December games. First up was a December 27 rematch against the Michigan College of Mines also known as the Houghton School of Mines. Gil Krueger was named acting captain in place of Don Meiklejohn who was in the Madison hospital fighting a serious case of influenza. In another close defensive matchup, each team was limited to only one goal. Krueger scored late in the game for Wisconsin to tie it at 1-1. The overtime period was unable to determine a winner so the tie stood.

On the following day, December 28, the UW boys were in Marquette, Michigan for a game versus the Marquette Owls at the Palestra rink. The Wisconsin skaters were beginning to bond as a team. It showed on the ice as they skated and passed well to one another on the way to a dominant 3-1 win over the Owls. Art Thomsen scored two goals in the first period for the Badgers while Gordon Meiklejohn scored the third goal midway through the third period. Wisconsin stayed in Marquette the day after beating the Owls in order to get in another practice.

Left to Right: G. La Budde (Mgr.), L. Peterson, H. Siegel, J. Gallagher, A. Thomsen, A. Frisch, G. Meiklejohn, captain D. Meiklejohn, captain G. Krueger, Coach Farquhar

1928–29 Wisconsin Varsity Hockey Team

The exhibition season continued on New Years Day when the Badgers visited the Wausau Cardinals Hockey Club. Coach Farquhar had scheduled his team to play against the club from Waterloo, Iowa, but a late cancellation had the team traveling to Wausau instead. The faceoff was set for 2:30 p.m. Sunday at the hockey rink on the Wisconsin River at Rothschild Park. This game was scheduled by the Wausau Frolic Committee. Last season, these teams played each other twice with the Badgers winning one and playing to a tie in the other game.

This contest had plenty of exciting action and consisted of fast skating, swift passing and hard shots that thrilled the crowd, which was estimated to be several hundred. The UW players continued to work well together and played a fierce style of hockey. Thomsen tallied an unassisted goal around six minutes into the first period after he skated straight down the ice at the Cardinal goalie and beat him with a shot. Wisconsin was on top 1-0 as the period ended.

Gordon Meiklejohn got the scoring going in the second period by sliding the puck between the Cardinals goalie's legs after getting a nice pass from Thomsen on the right side of the rink. A minute later Wausau was able to get on the scoreboard, making the score 2-1.

After gaining possession of the puck at center ice, Thomsen zig-zagged down the left side of the rink before making a perfect pass to Krueger who smashed the puck into the Wausau net. The score was 3-1 in favor of the Badgers. The final three UW goals happened in the first four minutes of the second period. Thomsen assisted on the two goals Gordon Meiklejohn scored and the other goal was scored by captain Krueger.

The Badgers went into a defensive mode after that and thwarted the attacks by the Wausau players. As time expired, the Badgers had another win with a 4-1 victory over the amateurs from Wausau. Art Thomsen was the MVP of this game, playing a part in all four Wisconsin goals and staying on the ice for the entire 60 minutes. Goalie Art Frisch also put on a spectacular display with his nontraditional techniques. Whether he was using his legs to kick away a shot, his hands to catch or deflect a shot, or his stick to block and deflect a shot, he was pulling off acrobatic moves the spectators had never seen before.

Also, of interest to the spectators was to see the two very different styles of play. The Wausau team would have one man skate the puck toward the Wisconsin net while the remaining players trailed behind the puck carrier. The Badgers would have three forwards wide, one in the middle and a winger on either side, working in tandem. This is similar to how hockey is played in the modern era.

Wisconsin Lineup: Gordon Meiklejohn (Center), captain Kreuger (Right Wing) and Thomsen (Left Wing), Gallagher (Right Defense), Rebholz (Left Defense) and Frisch (Goalie). Substitute: Peterson. Saves: Wisconsin 5, Wausau 11.

On Thursday, January 3, the Badgers ended their exhibition season in Illinois with a nighttime match against the Chicago Athletic Association club hockey team at the Chicago Coliseum. This hockey game was scheduled immediately following the conclusion of the National Hockey Leagues Chicago Blackhawks game versus the Toronto Maple Leafs, a unique opportunity for the UW. A crowd estimated at over five thousand stayed to watch the Badgers play the C.A.A. Fortunately, coach Farquhar's boys continued to play very well together and execute his game plans.

Back on the roster after being sidelined with the flu, Don Meiklejohn scored a goal in the first period for the Badgers when he got behind the Chicago defenseman and tipped in a shot on net. It was 1-0 in favor of Wisconsin after the first period.

Gordon Meiklejohn scored a goal with a long shot near the boards along blue line in the second. The UW now had a 2-0 lead.

C.A.A. was able to ruin the shutout by scoring on Frisch in the third period with a long shot of their own. The score was trimmed to 2-1 but Gordon Meiklejohn notched his second goal of the game with another long shot from within the Chicago zone to give the Badgers a two-goal cushion. The UW team earned another win by defeating Chicago 3-1. Frisch had a jaw-dropping 44 saves as he expertly defended the Wisconsin net.

Wisconsin Lineup: Gordon Meiklejohn (Center), captain Kreuger (Right Wing) and Thomsen (Left Wing), Gallagher (Right Defense), Rebholz (Left Defense) and Frisch (Goalie). Substitute: Peterson. Saves: Wisconsin 44, Chicago 21.

It was the first time a Wisconsin team had completed the holiday exhibition matches undefeated after winning every game before the regular season began. Gordon Meiklejohn and forward Arthur Thomsen led the team in scoring with three goals each to start this season. The Wisconsin hockey team continued to practice twice daily in preparation for their upcoming games against the North Dakota Aggies.

When Dr. Alexander Meiklejohn accepted a post at the University of Wisconsin as a professor, it was a decision that made an impact on the Badger hockey program. Until this time, the Wisconsin hockey team was routinely defeated by the top teams in the Western Conference. At the time Dr. Meiklejohn came to the UW, so did his highly talented sons Don and Gordon. Don would become the captain of the team and play center while his brother Gordon, an eventual Wisconsin captain, would play wing. Fortunately for the Wisconsin hockey program and its fans, the Meiklejohn's decided to leave their East Coast teams and made a new home in Madison.

On the weekend of January 11 and 12, the North Dakota Agricultural College hockey team, also known as the "Aggies" (later renamed the North Dakota State University Bison), visited the UW campus during their multi-college hockey tour. The Aggies were a rugged and hard skating hockey team. The Badgers were ready to give it right back to them.

The visitors scored first to take a 1-0 lead at the end of the opening period. Even though the UW had 16 shots in the first period, they were unable to score. The Aggies scored again in the second period to gain a 2-0 lead. In the third, Don Meiklejohn scored twice to tie the game at 2-2. His first tally was two minutes into the last period. Thirty seconds later he scored his second goal! Several minutes later,

Wisconsin's Gallagher picked up the puck in front of his own net and skated around the Aggies players before ripping a shot that beat the goalie to give the Badgers a 3-2 lead. During the last five minutes of the final period, Gordon Meiklejohn scored on a slick pass from Thomsen. Wisconsin beat North Dakota 4-2 in a classic battle of strength and skill.

Rebholz, Frisch and Gallagher

Wisconsin Lineup: Gordon Meiklejohn (Center), captain Don Meiklejohn (Right Wing), Thomsen (Left Wing), Rebholz (Right Defense), Nole (Left Defense) and Frisch (Goalie). Spares: Gallagher, captain Krueger, Bardes, Siegel and Wilson. Saves: Wisconsin 10, North Dakota 35. Referee: Jake Thompson from the Milwaukee Athletic Club.

In the second game of the series, the UW skaters figured out ways to expose the North Dakota defense and goaltending. A bitterly cold temperature of 10 degrees below zero, with a windchill of 30 below kept the crowd at home for this game. In fact, it was so cold that only Don and Gordon Meiklejohn's father and two reporters from different newspapers watched this game. Wisconsin pounded in eight goals while giving up four to the feisty Aggie squad. Siegel scored a hat trick, while Don Meiklejohn, Gordon Meiklejohn, Peterson, Krueger and Thomsen each scored a goal. Wisconsin held the lead by a score of 2-1 after the first period.

In the second period the floodgates opened as both Gordon and Don Meiklejohn, along with Thomsen and Siegel all scored for the Badgers. By the end of the second the score was in Wisconsin's favor, 6-2. The Aggies scored two more goals in the last period, but so would the Badgers. Both Siegel and Krueger tallied goals to push the score to 8-4.

This was the Aggies second loss of the weekend. The sweep came at as a cost as there was a serious injury to star winger Art Thomsen. He would be out of the Badgers lineup for an indefinite time.

Wisconsin Lineup: Gordon Meiklejohn (Center), captain Don Meiklejohn (Right Wing), Thomsen (Left Wing), Rebholz (Right Defense), Bardes (Left Defense) and Frisch (Goalie). Substitutes: Gallagher, Peterson, captain Krueger, Siegel, Dahlman and DeHaven. Saves: Wisconsin 13, North Dakota 19.

Art Thomsen's injury from the Aggies game was serious enough to prevent him from playing in the January 18 match against the Marquette University Hilltoppers. These rivals met at the Marquette rink for an 8:15 p.m. faceoff. The loss of Thomsen, along with the changing of some other line combinations, caused significant confusion and discord among the UW line mates. Despite the best efforts of the UW coach running practices focused on plans to devise defensive strategies in order to stop the Hilltoppers before the game, it was all for naught.

Neither team netted a goal through 10 minutes of play. The deadlock stopped in the twelfth minute when Marquette scored. The Hilltoppers tallied eight more goals in a row. Wisconsin was held off the scoreboard entirely. Consequently, the UW skaters suffered the worst loss of the year by a score of 9-0 against Marquette. This ended the Badgers five-game winning streak.

Wisconsin Lineup: captain Don Meiklejohn (Center), Siegel (Right Wing), captain Krueger (Left Wing), Rebholz (Right Defense), Gallagher (Left Defense) and Frisch (Goalie). Saves: Wisconsin 30, Marquette 13. Referees: Healy from Chicago and MacDonald from Toronto.

Art Thomsen

Art Thomsen came to the University of Wisconsin from Milwaukee and he was in his second year of a four-year degree majoring in physical education. He was an incredibly talented addition to the UW hockey roster playing at left wing. Thomsen initially came to Madison as a highly-skilled swimmer from the Milwaukee Athletic Club. As a freshman, he was a coveted member of the varsity swim team anchoring on the 160-yard relay squad. Fortunately for the Wisconsin hockey program, he left the swim team to participate on the ice this winter. Thomsen was a power forward known for his offensive attacks and also gained a lot of attention for his defensive efforts on the ice. While participating in the physical education program at the UW, he worked each weekday during the football season at one of the training tables assisting injured players with a variety of prescribed first aid and physical therapy. The Badger hockey program was fortunate to have such a player in the lineup. He was such an amazing athlete that he eventually decided to double roster this season participating on both the varsity hockey and swimming teams. Thomsen was torn when deciding to leave one of his sports for the other, so he elected to participate in both with the approval of his UW coaches.

Coach Farquhar went back to the drawing board to redesign custom plays and to revise his lines. He quickly appointed Art Thomsen and Gordon Meiklejohn to play defense on the Badger squad, joining fellow defensemen Russell Rebholz and Jimmie Gallagher. The four defensemen were intelligent and competitive players who were logical solutions to shore up the defensive needs of the team. The Badger hockey team was especially strong and ready to defend their zone.

In early February, the UW club headed to the Third Annual Wausau (WI) Winter Frolic Carnival to play some old foes and new competition. The Wausau round robin tournament games did not count as conference games for the Badgers. Rather, it was a fun tournament and the winner would be crowned Midwest Amateur Champions.

First up was a hockey game Thursday, February 7 against the host team from the Wausau Cardinals Hockey Club. This game would be held at the rink located on the grounds of Rothschild Park and an estimated five thousand fans were on hand to watch the event. While the Badgers were more skilled, their opponents would not roll over and had plenty of fight in them. At the final whistle, the Wisconsin skaters defeated the Wausau squad by a score of 6-1. Gordon Meiklejohn scored three goals while his brother and team captain, Don scored two goals. Gil Krueger had the other goal for the UW squad.

Wisconsin Lineup: captain Don Meiklejohn (Center), captain Krueger (Right Wing), Siegel (Left Wing), Thomsen (Right Defense), Gordon Meiklejohn (Left Defense) and Frisch (Goalie). Wisconsin Substitutes: Rebholz, Gallagher, Peterson, DeHaven and Ahlberg.

Next in their bracket was a rematch with Marquette (MI). On Friday, February 8, the Badgers faced off against the Marquette Owls, an equally skilled group of veteran skaters. This was an end-to-end game that was hard hitting and dominated by stellar goaltending and defensive action. During the first period, Wisconsin winger Howard Siegel tallied the first goal with a long shot on net from the far-right side of the rink to put his team up 1-0. It would be the game-winning goal as the Badgers defeated the Owls by a narrow 1-0 margin.

Wisconsin Lineup: captain Don Meiklejohn (Center), captain Krueger (Right Wing), Siegel (Left Wing), Thomsen (Right Defense), Gordon Meiklejohn (Left Defense) and Frisch (Goalie).

Wisconsin Substitutes: Rebholz, Gallagher, Peterson, DeHaven and Ahlberg.

On Saturday, February 10, the Badgers were paired up against Eveleth (MN) Junior College for a chance at the Winter Carnival championship. Also dubbed the Wisconsin Amateur Championship. The mighty skaters from Eveleth had what was considered to be one of the strongest teams in Midwest. Although the Wisconsin skaters were up for the challenge and matched the skating skills of the junior college challengers, the UW players were unable to find the back of the net. Eveleth, on the other hand, was able to slip two goals past the UW goalkeeper, Frisch. The Badgers barely lost by a score of 2-0 in this physically challenging game. Eveleth would win the Midwest Amateur Championship at the Winter Carnival by coming from behind to defeat St. Mary's College of Winona, Minnesota.

Wisconsin Lineup: captain Don Meiklejohn (Center), captain Krueger (Right Wing), Siegel (Left Wing), Thomsen (Right Defense), Gordon Meiklejohn (Left Defense) and Frisch (Goalie). Wisconsin Substitutes: Rebholz, Gallagher, Peterson, DeHaven and Ahlberg.

Next on the schedule were the Minnesota Gophers who returned to the UW Madison campus for a pair of games Wednesday, Feb and Thursday, February 14. Both games started at 7:30 p.m. on the Lower Campus Rink. Minnesota won the Western Conference championship last season and were just as tough this year with many expecting them to repeat as Big Ten champions. The Gophers arrived in the capital city with plans to make up for the loss suffered against Wisconsin last season. They tried to intimidate others with players named "Moosejaw" McCabe, "Big Foot" Tilton and "Saskatoon" Brown but the Badgers would not be bullied.

The Wisconsin rink was in fantastic condition, for a change, and ideal weather made for perfect ice. The Badger skaters were ready to play and took it to the Gophers as soon as the puck was dropped in the first game. An exceptionally loud crowd packed the bleachers of the home rink to watch this escalating rivalry. The UM squad had their hands full with a very feisty Wisconsin team.

Everyone in the crowd couldn't help but notice that two starting forwards, Don Meiklejohn and Art Siegel, wore unique leather hockey helmets to protect their prescription glasses. The protective gear was very high-tech for its time.

The Wisconsin offense was able to move the puck skillfully. Eleven minutes into the first period, Siegel scored the Badgers' first goal by smashing in a loose puck during a contentious pileup of players in front of the Gopher net. It was 1-0 Badgers after one period.

Early in the second period, captain Meiklejohn ripped a hard shot that the UM goalie stopped, but the rebound came right to Krueger. He immediately fired back on net and the Gopher goaltender blocked the attempt, but the deflection hit his defenseman in the shoulder and bounced into the back of the net. Krueger was credited with the second goal for the UW team to give the cardinal and white a rare 2-0 lead. Minnesota finally scored 10 minutes later. It was so cold that more than half the crowd that was on hand at the start of the game had departed so that they could unthaw.

The Gopher's plan was to repeatedly take long shots from center ice and chase down the puck to thwart the Badger defense, but it didn't work as planned. Wisconsin had completely outplayed Minnesota the entire match.

At a mere 120 pounds, "Baby Dynamite" (as Gil Krueger was also affectionately called by some fans) was hailed as a star of the game for his extraordinary hustle and the countless Gopher plays that he singlehandedly broke up. The same could be said for Thomsen. The two-sport athlete broke up numerous Minnesota rushes and brought the puck back into the opponent's zone on offensive attacks. The other UW star was the goalkeeper Frisch, hailing from Chisolm, Minnesota. He had 43 stops and kept the Gophers to only one goal. That one goal was scored when Frisch came out of his net to aggressively play the puck but found himself at least 8 feet from the crease when Minnesota put it in the net. The penalty boxes had a continual flow of players from each team due to many penalties handed out during the action. Even though the Gophers had a deep bench with several extra players, a determined Badger team skated to a well-deserved 2-1 victory. With this win, Wisconsin was the only undefeated Big Ten hockey team.

Wisconsin Lineup: captain Don Meiklejohn (Center), captain Krueger (Right Wing), Siegel (Left Wing), Thomsen (Right Defense), Gordon Meiklejohn (Left Defense) and Frisch (Goalie). Wisconsin Substitutes: Rebholz, Gallagher, Peterson, DeHaven and Ahlberg.

Not to be outdone, the Gopher team regrouped in preparation for the next game. Valentine's Day would be a heartbreaker for the cardinal and white skaters. The Badgers were clearly still exhausted from their game the night before. Another crowd of a couple of thousand spectators arrived for this night game and did the best they could to motivate the UW club with a variety of entertaining cheers, but the Minnesota team had other plans.

Around 15 minutes into the opening period, Minnesota capitalized on a nice three-man attack for a goal. To assist their efforts, Wisconsin defenseman Thomsen was serving a penalty at the time. The goal itself was a bit of a fluke as it found the back of the net only after glancing off the skate blade of Badger goalie Frisch. Minnesota was up 1-0 at the end of the first.

In the second period, a somewhat evenly matched game was broken up with yet another fluky Gopher goal. "Saskatoon" Brown gathered the puck at mid-ice and sent a wild shot toward the Badger net that skipped, slid, hopped and eventually careened with one last terrible bounce to find its way into the back of the Wisconsin net.

The third period was scoreless despite many attempts by the Badgers. Wisconsin's home crowd was in a frenzy as they tried to give their guys the hometown advantage. The game ended in a 2-0 loss for the Badgers. Coach Farquhar inserted big, bad Harold Rebholz to protect his smaller players and set a tone. Rebholz brought the crowd to their feet several times with enormous body checks and a couple of flying tackles upon the Minnesota opponents. Rebholz, alone, was called for three penalties. Both penalty boxes had frequent visitors as the Badgers and Gophers stretched and broke, the rules throughout the entire contest. With a revised game plan, the luxury of extra skaters to substitute in every few minutes and a couple of fluke goals, Minnesota was able to shut out the Badgers. Minnesota regained the lead of the Big Ten conference with the win.

Wisconsin Lineup: captain Don Meiklejohn (Center), captain Krueger (Right Wing), Siegel (Left Wing), Gordon Meiklejohn (Right Defense), Thomsen (Left Defense) and Frisch (Goalie). Substitute: Rebholz. Saves: Wisconsin 24, Minnesota 29. Referees: Wayne from Minneapolis and Healey from Chicago.

Top Row: Unknown Player, Hal Rebholz and Carl Peterson
Bottom Row: Art Thomsen, Don Meiklejohn and Unknown Player

Due to the demand for additional seating for spectators, the UW Athletic Department approved and added another section of bleachers on the north side of the hockey rink before the Michigan series. The extra seating was set up in order to accommodate the steady overflow crowds that surrounded the Lower Campus Rink this season to watch the Badger hockey team as they took on other challengers. Hockey at the University of Wisconsin was growing exponentially in popularity.

The Michigan Wolverines were next on the schedule to face the Wisconsin Badgers at the Madison outdoor rink. The February 18 and 19 games were sure to be well attended even though they fell on Monday and Tuesday nights. Another growing rivalry, the Badgers had no love lost when playing against the Wolverines. These games were guaranteed to be rough, fast-paced and contentious.

Several hundred fans showed up to watch the hockey game Monday, February 18 and to cheer on their Badgers. The Athletic Department intentionally pushed back the start time of this hockey game to 9 p.m. so it would not conflict with the UW versus Northwestern basketball game.

Michigan scored first at 15 minutes into the opening period to take a 1-0 lead. Gordon Meiklejohn tied it up at 1-1 for the Badgers two minutes into the second period on a beautiful counter after a pretty pass from Siegel. The Wolverines regained the lead again just five minutes later when their defenseman scored on a shot from center ice. Don Meiklejohn tallied the last goal of the second period after some fancy passing between his linemates to tie the game at 2-2.

Neither team was able to score in the third period so the two teams were forced to play an overtime period. The Wolverines got a lucky bounce and escaped with a 3-2 win over the Badgers after scoring the final goal four minutes into the OT period. By this time, late into the frozen Wisconsin evening, only a couple dozen Wisconsin faithful fans remained to see the end of the game.

Wisconsin Lineup: captain Don Meiklejohn (Center), Siegel (Right Wing), captain Krueger (Left Wing), Gordon Meiklejohn (Right Defense), Thomsen (Left Defense) and Frisch (Goalie). Substitutes: Rebholz, Peterson, DeHaven, Gallagher and Ahlberg. Saves: Wisconsin 20, Michigan 24. Referees: Ed Wayte from Winnipeg.

On the next night, coach Farquhar adjusted the game plan and had his skaters fired up for the second game against Michigan. Wisconsin outplayed the Wolverine squad and beat them to most of the loose pucks. The UW team was also able to win most of the faceoffs and control the puck a majority of the game. Siegel scored first for the Badgers on a nice passing play from Donnie Meiklejohn to give the home team a 1-0 lead 30 seconds after the game had started. Wisconsin buzzed the Michigan net for most of the period. The UW men thought they tallied another score, but the on-ice official waived it off as no goal. The score of 1-0 stood after the first period.

Wisconsin kept the pressure on Michigan during the second period. At one point, captain Don Meiklejohn was parked in front of the Wolverines net when a scrum of players started fighting for the puck. The UW captain banged in the loose puck for the second goal of the game. After two periods, the Badgers were in the lead by a score of 2-0. Peterson was able to get in the game on defense and put on a noteworthy display of his hockey skills.

During the third period, Wisconsin kept the pressure on the Michigan squad. Gordon Meiklejohn iced the game with one more goal for the Badgers during the final minute. Wisconsin won 3-0 and split the series with Michigan.

Goaltender Arthur Frisch's keen focus and superb display of athleticism helped him to turn away several quality Wolverine scoring attempts and helped secure a shutout in the 3-0 win over the Michigan squad.

Wisconsin Lineup: captain Don Meiklejohn (Center), Siegel (Right Wing), captain Krueger (Left Wing), Gordon Meiklejohn (Right Defense), Thomsen (Left Defense) and Frisch (Goalie). Substitutes: Rebholz, Peterson and Gallagher. Saves: Wisconsin 22, Michigan 19. Referee: Ed Wayte from Winnipeg.

*Wisconsin hockey back on **The Wisconsin Athletic Review.***

Wisconsin Goalkeeper Art Frisch

The Badgers were able to get a couple of days of solid practice in before their next game against a dangerous opponent in Marquette, who had a record of 9-2 at this point in the season. One of those wins was at the expense of the Badgers, who they trounced 9-0. Marquette had only lost one game to Minnesota and another to the Chicago Athletic Association hockey club this season.

With four conference games remaining and three nonconference games next on the schedule, the Wisconsin team welcomed back Marquette Thursday, February 21. One of the key UW defenders, Lawrence Peterson, was lost for the remainder of the season due to a serious illness. To add insult to injury, Art Thomsen, one of the best two-way players on the team made the interesting decision to depart early from the varsity hockey team this late in the season in order to focus on being an active member of the UW swimming squad. Despite losing two important players, the Badgers regrouped and were ready to take on Marquette. The Hilltoppers had won nine of their games to date this season and were expected to make easy work of the Badgers.

This game was the first feature attraction hockey match to kick off the University of Wisconsin Winter Carnival. Among the thousand or so spectators in attendance, several hundred had made the trip from Milwaukee to cheer on their Hilltoppers.

Once the game began it was a true back and forth battle with neither team able to score in the first period. When coach Johnny Farquhar wasn't barking out motivation and strategies in between periods, UW Athletic Director George Little was also observed yelling out orders at the Badger players.

Wisconsin's Gilbert "Baby Dynamite" Krueger finished a scoring chance on a crafty move 11 minutes into the second period to give his team a 1-0 lead. It all began with the Badgers blazing down the ice in a three-man wide offensive attack. Krueger passed to Don Meiklejohn, who immediately returned a pass to Krueger. The explosive skater deked to one side, pulling the Marquette goalie out of his net, before going the other way and softly sliding the puck through the vacated crease. It was a huge goal that would be the game winner.

Gallagher, the replacement for Thomsen in the lineup, thrilled the home crowd with some thunderous body checks. Almost every time the visitors made it inside the Wisconsin blue line, Gallagher would seek and destroy his opponent with body contact that put them on their pants. Multiple Marquette players were sent sprawling after venturing too close to the Badger zone.

Both teams were held scoreless in the final period. Goalkeeper Art Frisch played another stellar game in unison with his defensive core led by Jimmy Gallagher. The Badgers bettered Milwaukee with an impressive 1-0 shutout victory. Some were quick to call this the upset of the year! At end of the game Marquette coach and former UW hockey coach, Kay Iverson made a line toward Badger coach Johnny Farquhar in order to congratulate him on the victory. "I don't mind losing a game of that class. It was a great exhibition." Iverson said to Farquhar as they shook hands. (8)

Wisconsin Lineup: captain Don Meiklejohn (Center), Siegel (Right Wing), captain Krueger (Left Wing), Gallagher (Right Defense), Gordon Meiklejohn (Left Defense) and Frisch (Goalie). Substitutes: Rebholz and Peterson. Saves: Wisconsin 22, Marquette 19. Referees: Thompson and Healey.

On Saturday, February 23, the Chicago Athletic Club journeyed to Madison for a rematch. This 7:30 p.m. game was also a featured attraction during the UW Winter Carnival. The Wisconsin defense and goalie were able to shut the door on the visiting Chicago Athletic Club. During the first period, the Badgers made numerous attempts on the opposition's net, but were turned away by the defenseman or the goalie when they got close. Chicago elected to take every shot from a long distance and then to chase it down and try to regain possession. The same flow of play was evident in the middle period, too. Neither team scored during the first two periods.

Wisconsin was able to get on the scoreboard with less than three minutes left in the game. UW defenseman Jimmy Gallagher took the puck from his own zone and weaved through each Chicago player as he went the length of the ice. Gallagher capped off his display when he faked a move in one direction and brought the Chicago netminder out of his goal leaving the net exposed. The Wisconsin skater quickly went the other way and buried a hard shot, which would be the game winner. After scoring, coach Farquhar directed his men to go into a shutdown defense and forego any further offensive attempts. The UW squad notched a 1-0 win. Gallagher was clearly the MVP of the game. His defensive play broke up numerous scoring chances for Chicago while one of his best offensive attacks netted the game winner.

Wisconsin Lineup: captain Don Meiklejohn (Center), captain Krueger (Right Wing), Siegel (Left Wing), Gallagher (Right Defense), Gordon Meiklejohn (Left Defense) and Frisch (Goalie). Substitutes: Rebholz and Peterson. Referee: Wayte from Winnipeg.

Jimmie Gallagher

The last two victories boosted the confidence of the Badger skaters.

Wisconsin arrived the following weekend in Ann Arbor for games during the first couple of days of March. Adding to the challenge at hand, coach John Farquhar was forced to remain in Madison and unable to make this road trip to Michigan since he was too ill to travel due to the flu. Wisconsin freshman coach Ed "Spike" Carlson would take over as temporary head coach in the absence of Farquhar. As fate would have it, the Badgers also found themselves down to only one substitute player on their roster for the weekend series. The chances of clinching second place in the Big Ten didn't look very promising.

Prior to the start of the game, interim UW hockey coach Spike Carlson requested that each period be extended to 22 minutes, and not the traditional 20 minutes, by removing the timeout option. The opposing team and game official granted this odd request. Carlson thought he might be able defuse the Wolverines strategies by changing up the normal length of periods and eliminating the all-important timeout option. Arriving just as the game started, head coach Johnny Farquhar heroically made the journey by himself to Michigan so he could coach his team even though he was very weak after suffering from the flu.

Coaches Johnny Farquhar and Ed "Spike" Carlson

All of the Michigan goals were scored very late as time was close to expiring in each period. The extended period strategy requested by the UW backfired. Michigan's first goal was scored with 3:10 left in the opening period. A second goal scored by the Wolverines came in the final minutes of the middle period at 21:40. The same was true for the Wolverines third goal, which was scored with four minutes left in the final period.

At 8:44 into the third period, Don Meiklejohn got the Badgers on the scoreboard with a nice goal on a short shot from in front of the Wolverines net. The Badger skaters tried to defend their zone and get some much-needed offense going, but they were ultimately limited to the lone goal. Michigan gave Wisconsin a 3-1 loss. The Wolverines had not played a team that was nearly their size on the ice even though they acknowledged that the Badgers body checked harder than any other opponent they faced this season. The March 1 game was dominated by the Wolverines offensively. On the other hand, Wisconsin's reputation as a heavy hitting team, despite their overall small stature, kept true in this game.

Wisconsin Lineup: captain Don Meiklejohn (Center), captain Krueger (Right Wing), Siegel (Left Wing), Gallagher (Right Defense), Gordon Meiklejohn (Left Defense) and Frisch (Goalie). Substitute: Peterson.

On March 2, the Badgers were ready for revenge and played the Wolverines with a lot more intensity. It was a close battle dominated by defense, highlighted by fast skating and thunderous body checking. At the end of regulation time the score was knotted up at 2-2. The game ultimately ended in a tie even though two challenging overtime periods were played. The crowds were estimated between four thousand and five thousand in attendance for this series. Immediately after the game, the Wisconsin team headed to Minnesota for the final games of their season. Fortunately, Art Thomsen rejoined the team and was ready to play against the Gophers.

Wisconsin Lineup: captain Don Meiklejohn (Center), captain Krueger (Right Wing), Siegel (Left Wing), Gallagher (Right Defense), Gordon Meiklejohn (Left Defense) and Frisch (Goalie). Substitute: Peterson.

The final regular series conference matchup had the Wisconsin team in Minneapolis to face northern rival Minnesota at the Minneapolis Arena. These games would be played Monday and

Tuesday nights. The Gophers had a 5-1 record at this point of the season and their only loss was given to them by the Wisconsin Badger skaters. They had vengeance on their mind and were ready to capture the WIHL conference title.

From the start, the March 4 game was a furious match dominated by physical play, sharp passing and exceptionally fast skating. Even though the Badger bench was without a suitable number of substitutes, the UW team hung tough with the Gophers. The first period ended without either team netting any goals. Nearly three minutes into the second period, Minnesota got on the scoreboard. The goal was a result of the Gopher player intercepting a pass Don Meiklejohn intended for his brother Gordon and capitalizing on the opportunity. That score held up as the period ended. It was at nearly the three-minute mark of the third period that Minnesota scored again to go up 2-0.

Despite their best efforts, the Badgers were not able to get a win out of this first game in Minnesota and had to accept a 2-0 loss in front of over four thousand loyal Gopher fans. Minnesota clinched the WIHL conference championship with the win.

Wisconsin Lineup: captain Don Meiklejohn (Center), captain Krueger (Right Wing), Siegel (Left Wing), Gallagher (Right Defense), Gordon Meiklejohn (Left Defense) and Frisch (Goalie). Substitutes: Peterson and Thomsen. Saves: Wisconsin 17, Minnesota 24.

The second game that was played March 5 did not go any better for the Badgers. The Gophers, supported by an estimated five thousand fans in attendance sensed blood and went in for the kill.

It was scoreless after the first period, thanks in large part to quality goaltending from both sides. The second period was headed the same way until the Gophers scored on a rebound to take the lead after 16 minutes of play. At the start of the third period, it was still 1-0 and the Badgers had a chance. Minnesota netted another just after five minutes into the last period. About three minutes later, the Gophers scored again to go up 3-0. The final dagger was another Minnesota goal with just over three minutes left in the game. The Badgers played with great heart and competitive spirit, but could not find the back of the net. In the end, the Wisconsin lost 4-0. The Gophers would go on to win another championship this season.

Wisconsin Lineup: captain Don Meiklejohn (Center), captain Krueger (Right Wing), Siegel (Left Wing), Gallagher (Right

Defense), Gordon Meiklejohn (Left Defense) and Frisch (Goalie). Substitutes: Peterson and Thomsen. Saves: Wisconsin 21, Minnesota 24.

William Metcalfe

Below is a picture of Don Meiklejohn and Gil Krueger in front of the Red Gym in their Wisconsin hockey varsity uniforms. Long before the days of hard protective helmets, both players are wearing padded head gear made to be worn over prescription glasses while playing hockey. It was also used simply to protect the eyes, even if a player was not wearing glasses. These eye guards were the precursor to the modern hockey face shield and visor.

In fact, coach Farquhar had four players wearing spectacles and these protective eye masks that permitted glasses to be worn during hockey competition. Don Meiklejohn, Mike Murphy, Gil Krueger and John McCarter were the Badger players that wore eyeglasses while playing hockey.

200

Don Meiklejohn and Gil Krueger at the Lower Campus Rink.

L to R: Gil Krueger, Don Meiklejohn, Art Thomsen and Gordon Meiklejohn

By season's end, the Badgers had an impressive 11 wins. Many speculated that the cardinal and white skaters would have had even more wins if coach Farquhar had the luxury of qualified reserve players at his disposal. Numerous opponents had the good fortune of utilizing an abundance of spare skaters each period when they competed against Wisconsin.

As a result of several players becoming ineligible or unavailable midseason, and bouts of serious illness that sidelined a few other players, Wisconsin had a challenging season which prevented them from finishing as conference champions as coach Farquhar had envisioned. However, the Badgers accomplished a special milestone by recording its first 10-win season in 1928-29.

The special efforts and extraordinary skills of a few gifted Wisconsin hockey players throughout this season did not go unnoticed. The Wisconsin Athletic Review assigned their hockey writer O. Fred Wittner to rank the top players from the Northwestern Intercollegiate Conference (Wisconsin, Marquette, Michigan and Minnesota) into a First Team, a Second Team and a Spares roster. Gordon Meiklejohn was named to the First Team while his brother Don Meiklejohn and Lawrence Peterson were named to the Second Team. Goalie Art Frisch and Gil Krueger were selected as Spares.

Left to Right: Howie Siegel, Gordy Meiklejohn and Gil Krueger

In addition, Wisconsin hockey coach Johnny Farquhar selected an All-Star Team that would represent his version of an All-Western Conference hockey team. It was coach Farquhar's personal selection of the top collegiate hockey players in the Midwest. These were players from Wisconsin, Michigan and Minnesota. Farquhar's All-Midwest team included: Billings (Goalie) University of Minnesota, Gordon Meiklejohn (Right Defenseman) University of Wisconsin, Peterson (Left Defenseman) University of Minnesota, McCabe (Center) University of Minnesota, Gil Krueger (Left Wing) University of Wisconsin and Maney (Right Wing) University of Michigan.

Players that were awarded a varsity "W" letter for their accomplishments on the squad this season were Don Meiklejohn, Gil Krueger, Gordon Meiklejohn, Art Frisch, Howard Siegel and manager George LaBudde.

Junior "W" letters were awarded to Jimmie Gallagher, Lawrence Peterson and Art Thomsen.

Milton Bach, William Metcalfe, Robert Marty, and Richard Walsh of the freshman hockey team were awarded sweaters and numerals. Those individuals that were awarded numerals only were Alec Rohach, Warren Stromberg and team managers Harold Holbrook and Richard Jones.

Gil Krueger also became the hockey representative on the University of Wisconsin Athletic Board after winning a coin toss tie breaker against goalie Arthur Frisch during the May 1929 meeting.

Gordon and Donald Meiklejohn after practice on the Lower Campus Rink

Badger Brothers - Gordon and Don Meiklejohn

Gordon and Don Meiklejohn made a huge impact on the University of Wisconsin hockey program. Prior to arriving in Madison, these brothers began playing hockey days at Taft School, a private high school in Connecticut. Both were strong students and extraordinary athletes, proficient in hockey, tennis and soccer. They followed this path at the UW as both participated in varsity sports and carried a full academic load. Gordon and Don were both elected captain of the Wisconsin hockey team.

The Meiklejohn boys were following a similar path as the one their father paved in the 1890s while a student at Brown University. Dr. Alexander Meiklejohn was a highly gifted athlete and a star player on one of America's earliest collegiate ice hockey teams at Brown University. He was a center known for his speed and competitive nature. Dr. Meiklejohn was also a member of the American hockey team that participated in the first international hockey game between the USA and Canada in 1895. In fact, he also played in the first confirmed college hockey game played within the USA. On January 19, 1898, Brown defeated Harvard 6-0 at Boston's Franklin Park. His sons remarked that even while they were students at the UW, Dad was still pretty fast on his skates.

Dr. Meiklejohn was also a star tennis player while attending Brown University. Years later he could still defeat his sons who were in peak college shape at the UW. His son Don, who was ranked fifth on Wisconsin's championship tennis team in 1928, credited his father for the tennis skills that he and his brother Gordie possessed, but was quick to admit that their skills were nowhere near the elite level that their Father had.

In addition to hockey and tennis, Dr. Meiklejohn was also a gifted soccer player and played competitively for a few years following college on teams throughout the New England area. In 1928, his son Don attempted to get soccer recognized as a minor sport at the University of Wisconsin but his efforts were unsuccessful since the game was relatively unknown in the Midwest.

Gordon and Don's father never lost his passion for ice hockey and made certain to attend each and every home hockey game that Wisconsin played in Madison to watch his boys. This was admirable considering that oftentimes the outside temps dipped well below zero degrees during the matches. Dr. Meiklejohn was on the Wisconsin academic staff as a professor in the philosophy department and had numerous accomplishments as a well-respected scholar and educator. His theories on liberal learning earned worldwide recognition. In 1963, he was recognized for these contributions when President

Lyndon B. Johnson awarded him with the prestigious Presidential Medal of Freedom. This is the highest civilian honor a President can award during peacetime to those who have made significant contributions to the quality of American life.

Don Meiklejohn would also go on to excel in the academic world. After graduating from the University of Wisconsin, he earned a doctorate in Philosophy from Harvard University. During the Korean War, Meiklejohn served four years in the Army Intelligence Division. As a professor, he taught at Dartmouth College, the College of William and Mary, the University of Chicago and Syracuse University. He specialized in civil liberties, the First Amendment and political theories to name a few. At retirement, he had the distinguished title of Emeritus. A short time later Meiklejohn was awarded the Chancellor's Citation for Distinguished Contributions.

After graduating from the University of Wisconsin, Gordon Meiklejohn was selected to play on the United States hockey team at two different Winter Olympics. Since Adolf Hitler was in power and the 1936 Olympic games were being held in Germany, Gordon refused to participate. It was his way to protest the human rights issues involving segregation and exclusion at the Olympics under Hitler's regime. Four years later in 1940, Gordon was asked to be a part of the USA Olympic hockey team as they competed in St. Moritz, Switzerland. Meiklejohn decided that his duty to serve his country as a naval officer was more important than representing his country on a hockey team.

Gordon's lengthy medical career was legendary. He was a specialist in virology and is credited with playing a key role in researching, diagnosing and inoculating the influenza (flu) virus. His discoveries and problem-solving directly led to the modern-day flu shots that protect us from the illness today. Meiklejohn was also a catalyst in the eradication of smallpox. He also specialized in groundbreaking research that addressed issues caused by encephalitis, Rocky Mountain spotted fever, pneumonia and Q fever. Gordon Meiklejohn's storied medical career provided countless contributions to the health and well-being of mankind.

1928-29   Schedule and Results:
Coach John Farquhar
3-6-1 Tied for Second in WIHL   11-7-2 Overall

Date	Result		Opponent
December 27	Tie 1-1	OT	@ Michigan College*
December 28	Win 3-1		@ Marquette (MI)*
January 1	Win 4-1		@ Wausau*
January 3	Win 3-1		@ Chicago*
January 11	Win 4-2		North Dakota*
January 12	Win 8-4		North Dakota*
January 18	Loss 9-0		@Marquette (WI)
February 7	Win 6-1		Wausau**
February 8	Win 1-0		Marquette (MI)**
February 10	Loss 2-0		Eveleth Junior College**
February 13	Win 2-1		Minnesota
February 14	Loss 2-0		Minnesota
February 18	Loss 3-2	OT	Michigan
February 19	Win 3-0		Michigan
February 21	Win 1-0		Marquette (WI)
February 23	Win 1-0		Chicago*
March 1	Loss 3-1		@ Michigan
March 2	Tie 2-2	2OT	@ Michigan
March 4	Loss 2-0		@ Minnesota
March 5	Loss 4-0		@ Minnesota

*Exhibition Games

**Winter Frolic Tournament in Wausau, Wisconsin.

Chapter Eleven
Art Thomsen and Gil Krueger

1929-30 UW Hockey Team

The Wisconsin Athletic Board voted to renew coach John Farquhar's contract without question for the 1929-30 season. The hockey program faced a lot of adversity on its way to earning a second-place finish in the WIHL during the previous season.

Farquhar sent a telegraph reply to George Little, Director of Badger Athletics, indicating his acceptance of the contract sent to his home in Winnipeg, Manitoba. He agreed to his third season behind the bench and scheduled a return to Madison December 10. Behind Farquhar's leadership, Wisconsin was poised to have a strong season.

Coach Farquhar

At a team meeting held Tuesday, November 26, it was confirmed that the UW hockey program would again have some serious talent from the football squad. Four of the men—Bill Metcalf, Hal Rebholz, Jerry Secker and Al Eardes—were coming straight from a season with the football team and were in peak physical condition.

Other veterans returning this year included Don Meiklejohn, Gil Krueger, Art Frisch, Art Thomsen, John Gallagher and Howard Siegel. Each of these players received varsity letters last season. Swiderski, who was unable to play last year due to academic ineligibility, was back on the Badgers roster this season.

Krueger and Don Meiklejohn were elected to be the captains for the 1929-30 season. Both men had demonstrated their commitment to the sport and were seasoned veterans on the Badger hockey team.

Three experienced players from last year's team were not going to be lacing up the skates this season. The highly-talented captain Gordon Meiklejohn had decided to attend a university in China. It was feared this might end his storied career with the Badger hockey program. Substitute forward Lawrence Peterson was not enrolled at the start of the 1929 school year, so he was ruled ineligible although he indicated to school officials he planned to return in February. He would not be permitted to rejoin the hockey team due to his ineligibility. Jim Gallagher was also facing academic eligibility challenges and was working to get them resolved in order to rejoin the team.

The boards at the Badgers Lower Campus Rink had already been constructed and the first flooding of the ice happened Friday, November 30. Preparations were underway to give the players as much practice time as possible before the formal hockey season began. "Spike" Carlson, the freshman hockey coach, was overseeing the varsity practices until coach Farquhar returned to campus. Daily practices had been underway for a week and at least 12 men had reported to each on-ice workout. The players were divided into teams so they could simulate game experience. It was evident that this year's varsity squad would have plenty of speed and talent.

1929-30 Wisconsin Varsity Hockey Team
(Photo on the shoreline of Lake Mendota)

Unfortunately, the warm weather arrived when coach Farquhar did and only two on-ice practices had occurred since. That was hardly the ideal preparation before the exhibition game schedule began. The traditional Christmas break exhibition game schedule took the Badgers traveling to Michigan and Illinois before the regular season began.

On Thursday, December 19, the Wisconsin skaters arrived in Houghton, Michigan for a pair of games against the familiar foes at Michigan College, who were also called the Houghton School of Mines. The Badgers were clearly impacted by the potential loss of both captains, Don Meiklejohn and Gil Krueger, for this two-game series.

Captain Meiklejohn was in the infirmary with a badly infected foot as a consequence of attempting some home surgery to remove a nail he stepped on. Captain Krueger, who was injured in practice, had what was described as a "minor operation" scheduled for the following week in the infirmary and it would keep him out of seeing any game action until his recovery was complete. Some medical experts were predicting that Krueger would not be able to rejoin the hockey team this season. There was a slight chance the doctors would allow Meiklejohn to make the trip to Michigan and play.

Fortunately, Meiklejohn recovered faster than expected and he joined the team in Michigan. In the opening game, Wisconsin took control and executed set plays with precision. The Badgers scored first after 12 minutes in the opening period on a shot when spare player Siegel. A second goal was notched by the UW when captain Meiklejohn scored on a nice long blast in the second period. Midway through the third period, Metcalfe weaved in and out of the Tech players on a beautiful solo effort and scored off his full-ice rush.

The game was exceptionally clean and was dominated by speed and passing. The lone penalty was called on Swiderksi of Wisconsin. UW was able to out hustle and overpower the Huskies during the course of the game, finding the back of the net three times, Michigan College only scored a single goal. The Badgers would end up winning 3-1 over Tech and were pleased with earning a victory in their first preseason game.

Wisconsin Lineup: captain Don Meiklejohn (Center), Siegel (Right Wing), Thomsen (Left Wing), Swiderksi (Right Defense), Metcalfe (Left Defense) and Frisch (Goalie). Substitutes: Ahlberg, Toman and Secker.

The second game Friday, December 20, was a much closer affair and Michigan College was clearly looking to avenge the loss from the day before. The Huskies started out in clear control. In fact, they scored three goals in the first period! Siegel got Wisconsin on the scoreboard 10 minutes into the first period to make it 3-1. In the second period, Metcalfe made a nice solo rush down the boards and scored an unassisted goal on a fast, hard shot that beat the Michigan College goalkeeper. Later, Metcalfe was knocked out of the game by the Huskies with a stick to the face that required immediate medical attention. Fortunately, his nose was not broken. The Badgers were outscored 3-2 in the end and headed out of town with one loss and one win.

Wisconsin Lineup: captain Don Meiklejohn (Center), Siegel (Right Wing), Thomsen (Left Wing), Swiderksi (Right Defense), Metcalfe (Left Defense) and Frisch (Goalie). Substitutes: Ahlberg, Toman and Secker.

Coach Farquhar drops the puck for a face off between Metcalfe and Meiklejohn.

Coach Farquhar contacted his players to advise them of the upcoming game against the Chicago Athletic Association (CAA) and asked that they return to campus as soon as possible. Practice resumed December 30. They had a week before classes restarted at the University. This would afford the players around 10 days before their series with the Minnesota Gophers. The other players not yet back were told to report for hockey practice no later than January 2. Co-captain Gil Krueger was at his parents' home in Neenah, Wisconsin, recuperating from his recent surgery and was not expected to return to campus until classes began.

It was a long, cold ride to Chicago January 6 for a Monday night game against the all-star squad of skaters that comprised the CAA hockey team. Their roster was made up of former players from Princeton, Canadian teams and other high caliber hockey clubs. The match would be played at the new Chicago Stadium, which opened last year. Before their game, the Wisconsin players and staff were guests of the Chicago Blackhawks manager, Tom Shaughnessy, and they watched the Chicago Blackhawks play the Detroit Cougars.

The Wisconsin exhibition game was full of fast-paced action, impressive skating and powerful shots. In fact, the Badgers recorded 40 shots on the Chicago Athletic Association net minder. The game was extremely tight with lots of end-to-end action. CAA scored two goals in the first period and a third in the second period before Wisconsin was able to tally their lone goal. Siegel, Wisconsin's star forward, raced the puck down the ice and threaded a pass to teammate Gil Krueger who fired it as soon as he got the pass. It careened in the net off the Chicago goalies stick for the UW goal. Krueger, who was hospitalized for a health scare a few weeks prior, had rejoined the team for this scrimmage game. Shortly after scoring for the Badgers, he sustained a badly sprained wrist and had to leave the game.

CAA won the game and sent the Badgers back to Madison with a 3-1 exhibition loss. It is important to note that CAA had held the Chicago Senior Amateur Hockey Association title for the past three years. They were also considered to be the fastest amateur hockey team in the country. The preseason games were invaluable and the high level of competition was the only way to properly prepare the cardinal and white for the fast-approaching regular season.

Wisconsin Lineup: captain Meiklejohn (Center), Siegel (Right Wing), captain Krueger (Left Wing), Swiderski (Right Defense), Thomsen (Left Defense) and Frisch (Goalie). Substitutes: Krueger,

Ahlberg, Toman, Secker, Metcalfe and Bach.

Art Thomsen, who alternated between last year's Wisconsin varsity ice hockey team and the UW Swimming team, would again participate on both teams. The hockey players were happy to welcome him back as Thomsen rejoined the team and was ready to perform as one of the core veteran defensemen. He was a phenomenal athlete that was able to carry the load of being a star on two varsity teams while also a full-time student at the University of Wisconsin.

In order to fill the hole caused by the absence of injured player Gil Krueger, coach Farquhar moved sensational two-sport athlete Art Thomsen from defense to left wing. Krueger's injury during the game against Chicago would keep him out of the next match against division rivals Minnesota. Coach Farquhar also inserted Micky Bach into the lineup.

The game to formally kick off the 1930 WIHL conference regular season brought the top rivals from the north to Madison. Last season Minnesota won three of four games against Wisconsin. Even though the Gophers only had three returning varsity players on their team, they had highly skilled sophomores and freshman known for their elite skating. The UW squad was ready to prove they were a better team. The University of Minnesota Gophers made the trek to the UW campus for more than a simple hockey series. This was another chapter in the storied rivalry between the Badgers and the Gophers. A rivalry that is as fierce as they come in college hockey. Many would argue it was the beginning of the most storied rivalry in college hockey history.

The game Friday, January 2 at 7:30 p.m. was clearly dominated by the Badgers. A record crowd of over three thousand spectators packed the bleachers and standing room only to watch this anticipated matchup. Prior to this game, UW officials completed construction of a heated press box for those covering the game.

The cardinal and white skaters displayed an impressive defensive system that frustrated the Gophers. Although he wasn't expected to play, Gil Krueger got the scoring started on a beautiful pass from Siegel to give the UW a 1-0 lead after 14 minutes into the opening period. Don Meiklejohn notched another goal in the second period thanks to his extraordinary skating skills. After receiving a fine pass from Krueger, he worked his way down the boards and shredded the UM defense before ripping a powerful shot between the legs of the Gopher goalie to put the Badgers up 2-0 after only three seconds had ticked off the clock. Minnesota had not response. The Badgers blanked their northern foes, 2-0.

The Gopher squad was not happy with the shutout on the Wisconsin rink. It was quite rare when they lost to any opponent. This loss stung especially bad for Minnesota considering it was their season opener and it was against their border rival. Art Thomsen played a fantastic game and landed numerous pro-style body checks. Goalie Art Frisch played an impressive game and stopped 23 earning a shutout that was a huge testament to his athletic abilities as the goaltender.

Wisconsin Lineup: captain Meiklejohn (Center), Siegel (Right Wing), captain Krueger (Left Wing), Swiderski (Right Defense), Thomsen (Left Defense) and Frisch (Goalie). Substitutes: Toman and Bach. Penalties: Wisconsin: 5, Minnesota: 6. Saves: Wisconsin 23, Minnesota 39. Referees: Carlson from Milwaukee and Roberts from Chicago.

Left to Right: Gallagher, Bach and Krueger

Wisconsin Captain Don Meiklejohn

The second game between the Badgers and the Gophers took place the next day Saturday, January 11 at 3 p.m. The UW Athletic Department was forced to install more bleachers to accommodate the hockey-crazy crowds on the Wisconsin campus for this subsequent matchup. A driving snowstorm made things challenging for the players and fans the entire game. Minnesota jumped out to an early lead 12 minutes into the game but Wisconsin fought back when Siegel scored five minutes later. Minnesota spare Conway was forced out of the game after receiving a serious eye laceration from an errant puck midway through the first period. Moments after the puck cut him, Conway's eye was completely swollen shut. The Gophers scored a second goal with a minute to go in the first, giving them a 2-1 lead at the first intermission.

Minnesota scored again five minutes into the second period to make it 3-1. Wisconsin, playing again in front of a crowd nearing three thousand fans, refused to back down on their home rink. Almost eight minutes later, Metcalfe took off on a solo effort going end-to-end and scored. After trailing most of the game, the Badgers were able to tie it up at 3-3 when Meiklejohn netted a goal on a pretty pass from Gil Krueger with two minutes left in the period. Meiklejohn thrilled the crowd with his furious defense and quick-transitioning offensive game. Badger fans and teammates were thrilled to have Krueger back in the lineup since many thought he was lost for the season after his surgery and hospitalization. The game was stopped several times by the officials in order to shovel off the ice so that players could see the puck. Halfway through the third period, Meiklejohn worked his magic again and scored the fourth goal of the game for the Badgers. His admirable play directly resulted in the go-ahead goal for the UW squad.

Wisconsin versus Michigan on the Lower Campus Rink in Madison.

With five minutes left in the game, everyone in attendance, witnessed an exceedingly rare event when Wisconsin goalie Art Frisch was sent to the penalty box for two minutes. An incident in front of the net led one of the officials to call a minor penalty on the UW goaltender since it appeared Frisch had committed a foul against one of the Gopher skaters. A scrum in front of the UW net turned into a mass of fighting for possession of the puck. In an attempt to defend his crease against the Minnesota intruders, the ref decided Frisch was guilty of an egregious infraction and whistled him to the penalty box to serve his two minutes. Coach Farquhar and several of the UW players argued the call to no avail and Frisch found himself serving his own penalty, a requirement of the ice hockey rules at the time. During the six on five Minnesota failed to score on the empty net due to a tremendous defensive effort.

After Frisch returned to the net, the Badgers were able to fend off the Gophers while continuing their relentless attack. When time expired, the Wisconsin ice hockey team had earned another win by the score of 4-3. Coach Farquhar's focus on an impenetrable defensive hockey strategy this season was clearly paying dividends. This was a very rough game with Minnesota being called for 12 penalties while Wisconsin was charged with seven infractions. Harsh words and fisticuffs broke out several times during this battle.

For the first time in the history of the Wisconsin hockey program the Badgers swept the series and sent the Gophers back to Minnesota with a pair of losses! With the conference wins, Wisconsin now had sole possession of first place.

Wisconsin Lineup: captain Meiklejohn (Center), Siegel (Right Wing), captain Krueger (Left Wing), Metcalfe (Right Defense), Thomsen (Left Defense) and Frisch (Goalie). Substitutes: Swiderski and Bach. Penalties: Wisconsin 7, Minnesota 12. Saves: Wisconsin 12, Minnesota 20. Referees: Carlson from Milwaukee and Roberts from Chicago.

On the following weekend, the other major WIHL rival in the conference, the Michigan Wolverines, returned to the UW campus for a pair of games at Madison. More than three thousand spectators were in attendance to watch this hockey game January 17 at the Madison rink even though the outside temperature registered a bone-chilling 20 degrees below zero. To complicate matters, the game didn't start until 8:30 p.m. that evening.

The game time was pushed back so that it began after the Wisconsin vs Minnesota swim meet concluded. Art Thomsen, the UW dual-sport star, was putting on an iron man doubleheader performance as he was racing for the UW varsity swimming team in this meet against Minnesota earlier in the night. Thomsen swam in three events for Wisconsin. After the swim meet, he rushed to the Lower Campus Rink to suit up for the Badgers as a defenseman in this important conference matchup against Michigan. It was no small feat and he had a huge impact performing for both the swimming and hockey teams.

After participating in the UW swim meet, Art Thomsen rushes to put on his equipment so he can join the hockey game against Michigan that was already in progress.

The game was scoreless in the first period. Coach Farquhar gave his men a much-needed pep talk before the start of the second period. To the delight of the home crowd, Wisconsin scored first when captain Don Meiklejohn buried the puck with only three minutes left in the second period. At the end of the middle period the score was 1-0 in favor of the Badgers. Halfway through the third period, the Wolverines many attempts at the UW net finally paid off when Michigan scored to tie the game at 1-1. In a game dominated by defense, neither the Badgers nor the Wolverines were able to score more than one goal in regulation time. Each team had several quality scoring attempts, but the goalies and defensemen had other plans. Both teams were locked in a 1-1 tie.

It was on to overtime to decide a winner on this blustery night. Try as they might, neither team could score during the first five-minute OT, as both the Badgers and Wolverines went end to end and could not finish off their opponent with a goal. It wasn't until halfway into the second overtime that a centerman for Michigan was able to bounce the puck off the side of UW goalie Art Frisch's knee and into the net to end the game. The Wolverines won 2-1 in double overtime.

This was the first loss for the Badgers in a conference game this season. It didn't sit well with the Wisconsin squad since they had battled like warriors and still lost the game at home. The frigid weather wasn't enough to scare away fans and most of the crowd stayed to watch the entire game even though it didn't end until around 11:30 p.m.

Wisconsin Lineup: captain Meiklejohn (Center), captain Krueger (Right Wing), Siegel (Left Wing), Thomsen (Right Defense), Metcalfe (Left Defense) and Frisch (Goalie). Substitutes: Bach and Swiderski. Penalties: Wisconsin 8, Michigan 6. Saves: Wisconsin 14, Michigan 22. Referees: Fred Robertson from Milwaukee and Bob Williams from C.A.A.

Wisconsin versus Michigan as the Referee drops the puck for a faceoff.

The next day, on the afternoon of January 18, the Badgers and Wolverines took to the ice in the second match of the two-game series. The effects of the prior game were evident as every Badger player suffered from the bone-chilling cold which caused frostbite on exposed skin and frozen feet. Captain Don Meiklejohn and other Wisconsin players entered this game with their faces covered in a thick coating of protective cream intended to provide protection from further frostbite.

With last night's loss still fresh in their minds, the UW men played with a raised level of aggression and precision. Michigan scored first at 14 minutes into the opening period when the Wolverine forward pulled Frisch out of his net on a nifty deke and buried the puck into the wide-open goal. Badger captain Gil Krueger was able to tie the score on a nifty goal five minutes later. Prior to the Wisconsin goal, the UW skaters were buzzing the Michigan goalie. There was a notable amount of exceedingly rough play throughout the period and hostilities continued to rise. The Badgers defense stifled the Wolverines, and after one period of play the score was tied up at 1-1.

Wisconsin and Michigan all tied up with a score of 1-1 in the first period. The gentleman standing behind the goalie wearing the hood is the goal judge.

The spectators got quite a show during the second period of action. A majority of the hockey was centered on the Michigan net as the Wisconsin squad continued to penetrate the Wolverine's zone. The visiting goalie sprawled flat out on his belly at one point to cover the puck and snuffed out a fine scoring chance by captain Meiklejohn. Just over eight minutes into the period, UW player Micky Bach brought the puck up the ice and took a shot from the side that missed but it allowed Thomsen to gather the loose puck and score. It was the Badgers second goal of the period.

The physical action that was prevalent in the first period boiled over in the second period. Badger winger Howard Siegel was in the midst of a scramble for the puck when Wolverine forward Sam Hart violently slashed Siegel in the chest with his stick. Siegel dropped his stick tossed his gloves and began punching Hart. As both players locked up in a violent display of bare-knuckle fisticuffs, Badger star Art Thomsen came into the action, as did two more Wolverines followed by even more Badger players as the donnybrook was in full effect. For a time, it appeared that several spectators would also be a part of the on-ice brawl.

With players from both sides tangled up and sharing anything but pleasantries, even more punches were thrown as both coaches, the referees and numerous UW officials scrambled to break up the fights and restore order. Wisconsin Athletic Director George Little was right in the middle of the disagreements and was able to pry apart several willing combatants. At this point spectators began to spill on the ice and threaten to become active participants.

Several fights break out during the Wisconsin versus Michigan hockey game.

UW Athletic Director George Little and coach Johnny Farquhar rush onto the ice in order to separate the Badger and Wolverine hockey players fighting during the second period.

Referees, coaches, players and spectators restore the peace after the fights. Boys help return hockey sticks to college players that dropped them during the melee.

Once cooler heads prevailed, only Siegel and Hart were assessed minor penalties and were sent to the penalty box to serve two minutes for their role in the melee. Both players had the pleasure of each other's company as they sat side-by-side to serve their time.

Following the fight, the hockey game resumed and Bill Metcalfe was able to bang in Wisconsin's third goal of the game from in front of the Wolverine's net. By the end of the second period, the UW had a 3-1 lead and Wisconsin goalie Art Frisch was only required to make one save. The Michigan goalie had 11 saves and let in two goals.

Wisconsin vs. Michigan hockey game action on the Lower Campus Rink.

Just over five minutes into the third period, the Michigan hockey team was back on the scoreboard with a crafty half-ice shot that caught Frisch off guard and found the back of the Badgers net. The goal cut Wisconsin's lead to 3-2. UW's defense and game plan appeared to become vulnerable and for a moment it looked like the visiting Michigan squad was going to be able to tie it up and possibly win this game. But heroic efforts by Krueger, Meiklejohn, Thomsen and Frisch saved the day for the cardinal and white, who went on to win the game by a score of 3-2.

Wisconsin Lineup: captain Meiklejohn (Center), captain Krueger (Right Wing), Siegel (Left Wing), Thomsen (Right Defense), Metcalfe (Left Defense) and Frisch (Goalie). Substitutes: Bach and Swiderski. Saves: Wisconsin 14, Michigan 19. Referees: Williams from Milwaukee and Robertson from Chicago.

As a result of the 20-degrees-below weather and the added challenges from the frigid winds endured during both games against Michigan this weekend, co-captains Meiklejohn and Kreuger, along with forward Micky Bach suffered severe frostbite on their faces, hands and feet. All three of these Badger hockey stars were hospitalized for over a week due to the seriousness of their injuries.

These were significant frostbite wounds incurred playing the sport of ice hockey for the University of Wisconsin which would have impacts on these players for the rest of their lives.

During a week of intense practice, the Badger hockey team put in the necessary preparation ahead of an upcoming trip to Milwaukee to again face Marquette. It was also a much-needed break to heal injuries. Meiklejohn, Krueger and Bach remained hospitalized until Saturday. In fact, Wisconsin hockey officials made a request to the Marquette hockey personnel requesting that the game scheduled Friday, January 24 be postponed a day since these three players remained in the hospital. It was possible they would return to the lineup Saturday night in Milwaukee.

Marquette was having a fine season and the players were looking forward to the one-game matchup against in state rivals from the University of Wisconsin. As was often the tradition back in the 1920s and 1930s between competing schools, the Marquette Athletic Department and their team hosted a dinner with their guests from the UW hockey team prior to the game that Saturday evening January 25. There was a lot of laughs and joking around amongst the players, coaches and university officials at the dinner. Once game time arrived, both sides quickly returned to the task at hand.

Just over thirty two hundred fans were onhand to watch this game in Milwaukee. From the opening faceoff it was apparent Wisconsin had not healed from the Michigan series. Despite repeated offensive attempts, the Badgers were unable to get the puck into the net. Marquette, on the other hand, scored two minutes into the first period and then again three minutes later. Defensively, the Badger skaters played especially well, but it was the Milwaukee squad that was getting the lucky bounces and making the most of their passing and shot opportunities around the Badger net. Wisconsin was also hurt by the absence of star defenseman Art Thomsen, who elected to participate for the UW swim team in a meet against Chicago held in Madison this same weekend. Marquette scored again after twleve minutes into the third period and then again just three minutes later.

Late in the third period, a heated argument flared up between Micky Bach of the Badgers and Pauly Horrigan for Marquette. Bach had been in the penalty box for an infraction and returned to the ice after serving his two minute penalty. Horrigan loudly protested and insisted that Bach was cheating by returning to the ice too soon. Both players got nose-to-nose as their yelling was almost to the point of fisticuffs. The on-ice officials were forced to physically separate the two feuding skaters before any fight was able to materialize. In the end, Marquette dominated the Badgers and won the game. The UW players headed back to Madison after a painful 4-0 shutout loss.

Wisconsin Lineup: captain Meiklejohn (Center), captain Krueger (Right Wing), Siegel (Left Wing), Metcalfe (Right Defense), Swiderski (Left Defense) and Frisch (Goalie). Substitute: Bach. Penalties: Wisconsin 8, Marquette 9. Saves: Wisconsin 16, Marquette 15. Referees: Pinas from Minnesota and Cameron from Chicago.

Wisconsin had a couple of weeks of to prepare for their return trip to hostile territory. Next on the conference schedule was a visit to Minnesota to square off with the Gophers. Exams at the University of Wisconsin had concluded the first week of February. On Wednesday, February 5, as part of his ongoing preparations, coach Johnny Farquhar took his squad to Beaver Dam, Wisconsin to provide a live demonstration of the game of ice hockey. The Beaver Dam Kiwanis club hosted the UW players, who would put on an exhibition game for all those interested in watching. The Kiwanis were also actively trying to establish interest in a winter recreation program that included the game of ice hockey. Coach Farquhar took his varsity squad and reserve players to assemble two intermingled teams of equal strength to play this scrimmage game for the curious spectators. It was another way to grow the game and a way for Farquhar's players to get in some game-like experience for their ongoing conditioning.

The evening of February 8 had the always-dangerous Chicago Athletic Association hockey team returning to Madison for another match. This game was set for an 8:30 p.m. start. Poor weather and soft ice caused the postponement to Wednesday, February 12 at 7:30 p.m. However, the warm weather didn't leave and ultimately this game was canceled.

Coach Farquhar had the boys out for a 6:30 a.m. practice on the morning of Thursday, February 13, before the important Minnesota series in Minneapolis. The team planned to leave early Friday so they would have adequate time for another practice at the Minneapolis Arena before their first game Saturday.

The University of Minnesota had not forgotten how the Badgers swept them for the first time ever and sent them home with two embarrasing losses in their prior visit to Madison. On Saturday, February15, the Badgers stepped onto the Minnesota ice at the state-of-the-art Minneapolis Arena to face off against the Gophers. The Minnesota crowd of well over three thousand folks gave the hometown team a distinct advantage. The Badger skaters put up a heck of a fight, but the Gophers were first to score. It was 1-0 Minnesota after the second period. Each team went end-to-end with dazzling passes and fast skating the entire game.

Finally, in the third period the Badgers were able to get some offense going. Some crisp passing and aggressive skating set up an opportunity for Thomsen to log the only goal for the cardinal and white, tying the game at 1-1 on a nice unassisted effort halfway through the third period. The score remained tied at the end of regulation, so the two teams went to overtime.

After the first 10-minute overtime period, neither team was able to score, so a second overtime period was played. Midway through the OT period Wisconsin was shorthanded with two players in the penalty box. Minnesota was able to take advantage of the power play and scored the game-winning goal. In the end, the Badgers were handed a 2-1 loss in this double-overtime game. It was overshadowed with 15 penalties called and several more that were allowed as part of the game. Most infractions were primarily comprised of cross checks and boarding of players as these two teams played a highly aggressive and physical match.

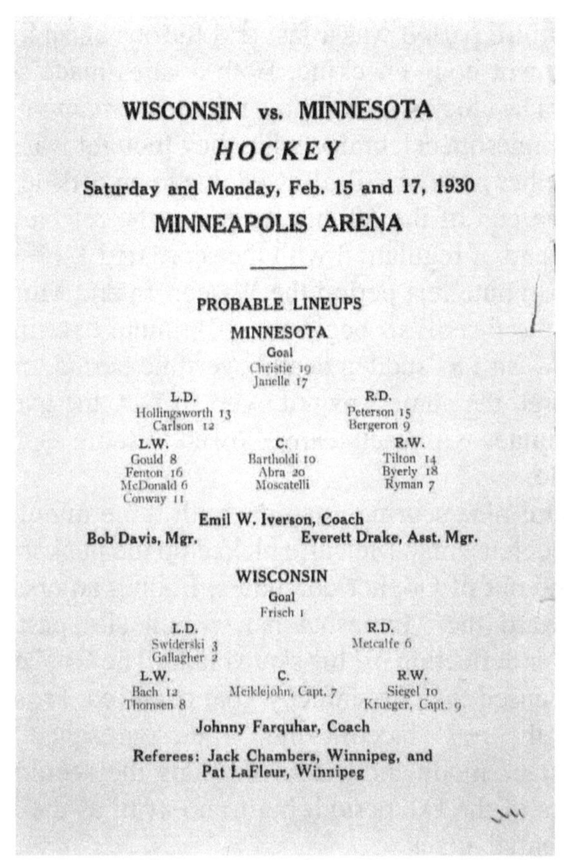

Image scan used by permission from VintageMNHockey.com

Wisconsin Lineup: captain Meiklejohn (Center), Thomsen (Right Wing), Siegel (Left Wing), Metcalfe (Right Defense), Swiderski (Left Defense) and Frisch (Goalie). Substitutes: captain Krueger, Bach and Gallagher. Penalties: Wisconsin 6, Minnesota 9. Saves: Wisconsin 20, Minnesota 27. Referees: Jack Chambers from Winnipeg and Pat LeFleur from Winnipeg.

A second game took place a few days later Monday, February 17. In front of over fifty five hundred hockey rowdy Minnesota spectators Wisconsin was first to score when Micky Bach was the recipient of some nice tic-tac-toe passing and buried the into the Minnesota net for the first goal of the game with just under a minute left in the first period.

As the battle continued throughout the second period, Minnesota was able to get a shot past Wisconsin goalie Art Frisch with a few minutes left in the middle period.

The entire third period was a fast and furious clash highlighted by hard and frequent body checking. Both goalies made several game-saving stops. The clock showed three minutes remaining in regulation time when Minnesota celebrated what they thought was the go-ahead goal. The Gopher goal was disallowed due to an offside called by the referee. At the end of the 60-minute game, the ref blew his whistle signaling the end of regulation with the score tied 1-1.

After a 10-minute rest period the Wisconsin and Minnesota teams lined up for the faceoff to begin the 10-minute overtime period. In these days it wasn't a "sudden death"overtime period, meaning when one team scored the game was not over. In fact, the game continued the full 10 minutes with each team allowed to score as many goals as they were able.

After several nice scoring attempts with three minutes elapsed in OT, Badgers defenseman Metcalfe picked up the puck in his zone and weaved in and out of Gopher defenders, finding an opening, he shot the puck toward the Minnesota net, which slid past the Gopher netminder after deflecting off his skate blade. The Gopher players and fans were incensed that the unlucky goal occurred. From the drop of the puck at the next faceoff, the Minnesota squad went into a heightened attack mode and tried everything they could for the final seven minutes of the OT period, but to no avail as the Badgers held off every potential attack.

With 18 seconds remaining on the game clock, Minnesota thought they scored to tie the game. This goal was waved off and declared no good by the official. The Gophers objected the ruling ad nauseam, and after a significant amount of time had passed Minnesota coach Kay Iverson ordered his team to leave the ice and return to the dressing room in protest. While the crowd howled, officials informed coach Iverson that if they left the game it would be ruled a forfeit in the record books and Wisconsin would be awarded the win. So Iverson sent his players back back onto the ice to play out the final seconds of the game.

Wisconsin won this OT game 2-1 as these two rivals split their two-game series. They were glad to get out of Minnesota with at least one win. Up to this point, the Badgers had never won a game on Minnesota's home ice. With the win, Wisconsin regained the lead in the league standings. This game went so long that it was necessary to hold the train at the station so the Wisconsin hockey team, coaches and fans could catch the return ride to Madison. All those in the Wisconsin camp were feeling the strenuous effects of two overtime games and found comfort in earning a win in the last contest. For the season, the Badgers won three out of four of the games against the Gophers. This was another record for the Wisconsin hockey program. Minnesota coach Emil Iverson left the Gophers hockey program at the end of this season to become head coach of the Chicago Blackhawks in the NHL.

Wisconsin Lineup: captain Meiklejohn (Center), Bach (Right Wing), Siegel (Left Wing), Metcalfe (Right Defense), Swiderski (Left Defense) and Frisch (Goalie). Substitutes: captain Krueger and Thomsen. Penalties: Wisconsin 9, Minnesota 4. Saves: Wisconsin 24, Minnesota 24. Referees: Jack Chambers and Pat LeFleur from Winnipeg.

Meiklejohn and Krueger

The Marquette Hilltoppers were up next, scheduled in Madison for a Wednesday night game. This was only a couple of days after the team returned home from their dramatic overtime win in Minnesota. Another frustrating bout of warm weather returned to plague the remaining season. Although the games were able to go on as planned, almost all of the practices on the outdoor ice were called off due to an unplayable surface caused by the warm temperatures. In addition to the troublesome weather, the club was challenged with several players suffering from injuries late in the season.

Wisconsin's game against Marquette set for Wednesday, February

19 was moved to Thursday, February 20 due to unseasonably warm weather turning the ice rink to soup. Then, the Thursday game was canceled due to the uncooperative weather. The game against the Chicago Athletic Association that was originally planned for Saturday, February 22 as a night game at the Lower Campus Rink, also had to be canceled due to soft ice.

Swiderski and Metcalfe

Swiderski – Frisch - Metcalfe

Still in first place, Wisconsin headed back to Ann Arbor, Michigan for the last two games of the season. For the first time in the history of the University of Wisconsin hockey program, the Big Ten hockey title was within reach. Both games at Michigan were scheduled on back-to-back dates. Coach Farquhar requested a day of rest for his Badger team between games. The Wolverines obliged and the games were changed so that they were played on Thursday and Saturday.

On February 27, the Badgers took the ice to challenge the Wolverines. Each team scored in the first period. Wisconsin's lone goal was a fluke that was the result of a Michigan player attempting to clear the puck with a kick of the skate, but he put it in the back of his own net. The Badgers had a very short roster due to several players being injured and the final score was indicative of their challenges. In the end, Wisconsin lost 5-1. A serious lack of decent ice to practice upon caused the Badgers to be dominated by the Michigan Wolverines. The loss propelled Michigan into first place along with Wisconsin.

Wisconsin Lineup: captain Meiklejohn (Center), captain Krueger (Right Wing), Thomsen (Left Wing), Metcalfe (Right Defense), Swiderski (Left Defense) and Frisch (Goalie). Substitutes: Bach, Gallagher and Siegel. Referees: Rankin from Waterville and Leaver from Windsor.

Two days later, coach Farquhar inspired his remaining players to face the challenge and play with pride and dignity for the University of Wisconsin. His men accepted the challenge and embraced their opportunity to represent the cardinal and white. A few thousand Michigan fans were on hand to cheer on their Wolverines as they battled the visiting Badgers. In a game packed with fancy passing, fast skating and unbelievable defensive stands, these two teams were unable to get anything past their opposing goaltenders. Each squad made countless offensive attempts, but could not get a point on the scoreboard. The game ended in a tie during regulation play. Both Metcalfe, who was injured in Thursday's game and Meiklejohn, who was hurt in the first period of this game, continued to play to the best of their abilities even though they were not 100%. Wisconsin and Michigan went through an entire 10-minute overtime period without scoring. A second 10-minute overtime was played and the game was deadlocked. Time expired and the referee signaled that the game was over. This match, the final game of the season, would end in a 0-0 tie. As a result, the Wisconsin ice hockey team lost the conference championship and was forced to accept second place in the Big Ten standings.

Wisconsin Lineup: captain Meiklejohn (Center), captain Krueger (Right Wing), Thomsen (Left Wing), Metcalfe (Right Defense), Swiderski (Left Defense) and Frisch (Goalie). Substitutes: Bach, Gallagher and Siegel. Penalties: Wisconsin 8, Michigan 2. Referees: Rankin from Waterville and Leaver from Windsor.

Gil Krueger

One of the key players on the 1927-30 teams was Gil Krueger. He was known as "Wisconsin's Mighty Atom" or the "Baby Cyclone" and was a highly talented and special player for the hockey program during his time at the University of Wisconsin. After the 1929 season, head coach, Johnny Farquhar, recommended Krueger for conference honors. In a letter to Gilbert's father Hugo, Farquhar remarked how Krueger is one of the finest players he's ever coached.

The recommendation for Krueger's conference honors from coach Farquhar read in part:

>"His conduct on and off the ice marks him as a sportsman of the very highest degree. Although weighing 115 pounds, he is absolutely full of fight and his value to our team this year has been greatly underestimated by the general public and only I myself, know-how much I appreciate his ever untiring efforts, 100 percent condition and, fast skating, and ability to stick 60 minutes in every game has made him in my estimate one of the best players in our Western conference. I do not hesitate

234

to select him for conference honor first
team. I am hoping that he will be honored
by the team to lead it next year and will
be very glad to recommend him and leave it
up to the boys for their acclamation..."

Krueger was named to the Big Ten All-Star team in 1929. He also
served as co-captain for the Badgers during the 1928-29 and 1929-30
hockey seasons. He graduated from the University of Wisconsin
shortly after the 1930 season concluded.

1929–30 UW freshman Hockey Team

*Pictured above on the far-right side of the freshman Hockey Squad photo is coach
"Spike" Carlson. It was Carlson who would be selected to be the head coach of
the 1930-31 UW Varsity hockey team. The freshman wore the Varsity jerseys
inside out for this photo since they had not yet "earned the privilege" of wearing
the cardinal and white Wisconsin sweaters.*

Each player on the Wisconsin team made significant contributions this
season. Co-captains Don Meiklejohn and Gil Krueger led the team
with their skating, goal scoring and tenacity of play. Howie Siegel,
one of the top performers, who had a scorer's touch and frustrated
many goalies with his combination of precise short and long shots on
net. Even though Art Thomsen was participating in both hockey and
swimming at the UW, his play on defense along with fellow
defenseman Bill Metcalfe was exemplary in nearly every contest.
Significant credit and recognition also went to goalkeeper Art Frisch,
especially when considering he had never previously played a game
of hockey prior to attending the University of Wisconsin. His hard

work allowed him to develop into one of the best goalies in the Big Ten conference.

The team had their end of season banquet March 11 at the Memorial Union. Bill Metcalfe, the standout defenseman, was elected team captain for the 1930-31 season during the banquet. He had just completed his third year of hockey at the UW and his first on the varsity squad. Metcalfe showed his brilliant ice hockey abilities and extraordinary defensive play this year. During the game against Minnesota, he was stellar and played an unheard of 80 minutes of hockey, which was the entire game including three regular 20-minute periods plus two 10-minute overtime periods. In his acceptance speech he thanked his teammates for the honor of being elected captain and hoped he would do as well as the prior captains had done leading the Badgers into competition.

Coach Farquhar selected his all-conference hockey team. This roster included two Wisconsin players: Metcalfe on defense and Meiklejohn at center. Wisconsin was ranked fifth nationally in the top college hockey teams according to the annual hockey guide issued to press outlets at the time behind only Yale, Marquette (WI), Harvard and Michigan.

Nine major letters were awarded to members of the UW team. They were co-captains Donald Meiklejohn and Gilbert Krueger, along with Arthur Frisch, William Metcalfe, Edward Swiderski, Arthur Thomsen, Howard Siegel, Milton Bach and team manager Stanley Krueger. In addition, James Gallagher was given a junior letter.

In May 1930, during the monthly meeting of the University of Wisconsin Athletic Council, Donald Meiklejohn was named the winner of the Big Ten Proficiency Award. He was also given the Conference Medal for proficiency in scholarship and athletics. Meiklejohn had starred for three years in hockey and tennis at the UW. He won the Kenneth Sterling Day award for scholarship, campus activity and high moral character. His grade-point average of 2.92 earned him a Phi Beta Kappa key his junior year, and that grade-point average was higher than any prior recipient of the award at the University of Wisconsin. The lowest grade he received during his academic career was a 93. In addition, he was president of Adams Hall, president of the dormitory senate, as well as a member of the "W" club, Arrowhead, White Spades, Iron Cross and Phi Beta Kappa.

Legendary Wisconsin hockey coach Johnny Farquhar departed the

UW following this season after accepting the position of general manager for the Chicago Shamrocks hockey club where he was quickly promoted to head coach. The Chicago Shamrocks were a professional hockey team in the startup American Hockey Association that began in 1930. Coach Farquhar was credited for the countless ways that he personally advanced the Wisconsin hockey program and its popularity.

1929-30   Schedule and Results:
Coach John Farquhar
4-4-1 Second in WIHL   5-6-1 Overall

Date	Result	Opponent
December 19	Win 3-1	@ Michigan College*
December 20	Loss 3-2	@ Michigan College*
January 6	Loss 3-1	@ Chicago*
January 10	Win 2-0	Minnesota
January 11	Win 4-3	Minnesota
January 17	Loss 2-1 2OT	Michigan
January 18	Win 3-2	Michigan
January 25	Loss 4-0	Marquette (WI)
February 15	Loss 2-1 2OT	@ Minnesota
February 17	Win 2-1 OT	@ Minnesota
February 27	Loss 5-1	@ Michigan
March 1	Tie 0-0 2OT	@ Michigan

*Exhibition Games

Chapter Twelve
"Spike" Carlson

1930–31 UW Hockey Team

On December 7, coach Edwin "Spike" Carlson was appointed head coach of the Wisconsin ice hockey team for the season by the UW Athletic Director George Little. Carlson was a player on the 1922 and 1923 Badger hockey teams. Carlson also played three seasons for the UW football team. Carlson suffered a horrendous injury when he broke his neck during a hockey practice as a member of the 1923 team. After many months of recuperating in a hospital, Carlson returned to play both football and hockey during his senior year at the UW. Last season, Carlson was Wisconsin's freshman hockey squad coach and he also assisted head coach Farquhar with the varsity team.

Coach "Spike" Carlson

HOCKEY

Carlson was a Madison-based architect and graduated from the University of Wisconsin in 1926 with a degree in civil engineering. He volunteered to serve in the Army during World War I, and quickly went from the rank of private to second lieutenant before accomplishing additional intermediate ranks. "Spike," as he was best known, was very familiar with the UW hockey personnel and was popular among all those that knew him. He stayed very close to the program and players after his graduation. Last season he was an assistant to varsity coach Farquhar and was the coach of the freshman squad.

In addition to taking over a team comprised primarily of veterans (a total of nine), he was one of the few UW hockey coaches for whom Mother Nature decided to accommodate with weather cold enough to keep appropriate ice at the Lower Campus Rink. An early cold spell in late fall meant the Badger team was able to skate on their home rink with a solid surface. This allowed coach Carlson to run daily practices from November into December. There were also tentative plans for another exhibition trip through the Iron Range of Minnesota to play the best teams in the area while the University was on Christmas break.

Longtime Wisconsin program supporter and former coach, Joe Steinauer, was lobbying on campus and in the press for the game of ice hockey to change its name. Steinauer strongly felt the name of the popular winter sport should formally change to "Ice-Box Golf." His efforts came up tremendously short of succeeding.

Returning Badger hockey players included; captain Bill Metcalfe, Howie Siegel, Art Thomsen, Milton Bach, Gordy Meiklejohn, Art Frisch and Ed Swiderski. Carlson was inheriting a strong set of hockey players. In the previous two years, the UW finished second in the league and they hoped to better that record.

Although Frisch was the starting goalie, he was expected to share time with Thayer Snavely later in the season. Snavely was eligible at the start of the second semester because the conference had a rule requiring that a player must put in a year's residence before he is eligible to participate in athletics. Snavely had transferred from Marquette to Wisconsin and was an experienced goaltender.

This seasons captain was Bill Metcalfe, a strong and aggressive defenseman. He had an extraordinary understanding of the game and was one of the top skaters in the nation. Ed Swiderski, a guard on the UW foobtall team, was slated to be the other defenseman. Art Frisch, the veteran goaltender who had played the past two seasons for the UW was back in net. Centerman Gordy Meiklejohn returned to the team this season after missing an entire year of hockey due to studying abroad in China. Starting wingers joining Meiklejohn on the line were Art Thomsen and Howie Siegel. Veteran spares were Micky Bach, Jim Gallagher and Leighton Ahlberg. The spares at the sophomore level were Roy Kubista and Gregory Kabat.

In planning for the exhibition games slated for the Christmas break, coach Carlson tentatively scheduled his boys to play against some unusually stiff competition. The teams were thought to be some of the strongest amateur clubs in North America at the time. The tour included Hibbing, Minnesota; Fort Frances, Ontario in Canada; the Kelly-Duluth hockey club; the Michigan School of Mines and the team at Marquette, Michigan. The Hibbing City hockey team was well known for their offensive proficiency and stodgy defense.

On December 22, the Hibbing City team gave the Badgers anything but a warm welcome. Although the UW played an excellent exhibition game, they were unable to earn a lead against Hibbing and fell hard by a score of 4-2. Sammy Phillips, of the Hibbing City team, formerly played with the Duluth Hornets, and scored all four of their goals. He scored twice in the first period and once more in both the second and third periods.

Wisconsin Lineup: Meiklejohn (Center), Thomsen (Right Wing), Siegel (Left Wing), captain Metcalfe (Right Defense), Swiderski (Left Defense) and Frisch (Goalie). Substitutes: Bach, Gallagher, Kabat and Kubista. Referee: Helmer Grenner from Duluth.

The next day Tuesday, December 23, the Hibbing City team played the Badgers in their second game. Wisconsin jumped out to a 2-1 lead. Early in the second period, the UW skaters extended their lead to 3-1. But Hibbing City was able to net two consecutive goals by the middle of the period to tie the game at 3-3. Early in the third period Hibbing City took the lead 4-3and scored one more to soundly defeat the Badgers again by a score of 5-3.

Wisconsin Lineup: Meiklejohn (Center), Thomsen (Right Wing), Siegel (Left Wing), captain Metcalfe (Right Defense), Swiderski (Left Defense) and Frisch (Goalie). Substitutes: Bach, Gallagher, Kabat and Kubista. Referee: Helmer Grenner from Duluth.

On Christmas Day 1930, the UW team arrived in Fort Frances, Ontario to face a team that also had a reputation which struck fear into most challengers. Last season the Fort Frances Ontario Tigers made a serious run for the Allan Cup, a Canadian championship trophy. The Badgers refused to back down as coach Carlson had them well prepared for this battle at the Arena Rink with the Tigers. The UW skaters fought end-to-end with Fort Frances. Art Frisch was memorable in goal and his defensive duo, Thomsen and Swiderski, were equally up for the challenge against the swarming Canadians.

Fort Frances scored 14 minutes into the first period. Nicklin, the referee, only called one penalty in this game and it was against the Tigers in the first period. The penalty was on a Fort Frances defenseman that hammered Badger captain Bill Metcalfe into the boards. Metcalfe would eventually return to the game after receiving first aid on the Wisconsin bench.

The Tigers would score again nearly six minutes into the second period for a 2-0 lead. "Swede" Swiderski, a Wisconsin defenseman, was able to score nearly 12 minutes into the second period but it would be their only goal. It was a spectacular goal for the Badgers, however, a local reporter covering the game referred to Swiderski's tally as "one of the classiest solos seen on the Arena ice." (9) The Fort Frances Tigers were able to outlast the UW squad with a scoreless third, winning 2-1.

Wisconsin Lineup: Meiklejohn (Center), Thomsen (Right Wing), Siegel (Left Wing), captain Metcalfe (Right Defense), Swiderski (Left Defense) and Frisch (Goalie). Substitutes: Gallagher, Kabat and Kubista. Saves: Wisconsin 38, Fort Francis 23. Referee: Nicklin from Ontario.

CAPTAIN METCALFE
Defense

The remaining exhibition games against Kelly-Duluth, the Michigan School of Mines and Marquette, Michigan were canceled by coach Carlson so the boys could return home to rest up and heal their injuries before the regular season began in early January. First up was the all-important series against border rival Minnesota.

Aside from sharpening their hockey skills, endurance and playing some challenging teams, the exhibition games greatly helped accelerate team chemistry. Friendships lasting a lifetime were forged on these Christmas break schedules each season.

Wisconsin, along with nearly every other top hockey team in the country, had more than a conference championship in mind for their ultimate goal by season's end. For the first time in Olympic history, America would be entering a hockey team to participate in the 1932 Winter Olympics. College teams had the understanding that the top performing team would largely make up the roster that the USA would send to represent our country in Olympic hockey competition.

Varsity Squad
Top Row: Carlsen, Coach; Meiklejohn; Swiderski, Gallagher, Kubat, Erler, Manager
Bottom Row: Frisch, Kubista, Siegel, Thomsen, Metcalfe, Bach, Ahlbergh

1930–31 UW Varsity Hockey Team

UW captain Bill Metcalfe challenged his teammates to focus on the upcoming series since their northern rivals from the University of Minnesota were scheduled to return to Madison January 9 for a scheduled two-game matchup. In the first game of the New Year, this series was the formal kickoff of the inaugural Big Ten season. A week before Minnesota arrived, coach Carlson toyed with the tactical decision to move Metcalfe from defense to offense in hopes of getting some additional scoring opportunities. Gordon Meiklejohn was moved back to defense to fill the void.

Meiklejohn spent last year studying at a university in China and caught amoebic dysentery, a serious virus, while he was abroad. The illness drained him of his strength and his ability to play hockey at one hundred percent. He also dropped 15 pounds. However, coach Carlson made a last minute change to move Metcalfe back to defense where he excelled and returned Meiklejohn to forward since he seemed to regain his legs and stamina in the last few practices leading up to the weekend games.

Wisconsin Lineup:

Jersey #	Player	Position
#13	Bach	Center
#3	Meiklejohn	Right Wing
#8	Thomsen	Left Wing
#11	Swiderski	Right Defense
#12	Metcalfe (capt.)	Left Defense
#2	Frisch	Goal

Substitutes:

#4	Siegel
#1	Kabat
#6	Ahlberg
#7	Gallagher
#10	Kubista

In a revolutionary move that would bring Wisconsin hockey to fans statewide, WIBA Radio based in Madison set up a broadcast booth at the UW Lower Campus Rink in an attempt to test the interest with hockey listeners around the Badger state. The radio announcer calling the game was Joe Steinauer, former Wisconsin club hockey coach and long time advocate for ice hockey at the University.

The puck dropped at athletic director in front of a home crowd estimated to be over thirty five hundred students and townspeople. Wisconsin led by Bach and Meiklejohn, outplayed the struggling Gophers. The match was played on soft ice making the flow of the game a lot slower and much more difficult. After a tightly played first period, the score was 0-0.

Wisconsin jumped out to a lead nine minutes into the second period when Micky Bach's scored on a nice pass from Seigel, was just after nine minutes into the period. Wisconsin was up 1-0. After the ensuing faceoff, Bach, a strong and tough center for the Badgers, took issue with an offending Gopher and dropped his gloves in front of the Minnesota goal to fight. He quickly pummeled his opponent and sent him sprawling on the ice. The defeated Gopher player was forced to leave the ice in order to address his injuries and to question the wisdom of starting an altercation with the feisty Badger. Both players were assessed major penalties for their role in the fight.

Bach served his fighting major and returned to the ice eager to inflict more damage on the Gophers. He teamed up again with Siegel to net his second goal, this one registered with just 20 seconds left in the period. Bach was a one-man wrecking crew. Wisconsin had a 2-0 lead going into the third period.

Minnesota finally got on the board with two-and-a-half-minutes left in the game. Whatever rally they were hoping to mount was squashed by the Badgers after the home team netted their third goal 30 seconds later when Art Thomsen scored. Wisconsin outmuscled and outscored Minnesota for the impressive 3-1 win. In addition to Bach, Wisconsin's stellar defenseman "Tough as Pig Iron" Swiderski played a stellar game. Art Frisch was also fantastic in net for the Badgers.

Wisconsin Lineup: Bach (Center), Meiklejohn (Right Wing), Thomsen (Left Wing), captain Metcalfe (Right Defense), Swiderski (Left Defense) and Frisch (Goalie). Substitutes: Gallagher, Siegel and Kubista. Saves: Wisconsin 12, Minnesota 14. Referee: Jack Thompson from the Milwaukee Athletic Club.

The second game January 10 was scheduled in the morning at 9:30 a.m. to increase the probability of decent ice so that the contest would be played. More warm temps the prior evening and a chewed-up ice surface that was unable to be adequately repaired due to the weather forced UW Dean Goodnight to cancel this game. Minnesota then traveled to Milwaukee to play two games against Marquette.

The game was tentatively rescheduled for Wednesday, January 14 as the Gophers made their way back from Milwaukee. However, Minnesota officals canceled this game before it was played. Even though the ice at the Lower Campus Rink in Madison was nearly perfect, Minnesota officials gave no explanation for the cancellation when they notified Wisconsin. It was later revealed that the Gopher squad was ordered home by University of Minnesota Athletic Director Fritz Orisler since the players had missed a considerable amount of classes and he did not want them to miss another day. These two teams would have to wait to play until Wisconsin's scheduled roadtrip to Minnesota in February.

Up next for the Badgers was another two-game series in Madison against the University of Michigan Wolverines. Michigan was the WIHL champions of the 1929–30 season and had been ranked second in the nation. Wisconsin wanted nothing more than to beat them at home and they would have their chance on the weekend of January 16 and January 17.

"Micky" Bach
Center

"Gordy" Meiklejohn
Wing and Defense

A huge crowd of around three thousand spectators packed the bleachers and overflow areas to take in Friday nights game. Faceoff was set for 7:30 p.m. During the game, Frisch's goaltending acrobatics gave the Wolverines fits. The Badgers' offense was powered in part by Micky Bach and Gordy Meiklejohn. Throughout the first 10 minutes, the teams were feeling each other out, playing cautiously so they would not be the one to make the first defensive error. Gordy Meiklejohn started a solo rush up the ice weaving through the Michigan defense and curled toward the boards in the Wolverines' zone. From there he made a fantastic centering pass to Gallagher, who was keenly aware the puck would be coming to him.

Gallagher actually missed the puck when he tried to shoot from his right side, but was agile enough to quickly try again by instantly shooting from his left side while off balance and was able to rip a high, hard shot into the top of the net since the UM goalie was faked out of position by the unitended and creative double-clutch shot. The Badgers had a 1-0 lead.

Four minutes later, captain Metcalfe received a precision pass onto his stick from Siegel and scored Wisconsin's second goal by ripping a shot past the Michigan goalie, Tompkins. The boys sporting the cardinal and white colors were able to get two huge goals in the first period. The second period was scoreless.

The Badgers dominated their rivals with fast skating, impressive stickhanding and physical play. As expected, the game got rougher as the clock ticked away. Halfway into the third period, the referees whistled off both Thomsen and Metcalfe for unnecessary roughness. Michigan again swarmed the UW net but was unable to score. Wisconsin alternate Kabat was substituted into the game and participated in his first official conference hockey game donning the cardinal and white sweater. Star defenseman Ed "Tough as Pig Iron" Swiderski continued with thunderous body checks, breaking up any chances the Wolverines tried to muster. The Badgers defense and standout goalie Art Frisch were able to deny every offensive attack from the Wolverines. The game ended in a 2-0 win for the UW squad.

Wisconsin Lineup: Bach (Center), Meiklejohn (Right Wing), Thomsen (Left Wing), Swiderski (Right Defense), captain Metcalfe (Left Defense) and Frisch (Goalie). Substitutes: Siegel, Gallagher, Ahlberg, Kabat and Kubista. Saves: Wisconsin Frisch 18 and Ahlberg 2, Michigan 12. Penalties: Wisconsin 10, Michigan 3. Officials: Jake Thompson from the Milwaukee Athletic Club and Russ Rebholz from Wisconsin.

The next day's faceoff was set for 2 p.m. Concerns that the daytime sun would thaw the playing surface caused the game to be moved to 9 p.m. that night. Another enthusiastic crowd estimated around 3,000 was on hand to watch as the two teams picked up where they left off from the prior game. Many UW fans were very concerned about the "Michigan Jinx" that usually crept up in every Wisconsin versus Michigan series. Attempt after attempt to score on both the Badger and Wolverine nets were denied. The Badgers halted any plans the Wolverines had for revenge. The UW skaters had control of the game and were able to turn back every offensive play the Michigan boys made. As the ice was becoming soft and difficult to play, the game remained scoreless after both the first and second periods. In beween each period, the crowd continued their own entertainment by participating in snowball fights and Wisconsin-themed cheers.

Neither team scored in regulation so the game was sent to overtime. Many in attendance wondered if the jinx would return. Coach Carlson gave his boys an inspirational pep talk before the extra period and made sure they were ready to compete even harder to earn a win. The UW skaters played with deeper determination. At 5:35 into the overtime period, UW forward and spare player Howie Siegel took possession of the puck from the Wolverines corner and skated into the slot area. Siegel then did a head fake on the Michigan goalie as if he was going left and immediately after the Michigan goalie bit on the fake, he went right and ripped a shot from in close that found the back of the net for the monumental 1-0 win! Wisconsin had swept the Wolverines, the WIHL champs of the prior season, by winning both games of their series this weekend. Remarkably, Frisch recorded his second straight shutout by holding Michigan scoreless.

"ART" FRISCH
Goal

On January 20, Marquette came to Madison to continue their annual competition. In the days prior to this outing the Badgers were frustrated by a warm weather spell that hampered their on-ice workouts. However, the men who cared for the Madison rink on the University of Wisconsin campus had the ice in near-perfect condition for this game. The skating surface was rock hard and it was nearly as smooth as glass. Perhaps the biggest single advantage the Badgers had against the Hilltoppers was their goaltender, Art Frisch. To date, he had been solid and had only allowed one goal to be scored against him in three conference games this season.

WIBA Radio set up to broadcast the live action of this game across the air waves. The station received hundreds of favorable requests after its first-ever radio broadcast of the Wisconsin versus Minnesota game two weeks earlier. Beloved coach and hockey expert Joe Steinauer was again selected to announce the game.

Game time was set for 8 p.m. and Wisconsin Lieutenant Governor Henry Huber had the honor of dropping the puck for the ceremonial faceoff to begin the match. The thirty five hundred or so spectators were treated to exciting offensive rushes and remarkable defensive displays during the hockey game. They also watched the game in bitterly cold temperatures that hovered around zero degrees.

Coach Carlson had his defense delivering ferocious body checks and it was routinely demonstated by team captain and defenseman Metcalfe along with fellow defenseman "Tough as Pig Iron" Swiderski and most of the other varisty players on the Wisconsin roster who understood the importance of checking in ice hockey. Both teams were undefeated in regular season play. Meiklejohn led the offense while Thomsen shored up the Badgers defense in front of crafty and intelligent goalie Art Frisch. A scoreless first period had spectators on the edge of their seats.

Marquette scored in the first two minutes of the second period by beating Frisch through his five hole. Two minutes later, Badger forward Meiklejohn scored on an identical shot to beat the Hilltoppers' goalie between the pads. Just like that, the UW were able to tie the game at 1-1. After a goal-free third period, the game required overtime in order to determine a winner. Lots of altercations among rival players throughout the game thoroughly entertained those in attendance.

Five minutes into the extra session, Jimmy Gallagher, a creative and dangerous forward for the Badgers who played both center and winger, picked up the puck near center ice from the boards and quickly skated down the side until he cut back to the center slot. He weaved through the Marquette defense and ripped a rocket at the opponent's net. The shot was so hard that it flew back out of the net instantly and many doubted it was in fact a goal. The Hilltoppers argued that the puck never went into the net and should not count as a goal. "Buster" Shimek, the assistant track coach at Marquette, had a perfect view of the score and confirmed the shot was a legal goal to the game officials. Gallagher scored the game-winning goal in overtime to give the UW a 2-1 win over the visiting Hilltoppers.

Wisconsin Lineup: Bach (Center), Meiklejohn (Right Wing), Thomsen (Left Wing), Swiderski (Right Defense), captain Metcalfe (Left Defense) and Frisch (Goalie). Substitutes: Gallagher and Siegel. Saves: Wisconsin 28, Marquette 19. Penalties: Wisconsin 7, Marquette 0. Officials: Referee Tobin from Chicago and Umpire Jake Thompson from Milwaukee.

After starting the season with an impressive five game winning streak against Fort Frances, Michigan, Minnesota and Marquette, Wisconsin's luck promptly took a turn for the worse. Mother Nature was not in a pleasing mood for ice hockey and she brought in a treacherous warm spell. The weather eliminated the ice surface at the rink. Badger hockey players were frequently greeted at the rink by a discouraging sign that simply read: **No Ice Today**. Skating was impossible in these conditions and resulted in the cancellation of numerous hockey practices.

"SWIDER" SWIDERSKI
Defense

On top of that, exams at the University of Wisconsin took a toll on star Badger defenseman Swiderski. "Swider" or "Tough as Pig Iron," as he was affectionately called by teammates and fans, cited the pressures of school as the reason he didn't pass his exams and the reason why he immediately departed the Wisconsin hockey team. Coach Carlson understood Swider's situation and wished him well in his endeavors.

Members of the hockey team began working nights to maintain the ice at the Lower Campus Rink following recent bouts of warm weather, several of the players gathered around midnight most nights to take turns working several hours at a time as they handled the hose to flood the ice and repair imperfections on the playing surface. The typical UW employees that maintained the rink worked the day shift. With finances being so tight and the hockey budget strapped, these extra efforts by the hockey players were critical to maintain the rink surface. Coach Carlson had also been forced to hold practices at 7 a.m. in the morning so the boys had sufficient ice before the mid-day thaw set in each afternoon.

On Wednesday, February 11, the UW skaters traveled back to

Milwaukee for a single game against the Marquette Hilltoppers. The Badgers would be without Art Thomsen and Ed Swiderski for this game. Thomsen was nursing a lower body injury while Swiderski had been declared academically inelegible and left the hockey progam. Joining the team were several hundred Badger fans that made the trip in order to watch the game.

This hockey game was anything but typical as the skaters fought through the game playing on an uncompromising skating surface consisting of mud, snow and slush! The first period was scoreless. Both teams were trudging through the water covered ice surface at the Marquette University rink for the entire game.

UW Badgers players poke at the puck while the Hilltoppers defend their net

Marquette recorded the only goal of the game on a freak shot from mid-ice that flipped sideways as it went past Badger goalie Frisch. The Hilltopper that notched the lone goal had picked up the puck from mid-ice late in the second period, skated a few strides and then fired the long, wobbly shot toward the Badgers' net. The puck hopped, slid and finally skipped over Frisch's goalie stick and found the back of the net. By the end of the second period, it was 1-0 in favor of Marquette.

With less than four minutes on the game clock, the Wisconsin skaters ramped up their attack and repeatedly buzzed the Marquette

251

net with attempt after attempt. The Hilltoppers turned away every attempt and would not allow the Badgers to tie the score or to take the lead. Wisconsin left Milwaukee with a lousy 1-0 loss.

Wisconsin Lineup: Gallagher (Center), Siegel (Right Wing), Bach (Left Wing), Meiklejohn (Right Defense), captain Metcalfe (Left Defense) and Frisch (Goalie). Substitutes: Kubista and Kabat. Saves: Wisconsin 13 , Marquette 15. Officials: Williams and Carlson from the Milwaukee Athletic Club.

The Badgers took the train from Milwaukee to Minneapolis for the upcoming two-game series against the Gophers scheduled for February 13 and 14 at the Minneapolis Arena. The hockey Gods were playing a cruel joke on the UW team during the first game against UM. Goalie Art Frisch mistakenly knocked the puck into his own net for the first Gopher goal eight minutes into the first period. Wisconsin put agoal into the University of Minnesota net five minutes later when Bach took a nice pass from Thomsen and faked out the Gopher goalie to tie the game. The score stood at 1-1 after the first.

Six minutes into the second period Minnesota benfitted again when the puck richocheted off Badger defenseman Gordy Meiklejohn's skate blade and went into the UW net. It was their second goal of the game. The third period was scoreless despite the best efforts of both teams. As their luck would have it, Wisconsin scored three times and **lost** 2-1! It was a largely disappointing defeat for Wisconsin.

Wisconsin Lineup: Bach (Center), Siegel (Right Wing), Thomsen (Left Wing), Meiklejohn (Right Defense), captain Metcalfe (Left Defense) and Frisch (Goalie). Substitutes: Gallagher, Kubista and Kabat. Saves: Wisconsin 16, Minnesota 17. Penalties: Wisconsin: 6, Minnesota 6. Official: Nick Kahler.

In the second game, Wisconsin was clearly outplayed despite their best efforts. The rowdy crowd, estimated to be over five thousand fans, watched their Minnesota team pick apart the Wisconsin squad to get lots of great shots on net. In addition, the Gophers had a deep bench with several extra reserve players that proved to be too much for the UW squad.

With less than two minutes left in the opening period, Minnesota took a 1-0 lead. They netted another goal halfway through the second to extend the lead to 2-0. The Badgers scored when Thomsen made good on a nice pass from Bach to make the score 2-1.

In the third period, star forward Art Thomsen suffered a deep laceration above his eye that took him out of the game. With just over a minute left in regulation the Gophers scored again to extend their lead to 3-1. The game clock showed 10 seconds left in the match when Minnesota scored their fourth goal. The Badgers fought on to the bitter end and the game concluded with a 4-1 loss.

Wisconsin Lineup: Bach (Center), Siegel (Right Wing), Thomsen (Left Wing), Meiklejohn (Right Defense), captain Metcalfe (Left Defense) and Frisch (Goalie). Substitutes: Gallagher, Kubista and Kabat. Saves: Wisconsin 21, Minnesota 20. Penalties: Wisconsin 7, Minnesota 4. Official: Nick Kahler.

"Art" Thomsen
Defense

"Jim" Gallagher
Wing and Center

"Howie" Siegel
Wing

Wisconsin returned home to recover and regroup. The upcoming weekend had them returning back to Ann Arbor, Michigan to take on the Wolverines for the last two games of the season. Michigan was eager to welcome Wisconsin back to town. They had not forgotten how the Badgers beat them twice in January. Coach Carlson had the Badgers prepared as best he could for the matchup. With a win, the Badgers would clinch the conference title outright. All Wisconsin had to do was prevent the Wolverines from getting a win or a tie.

On February 19, Wisconsin and Michigan played the first game on the docket. In a suprisingly even game, both teams were unable to get any offensive scoring going. The UW skaters were unable to capitalize on any opportunities and even had two ideal shots at a wide-open net with each one clanking off the post as the puck bounced harmlessly into the corner. Michigan was able to get the puck into the Wisconsin net, but the goal was disallowed due to an offside call by the referee. Defensively, each team was able to effectively diffuse their opponents and each goalie turned away every shot on net. Even with two overtime periods for extra time, neither team was able to get a point on the board and the game ended in a 0-0 tie after five periods covering 80 minutes of play.

Wisconsin Lineup: Bach (Center), Siegel (Right Wing), Thomsen (Left Wing), Meiklejohn (Right Defense), captain Metcalfe (Left Defense) and Frisch (Goalie). Substitutes: Gallagher, Kubista and Kabat.

In the final game February 21, Wisconsin was again facing the boys from Michigan. This final contest of the season was crucial for both teams since they were playing for the WIHL title. Greg Kabat elected to miss the UW track meet in Illinois where he would have been representing the school as a shot putter so that he could play in this hockey game. Unfortunately, subpar officiating interfered with a fair game and heightened frustrations. Notably, a shot in the second period by a Michigan forward was counted as a goal even though there was significant disagreement on whether or not the puck actually went into the UW net. Early in the third period a perfectly shot puck by UW forward Meiklejohn clearly went into the net, but was disallowed by the referees to the disbelief of the Wisconsin players and coach.

As a result of the boiling rivalry and referees losing control early in the game, tensions quickly escalated to dangerous levels between the Badgers and Wolverine players causing several fights to break out.

They went from one-on-one fights, to several players on both teams fighting each other at the same time. With tempers running hot there was a lot of harsh words tossed back and forth during the handful of scuffles as well throughout the remainder of the match. One huge fight revolved around UW skater Jimmy Gallagher. He responded to the challenge by the Wolverines player to settle the score and several punches were thrown. Several other players joined the fracas and officials needed a few minutes to stop the battling players and to restore order to the game. Clearly the Wisconsin players agitation was a direct result of getting homered by the referees in Michigan.

There were even two more occasions when the Badgers were certain they had scored since the puck was in the Wolverines net yet the referees waved off the goal for reasons unknown. Michigan put the puck into the Wisconsin net two more times and those goals were allowed, giving the Wolverines a 3-0 lead.

UW defenseman Art Thomsen gave forward Kabat a perfect pass through traffic and he scored a beautiful goal. This tally was also disallowed after the referees ruled that Wisconsin had too many men on the ice. Apparently, Bach was sent off the ice to serve a penalty and he went to the players bench in protest rather than to the penalty box. One of Bach's teammates saw him come on to the players bench and assumed it was a substitution so he joined the game which caused the Badgers to have too many players on the ice. Sadly, the Badgers were not going to get on the scoreboard in this season-ending game. On the scoresheet, Michigan won 3-0 even though Wisconsin had "scored" no fewer than four goals that had been were disallowed for various reasons.

Wisconsin head coach Spike Carlson was on his way to the UW locker room after the game when he was taunted and attacked by a spectator. Coach Carlson traded punches with the Michigan fan until the police separated the two combatants. The Badgers prepared to head home to Madison while the Wolverines celebrated another championship.

Wisconsin Lineup: Bach (Center), Siegel (Right Wing), Thomsen (Left Wing), Meiklejohn (Right Defense), captain Metcalfe (Left Defense) and Frisch (Goalie). Substitutes: Gallagher, Kubista and Kabat.

Warm weather during the month of February and a serious lack of ice destroyed what should have been a championship season for the

Badgers. Without ice for hockey practices the team would lose the remaining games during the last half of the season this month.

At the end of this season, five key seniors were scheduled to graduate; captain Bill Metcalfe, Art Frisch, Jimmy Gallagher, Howard Siegel and Arthur Thomsen. Only four varsity hockey players would be returning next year: Bach, Kabat, Kubista and Meiklejohn. The freshman squad was the biggest one to date in the history of the Wisconsin hockey program and would produce some quality players to round out the roster next season.

Captain Bill Metcalfe was named to the All-Western Hockey Team selected by Marquette coach John Hancock. Metcalfe would be the only Badger selected for this distinction and was also picked for Second Team All-American honors in the May 1931 issue of College Humor. Les Gage (Wisconsin alumni class of 1923), the sports editor of College Humor, recognized the Wisconsin hockey team and the four stars:

Thomsen, a forward, Metcalfe and Meiklejohn, both defense players and Frisch, goalie, were the ranking members of the Wisconsin squad. Metcalfe was unquestionably the best defense man in the section and was commended highly by Coach Hancock of Marquette; "The Badger player was big and strong and an ideal man for his position.He was smart, good on quick breaks, fast and fearless." (10)

At the annual hockey postseason banquet held March 10, Gordon Meikljohn was elected to be captain of the team for next season. Gordon is carrying on the tradition started by his older brother Don Meiklejohn, who was previously the Wisconsin hockey team captain for two years. In addition to the varsity captain, the freshman team elected teammate Vernon Stehr as the honorary captain for the 1930-31 season that just concluded. All of the departing seniors made sure to share their advice with the younger players to ensure the success of the hockey program going forward.

Most notably, standout goalie Art Frisch addressed the varsity candidates and eloqently expressed how challenging it was to make the UW hockey roster, and that it is all worthwhile as everyone who succeeds creates fantastic memories that last a lifetime. His prophetic words still ring true today. Frisch said, "You will find your jobs next winter to be harder than the jobs of any set of incoming varsity men. You will have to work and fight continually to uphold a never-say-die tradition that has been built up by Wisconsin hockey teams. You will find Minnesota and Michigan stronger than they were this season but if you will give your best you will have done all that is asked of you." (11)

To end the banquet, coach Carlson thanked all the men on this year's team for all of their efforts to make it a great season. He also wished the seniors good fortune in their new endeavors after graduating from the University of Wisconsin. Coach Carlson concluded his remarks with a special thank you to Art Thomsen for his accomplishments in his role as coach of the freshman team and for promoting the game of ice hockey among the high schools in the Madison, Wisconsin area.

1930-31   Schedule and Results:
Coach Spike Carlson
4-4-1 Tied for second in WIHL   4-7-1 Overall

Date	Result	Opponent
December 22	Loss 4-2	@ Hibbing*
December 23	Loss 5-3	@ Hibbing*
December 25	Loss 2-1	@ Fort Frances (Ont.)*
January 9	Win 3-1	Minnesota
January 16	Win 2-0	Michigan
January 17	Win 1-0 OT	Michigan
January 20	Win 2-1 OT	Marquette (WI)
February 11	Loss 1-0	@ Marquette (WI)
February 13	Loss 2-1	@ Minnesota
February 14	Loss 4-1	@ Minnesota
February 19	Tie 0-0 2OT	@ Michigan
February 21	Loss 3-0	@ Michigan

*Exhibition Games

Chapter Thirteen
Greg Kabat

1931–32 UW Hockey Team

Art Thomsen, the former UW varsity ice hockey player and swimmer, would take over as head coach this season after the University of Wisconsin Athletic Board confirmed his appointment. Coach Thomsen faced an uphill battle with every necessary aspect of fielding a qualified and competive hockey squad. The challenges included funding issues as a reasonable budget was needed to cover the numerous expenses the program incurred each season. On top of that was the struggle with decent playing ice which they would face all season long and the lack of experienced players.

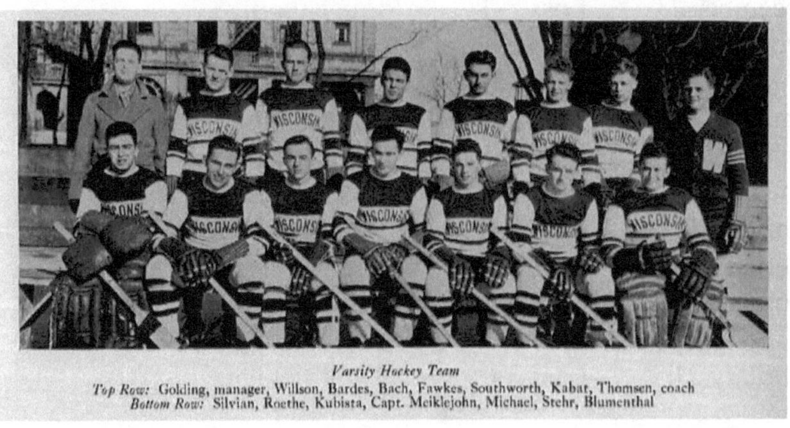

Varsity Hockey Team
Top Row: Golding, manager, Willson, Bardes, Bach, Fawkes, Southworth, Kabat, Thomsen, coach
Bottom Row: Silvian, Roethe, Kubista, Capt. Meiklejohn, Michael, Stehr, Blumenthal

One of the top returning veterans was captain and All-American defenseman Gordy Meiklejohn. Fortunately for coach Thomsen and the Badger hockey team, Meiklejohn was an extraordinarily gifted skater and a player that possessed an unusually high hockey IQ.

He frequently received accolades from the press as well as from opposing coaches and players. Meiklejohn had a reputation as a ferocious body checker and an intimidating defenseman that was highly skilled in all aspects of the position. He was considered to be one of the most prolific scoring players at the position of defense. Known as an offensive defensman that was a particularily fast skater, he was also blessed with an exceptionally hard shot. It was no surprise that Meiklejohn led his team in scoring this season and was unanimously regarded as the most outstanding player in each of the games he played.

Greg Kabat was another key veteran returning to the cardinal and white lineup. He had just finished the fall season as the captain for the Wisconsin football team. He was a natural athlete that would play a vital role on the hockey team this season. One of the varsity goalies on the Badgers hockey team was Paul "Piggy" Blumenthal. He had never played ice hockey or held a hockey stick in his life until last fall when coach Thomsen took him aside for instruction and some pointers on how to play the position of goalie in ice hockey. Blumenthal was such a natural at the position that he would eventually surpass Les Silvian, the starting goalie on the Wisconsin hockey squad, and became the No. 1 goalie on the varsity team. Other members of the team included: Robbie Halverson, John Roethe, Roy Kubista, Bruce Michael, Billy Southworth, Vernon Stehr, Jim Lyke, Bill Riley and Richard Fawkes.

The winter months between November and March during this hockey season experienced several days with temperatures in the high 40s, 50s and even into the 60s. Decent ice was nonexistent for weeks at a time, leaving the Wisconsin players without critical practices, scrimmages or even games. It was impossible to maintain ice on the Madison rink and Lake Mendota was chunky slush on a good day. The varsity hockey team had less than six on-ice practices before heading off to play Minnesota and Michigan. In addition, the nation was still in the harsh grip of the Great Depression. Consequently, the hockey budget was slashed so significantly that travel and players equipment were not adeqately compensated.

Several people again tried to rally support for the construction of a rink with a roof and artificial ice in Madison. One would think the number of students and citizens around the Madison area that frequently attended the Wisconsin hockey games at the Lower Campus Rink would indicate that funding an indoor rink was entirely feasible, especially when considering that game time temperatures were often hovering around zero degrees. But such an investment gained little traction due to the shaky economical climate that had a hold of the United States during these years.

Roy Kubista   **Gordy Meiklejohn**   **Greg Kabat**

This season the Badgers played an unusually early exhibition game against the Wausau Hockey Athletic Club, also known as the Veterans of Foreign Wars hockey team, in Wausau December 5, 1931. This match was intended to be a tuneup before the regular season. The 3 p.m. game was set to be played at the City Market Square Rink in Wausau and just over three hundred people showed up to watch their local hockey team take on the college boys from Madison.

Neither side was able to muster up much offense, especially since the goalies and defensemen on both sides were highly talented players. When offensive attacks were set up, the defense and superb goaltending squashed their efforts. After one period, the game was scoreless. The Vets appeared to be outplaying the UW squad, but the Badgers were not overly dominated. In the second period, Wausau captain Ray Walters took a nice pass from his brother Gordon and tallied the first score of the game. The Vets took a 1-0 lead. The reserve players for both teams were able to get some decent ice time during this contest. At the final whistle, the amateur players from the Wausau team claimed a 1-0 victory over the visiting University of Wisconsin Badgers hockey team.

Wisconsin Lineup: Kubista (Center), Halverson (Right Wing), Michael (Left Wing), Bardes (Right Defense), captain Meiklejohn (Left Defense) and Silvian (Goalie). Substitutes: Stehr, Kabat, Lyke, Roethe, Fawkes and Blumenthal. Saves: Wisconsin 18, Wausau 12.

Coach Thomsen scheduled a a pair of games with the Michigan College Huskies to both end calendar year 1931 and to begin 1932 as the games were scheduled for December 31 and January 1. Both games were played at the Jack O'Lantern Rink located in Eagle River, Wisconsin These games were part of the attractions at the Jack O'Lantern Lodge Ice Carnival and New Years celebration hosted by lodge owner Charles E. Taylor.

In front of one hundred plus enthusiastic hockey fans, the teams played a fast back-and-forth game on New Years Eve. Historically, the Huskies were a strong hockey team that had skilled skaters with a high compete level. During the opening period, Wisconsin scored on their first shot on net. UW right winger Rob Halverson got a pass from teammate Bruce Michael and buried the short shot to put the Badgers up 1-0. Toward the end of the first period Michigan scored to tie the game at 1-1.

The action was tight throughout the second period but the Huskies pulled ahead 2-1 with a late goal. Wisconsin came out strong for the third period and tied the score a few minutes in to the final period when Meiklejohn scored on a clever shot from the side of the net. With under five minutes left in the third period, the Huskies scored again, taking a 3-2 lead. Wisconsin could not counter before the final buzzer. As a result, Michigan College bettered the UW by one goal and the Huskies ended up on top with a 3-2 win in this opening match.

Wisconsin Lineup: Kubista (Center), Halverson (Right Wing), Michael (Left Wing), Bardes (Right Defense), captain Meiklejohn (Left Defense) and Silvian (Goalie). Substitutes: Stehr, Kabat, Lyke, Roethe, Fawkes and Blumenthal.

On New Years Day the Badgers again took the ice at the Jack O'Lantern Rink. This time the crowd doubled to nearly two hundred spectators. Wisconsin had regrouped and played evenly with the Huskies in this rematch, which was the second of the two-game series. At the end of regulation, the game was even at 2-2. An additional overtime period was unable to determine a clear winner. The game went down in the record books as a 2-2 tie.

Wisconsin Lineup: Kubista (Center), Halverson (Right Wing), Michael (Left Wing), Bardes (Right Defense), captain Meiklejohn (Left Defense) and Silvian (Goalie). Substitutes: Stehr, Kabat, Lyke, Roethe, Fawkes and Blumenthal.

Jack O'Lantern lodge owner, and local hockey supporter, Charles E. Taylor would later commission and finance the Eagle River

Hockey Stadium, also known as "the Dome" which would not be completed until 1933.

Wisconsin's schedule had another nonconference team coming to Madison for a game. The amateur skaters of the Milwaukee Rowing Club hockey team were next on the schedule for a Saturday, January 9 battle. Coach Thomsen's cardinal and white team was ready to play. As a surprise to many, the Lower Campus Rink was in decent shape and the game would go on as planned. Players and fans had waited nearly a month for decent ice for a home hockey game. Due to unseasonably warm weather, the rink didn't have ice all of December and this season would be one of the worst for playing ice hockey in many years. This game was only possible due to a wintery cold snap that dropped temps below freezing for a couple of days.

The Badgers got their offense rolling when Kubista scored halfway into the first period. They added to their one-goal lead with a flurry of three more goals in the middle period. Gordy Meiklejohn scored in the first minute of the second period to extend the Badger lead to 2-0. Two minutes later Kubista netted his second goal of the game to push the lead to 3-0. With three minutes left in the second period, Meiklejohn scored his second goal of the game to make the score 4-0 in favor of the Badgers.

The pace of the game was noticeably faster in the third period. The Milwaukee Rowing Team scored 11 minutes into the final frame. Four minutes later, the UW scored their fifth of the game when Meiklejohn recorded his third goal of the game to complete the hat trick and take a 5-1 advantage. Wisconsin's defense and goaltending were exemplary in this match, helping them to a 5-1 victory.

Wisconsin Lineup: Kubista (Center), Halverson (Right Wing), Michael (Left Wing), Bardes (Right Defense), captain Meiklejohn (Left Defense) and Silvian (Goalie). Substitutes: Stehr, Kabat, Lyke, Roethe, Fawkes and Blumenthal. Saves: Wisconsin 12, Milwaukee 30.

A serious lack of ice forced coach Thomsen to cancel the weekend home series against the Michigan Wolverines which was scheduled for January 15 and 16. Record high temps for wintertime in January made the efforts of making any ice impossible on the Madison rink. In order to adapt to the less than ideal weather conditions, Coach Thomsen had his players reporting to Lake Wingra in Madison to practice on the lake ice. It was the only option to allow the players to put time into their ice skating, shooting and teamwork.

Next on the schedule was a trip to play the Gophers Tuesday, January 19. The Wisconsin team would leave late Monday night and head north. This was the first game of the Big Ten season and the contest was to be played at the newly opened St. Paul Auditorium that was complete with artificial ice, a rare commodity in these days. The Badgers received a special invitation from the University of Minnesota hockey officials to participate in the formal dedication of the St. Paul Auditorium. Immediately following the ceremony was the Wisconsin versus Minnesota hockey game starting at 9 p.m.

As expected, this inaugural game was clearly a Minnesota-dominated event as the UM squad wanted to make the most out of the St. Paul Auditorium dedication and promptly creamed the Badgers. It started out like it would be a great game for the UW. The first period remained scoreless until six minutes left in the period when the Gophers scored. They were able to add two more and by the end of the first period Wisconsin was down 3-0.

Nearly four minutes into the second, Minnesota added another goal to push their lead to 4-0. Wisconsin forward Greg Kabat scored a beautiful goal to put the Badgers on the board making the score 4-1.

Kabat, who was also a talented guard on the UW football team, had a reputation as a rough hockey player. His reputation preceeded him in this game. Kabat singlehandedly knocked down countless Minnesota players with his extraordinarily violent body checks. However, up North they let the boys play. Kabat was only called for one penalty and it was also the only infraction called on the Badgers during the entire game.

Overall, the game was a shellacking for the visitors. The Gophers scored three more goals in the second to make the score 7-1. They would keep the pressure on and added three more goals in the third period. At the end of regulation, Wisconsin had been soundly defeated by a final score of 10-1. It was one of the worst defeats of a Big Ten hockey team in the short history of the league.

Wisconsin Lineup: Kubista (Center), Halverson (Right Wing), Michael (Left Wing), Bardes (Right Defense), captain Meiklejohn (Left Defense) and Blumenthal (Goalie). Substitutes: Stehr, Kabat, Lyke, Roethe, Silvian and Fawkes. Saves: Wisconsin 29, Minnesota 10. Penalties: Wisconsin 1, Minnesota 9.

Wisconsin returned home and the unseasonably warm weather

conditions impeded any consistent opportunties to practice on the ice. Their dryland sessions and calisthenics were great at building up their physical and cardio strength, but without skating time on the ice the Badgers remained at a huge disadvantage, especially when compared to other top schools like Michigan and Minnesota that had the luxury of indoor artificial ice.

Coach Thomsen received correspondence from officials with the Polish Olympic Hockey Club. The international team was in the Chicago area preparing for the upcoming Winter Olympic games at Lake Placid. In the proposal, the Badgers were requested to play the Polish squad on February 15 at Chicago Stadium. A decision was dependent upon approval from the UW Athletic Council. Ultimately, the request was denied and the Badgers did not play the Polish Olympic team.

In mid-February, coach Thomsen brought his men for a return visit to northern Wisconsin to play the Wausau Hockey Athletic Club, also known as the Veterans of Foreign Wars hockey team. Greg Kabat, a three-sport athlete on the team, decided he would rather play in this game in Wausau than represent Wisconsin at shot put during the track meet back in Madison. Kabat was also the captain and an All-American guard on the football team. His pro-style body checks during every hockey game delighted fans wherever he went. Opponents had good reason to fear him. If he caught you with a body check you were likely to have to leave the game for a spell.

The Badgers narrowly lost to Wausau 1-0 in their first game of the seaon back on December 5. They wanted to prove conclusively that they were a far better team than their northern adversaries. This game was set to be played at the local City Market Square Rink in Wausau on the night of February 13. A few hundred townspeople showed up to watch the Badgers play the Vets.

Wisconsin right winger Robbie Halverson started the scoring for the Badgers with a nice un assisted goal early in the first period. A short while later, Gordy Meiklejohn pushed the Wisconsin lead to 2-0 with another unassisted goal. The visitors led 2-0 at the end of the first period.

Meiklejohn notched another to give Wisconsin a 3-0 advantage in the second. In the final period, the Vets scored their first two goals to make the score 3-2. UW spare Billy Southworth made the most of his substitution into the game and scored the fourth goal unassisted for the Badgers. A few minutes later, Badger center Roy Kubista scored on a nice pass from Bruce Michael, the crafty Badger left winger. At the end of regulation, the Badgers had defeated the Veterans of Foreign War by a score of 5-2. Wisconsin's goalie, Wes Silvian, was the MVP of the game. He turned away a mind-boggling 46 shots from the Wausau Vets.

Wisconsin Lineup: Kubista (Center), Halverson (Right Wing), Michael (Left Wing), captain Meiklejohn (Right Defense), Fawkes (Left Defense) and Silvian (Goalie). Substitutes: Stehr, Kabat, Lyke, Roethe, Riley, Southworth and Blumenthal. Saves: Wisconsin 46, Wausau 17. Penalties: Wisconsin 10, Wausau 5.

The UW boys returned to Michigan for the last series of the season. These games were scheduled for February 19 and February 20. The Michigan Wolverines were a powerhouse team in the college hockey ranks. It didn't take long for the UM players to show off their skating and stickhandling skills. The Wolverines were in full control of the game from the opening faceoff.

Wisconsin was hanging tough at the beginning of this game, but it didn't last long. The Wolverines scored their first goal halfway through the first period. Around 50 seconds later they scored again. Less than a minute-and-a-half later Michigan had a 3-0 lead. That was the end of scoring in the opening period. Although Badger goalie Les Silvian started this game, coach Thomsen pulled him after one period. He inserted Paul Blumenthal to guard the net for the remainder of the game.

Just over a minute into the second period the Wolverines scored again to take a 4-0 advantage. The Badgers responded just under 20 seconds later when captain Gordy Meiklejohn scored. He pulled the puck out of a mix-up of bodies in front of the Michigan net and quickly shot it in the Wolverines goal to make the score 4-1. It would be 10 minutes later before the maize and blue scored another goal. With five seconds left in the middle period, UM made it 6-1. The third period was a much tighter battle as the two rivals battled back and forth. The Wolverines again found the back of the net with less than 90 seconds to go in the game. Once regulation time concluded, Michigan had easily defeated Wisconsin by a score of 7-1.

Wisconsin Lineup: Kubista (Center), Halverson (Right Wing), Michael (Left Wing), Fawkes (Right Defense), captain Meiklejohn (Left Defense) and Silvian (Goalie). Substitutes: Stehr, Kabat, Lyke, Roethe, Riley, Silvian and Southworth. Penalties: Wisconsin 3, Michigan 7. Referee: "Puss" Traub from Windsor.

The next night wasn't much better for the Badgers. Silvian was back in net for the Uw and held the Wolverines scoreless until seven minutes into the first period. Michigan was up 1-0 at the end of the period. The Wolverines ramped up the scoring machine two minutes into the second period and scored their second goal. Around seven minutes later, Michigan pushed their lead to 3-0. Understandably, this game was extraordinarily physical since the rivalry was boiling over. The heightened physical play continued to increase in intensity every shift. The third period was filled with ferocious body checks by both teams. Three minutes into the final period, the UM squad was up 4-0 and they scored their final goal a handful of minutes later to take a commanding 5-0 lead.

No matter what they tried, the UW boys were unable to put any pucks in the net. While the Wolverines scored five times, they also held the Badgers scoreless and earned a shutout. Michigan won 5-0 and the hockey season had a dismal ending for the University of Wisconsin.

Wisconsin Lineup: Kubista (Center), Halverson (Right Wing), Michael (Left Wing), Fawkes (Right Defense), captain Meiklejohn (Left Defense) and Silvian (Goalie). Substitutes: Stehr, Kabat, Lyke, Roethe, Riley, Silvian and Southworth. Penalties: Wisconsin 2, Michigan 7. Referee: "Puss" Traub from Windsor.

Top Row: Golding (Manager), Allan Willson, Al Bardes, Micky Bach, Richard Fawkes, Billy Southworth, Greg Kabat, Art Thomsen (Coach)
Bottom Row: Les Silvian, John Roethe, Roy Kubista, Gordon Meiklejohn (Captain), Bruce Michael, Vernon Stehr, Paul Blumenthal

The 1931-32 UW varsity hockey team pictured above. Coach Art Thomsen is on the far right of the photo wearing his Wisconsin letterman sweater earned while playing for the Badgers in the three prior seasons. The third, fourth and fifth players seated in the front row of this photo have their jersey numbers written on the top of their hockey sticks. They are Roy Kubista #2 , Gordy Meiklejohn #10 and Vernon Stehr #12. Les Silvian, the goalie in the front row on the left, is wearing "bear paw" goalie gloves which were common in the 1930s. Both goalies and several players, have Northland brand hockey sticks. These were very popular sticks among youth, college and pro hockey player and were manufactured in Hastings, Minnesota.

This team photo was taken on the University of Wisconsin Lower Campus Rink. The YMCA building is visible in the background of this varsity team photograph.

During the 1931-32 season, numerous games were canceled even before visiting teams arrived in Madison. The weather was so uncooperative that the Badgers were rarely able to practice on their home rink and only played a total of three conference games! With a greatly reduced season, their record was a dismal 0-3-0 in the league. Overall, the Wisconsin team put together an unimpressive 2-5-1 record, good for last place in the WIHL.

1931-32   Schedule and Results:
Coach Art Thomsen
0-3-0   2-5-1 Overall

Date	Result	Opponent
December 5	Loss 1-0	@ Wausau*
December 31	Loss 3-2	Michigan College*#
January 1	Tie 2-2 OT	Michigan College*#
January 9	Win 5-1	Milwaukee*
January 19	Loss 10-1	@ Minnesota
February 13	Win 5-2	@ Wausau*
February 19	Loss 7-1	@ Michigan
February 20	Loss 5-0	@ Michigan

* Exhibition Games

#Played at Eagle River, Wisconsin.

Chapter Fourteen
Not Less Than Zero

1932–33 UW Hockey Team

Coach Art Thomsen's Wisconsin hockey team was pummeled by weather and opponents alike this season. Captain Roy Kubista and his teammates racked up a dismal record against in-state and out-of-state rivals. They recorded just six goals this season and allowed 43 goals against. Five shutouts were also recorded against the Badgers.

Budgeting challenges almost canceled the UW hockey program. The economy was still in the grips of the Great Depression. Coach Thomsen's team was unable to catch a break and the challenges continued to grow. Minor sports, including ice hockey, were dropped from the formal Wisconsin Athletic Department. UW Football agreed in principle to share a portion of their gate receipts to help fund the desperate hockey program.

There were plenty of men that came out to play hockey again this year at the University. Varsity players included captain Roy Kubista, David Greeley, Billy Southworth, James Lyke, Robert Mercer, Robert Halverson, Richard Fawkes, Maurice Jansky and Vernon Stehr. The freshman squad players included Charley Heyer, James Gillies, James Fallon, Don Maxwell, Harry Quinn, Richard Muther and Herbert Terwilliger.

Coach Thomsen was determined to see hockey continue at Wisconsin. News of selecting a varsity team quickly spread around campus and potential players were urged to join the intramural hockey leagues. The top players in those student leagues would be selected to join the Wisconsin varsity hockey roster. To make matters worse, star player and last season's leading scorer, Bruce Michael, made the difficult decision to depart from the team in order to return home and support his struggling family. Fortunately, he would return to the roster later in the season.

Mother Nature was in an equally bad mood and ruined many practices, scrimmages and games. Winter arrived in late December and temps cold enough for decent ice in the last month of 1932 were long overdue. The weather delayed regular practice time for the Badgers and opponents had no problem taking advantage of the ill prepared UW squad.

Coach Thomsen's team was unable to catch a break and the challenges took many forms this season. Minor sports, including ice hockey, had been dropped from Badger Athletic Program, but Director of Intramural Athletics, professor Guy S. Lowman, had a unique plan to cover these abandoned sports and to get them funded as "extramural" sports. Mr. Lowman intended to arrange a minimum schedule to keep hockey, and the other disenfranchised minor sports, alive on campus.

Financial incentives and other inducements were proposed in order to get the University of Minnesota hockey team to stop in Madison to play the Badgers on their way to and from Ann Arbor, Michigan for their scheduled games against the University of Michigan. In addition, a home and home game arrangement with Marquette University was proposed to relieve some of the financial burden the program was experiencing. A lack of decent funding, due to severe budget cuts had a ripple effect on the UW hockey program. The team was unable to get new equipment, were forced to play fewer games overall and their travel was negatively impacted.

The weather continued to be a large factor hampering progress for the club, from the preseason all the way through to the end of the regular season. Frequent warm spells caused undesired thawing of the Madison ice rink and the cold days brought frigid temps which produced inordinate amounts of snow. As luck would have it, the other teams Wisconsin was scheduled to play got sufficient practice times on suitable natural ice and/or artificial ice, so their home games were not impacted by weather-induced cancellations.

Coach Art Thomsen was able to negotiate arangements for away hockey games involving Michigan College and the University of Minnesota. Part of the deal involved generous revenue guarantees for each of the away two-game series and allowed the Badgers to travel by train in order to meet their opponents.

In order to prepare for their upcoming away game in Houghton, Michigan, the Wisconsin squad prepared with on-ice workouts and planning sessions. Coach Thomsen realized he needed to revise his lineup in order to produce a faster offensive threat. To do so, he created two forward lines that would alternate playing time during games. The first line trio included team captain Roy Kubista, Robert Halverson and Vernon Stehr. A second forward line was comprised of Bob Mercer, Dick Fawkes and Maurice Jansky.

Early in the season, Billy Southworth began to shine. Southworth was an extremely fast skater that could often go on a solo rush which usually ended up with a goal for the cardinal and white team. He was also a skilled stickhandler that enabled him to weave in and out of opponents.

Coach Thomsen lined up the semi-professional Milwaukee Rowing Club hockey team as the first opponent in January this season. Last year, the Milwaukee team won the tri-state championship in Chicago by beating teams from Michigan, Wisconsin and Illinois. They were an exceptionally talented team made up primarily of veterans that already completed their college hockey careers while other players on the team were simply superior hockey playing veterans. A pair of games scheduled for Friday night January 6 and Saturday afternoon January 7 were to be played in Madison at the Lower Campus Rink.

These games were intended to be the first test of the extramural plan. Since mens hockey was no longer a minor sport at the UW, it didn't have financial backing and was required to be self-supporting. The team would still be playing intercollegiate hockey under the conference rules of eligibility. Students were not happy to find out that the coupon books with tickets for a variety of Wisconsin sporting events would not be honored at home Badger hockey games since the team no longer earned any money from the coupons as they did in prior years. Admission for all hockey games this season would be twenty-five cents at the door. Gate money would go toward defraying costs of the sport so the hockey team could continue to play.

Everything was ready to kick off the season and institute this new admission structure, except the weather. Warm temps caused terrible ice conditions. As a result, both games against the Milwaukee Rowing Club were canceled. A rematch was tentatively in the works for later in January.

On Thursday January 12, the hockey team packed up several automobiles so that they could caravan to Houghton. The Michigan College of Mining and Technology was the first away conference series Wisconsin had scheduled. Badger right winger Rob Halverson was injured in the final practice of the week and was unable to play. A star forward, Halverson sustained a deep ankle cut from a teammate's skate in an accident during practice. He was out indefinitely. As a result, Dick Fawkes or Greg Kabat were picked to fill the void on the first offensive line by playing the starting position on right wing.

Coach Thomsen selected nine men to make the trip to Michigan. Among them were goaltenders Dave Greeley and Wayne Lewis along with captain Roy Kubista, Dick Southworth, Dick Fawkes, Vernon Stehr, Maurice Jansky, Rob Mercer and Greg Kabat. The first game was set for Friday, January 13. This Wisconsin team had two challenges: lack of sufficient practice time due to poor ice and the fact that neither of their goalies had any prior game experience.

Michigan College was an incredibly strong hockey team. Although the UW squad held Tech scoreless in the first period, it would not be enough. One of the Huskies' forwards eluded the Badgers defense and ripped a high shot that beat UW goalie David Greeley over his shoulder for the first goal of the game. Wisconisn was able to stop Tech from scoring any more goals in the middle period, but they couldn't score any of their own. At the end of the second period, the Michigan School of Mines had a 1-0 lead.

The Michigan College players opened the flood gates in the third period and scored four unanswered goals. In what was deemed a clean and hard fought game, each team only received three minor penalties. Wisconsin's penalty box visitors were Jansky, Kabat and Fawkes. Without a doubt the home crowd of two thousand plus spectators in attendance enjoyed the hockey action and the final score of 5-0. The score could have been a lot worse. Fortunately, new Wisconsin goalie Dave Greeley played a spectacular game in net.

Wisconsin Lineup: captain Kubista (Center), Fawkes (Right Wing), Stehr (Left Wing), Southworth (Right Defense), Kabat (Left Defense) and Greeley (Goalie). Substitutes: Mercer, Jansky, Baumgart and Lewis. Referee: Jack Mahan.

On the afternoon of Saturday, January 14, it was nearly an identical match against the Huskies. The cardinal and white skaters were out hustled and dominated by the boys from Michigan. Tech's first goal came with just over five minutes left in the opening period. By the end of the period it was 1-0. At seven minutes into the second period,

Michigan College increased their lead to 2-0. Two minutes later, it was 3-0.

Coach Thomsen yanked Greeley even though he was playing considerably well and had made 23 saves to that point. He put in his other goalie, Wayne Lewis, to start the third. The final period wasn't much better for the Badgers. Five minutes into the third the Huskies scored again. The Huskies were able to score in every period while the Badgers offense was still missing. At the final buzzer the Huskies had completed the two-game sweep by shutting out the Badgers 4-0 in this game. It was another clean game with the referee only calling one penalty on each team during the 60 minutes of play.

Wisconsin Lineup: Mercer (Center), Fawkes (Right Wing), Stehr (Left Wing), Southworth (Right Defense), Kabat (Left Defense) and Greeley (Goalie). Substitutes: Fawkes, captain Kubista, Baumgart and Lewis. Referee: Jack Mahan.

The previously postponed match against the Milwaukee Rowing Club hockey squad was rescheduled for Tuesday, January 17 at 8:15p.m. at the Lower Campus Rink. Again, it was solely dependent upon the weather allowing for decent ice. At game time, it was decided the game would be played as scheduled.

The Rowing Club was primarily a band of amateur hockey players that were highly skilled and very competitive. An interesting combo on the roster for this Milwaukee team featured a father-son duo on the same line. Jack Thompson was the right winger for Milwaukee and his son, Al, played left defense.

Milwaukee got on the board first, scoring in the opening period. Wisconsin was unable to tally one of their own. In the second period, both Southworth and Stehr scored for the Badgers to take a 2-1 lead. They also held Milwaukee scoreless in this middle period which set up an epic battle in the third period. It was a very tight, back-and-forth defensive battle.With just under two minutes left in the game, the visitors scored their second goal to tie it up at 2-2 and force overtime.

After a 10 minute rest, both teams lined up to determine a winner. In these days, overtime periods were not sudden death, where the team that scores first is declared the winner and the game is over. Instead, the full 10 minutes of the overtime was played and both teams could score as many times as possible. Milwaukee scored twice during OT and the Badgers were unable to net any goals. At the end of the extra period, the Milwaukee Rowing Club defeated Wisconsin by the score of 4-2. Although a two-game series was scheduled, the second game was canceled due to soft ice caused by the unseasonably warm weather.

Wisconsin Lineup: Mercer (Center), Jansky (Right Wing), Stehr (Left Wing), Southworth (Right Defense), Kabat (Left Defense) and Greeley (Goalie). Substitutes: Fawkes and captain Kubista. Saves: Wisconsin 23, Milwaukee Rowing Club 13.

Significant lack of ice forced the postponement of the two-game series Wisconsin was supposed to play against Marquette in Milwaukee January 20 and January 21. Coaches from both teams agreed to attempt to find makeup dates as soon as the weather cooperated.

Three weeks after their last game, the Badgers traveled to Eau Claire, Wisconsin for one of the two games they would play at the Winter Carnival. In the first game February 2, they were slated to play the home team, the Eau Claire City Hockey Team at the Birch Street Rink. On a bitterly cold night, a large and rowdy home crowd was on hand to watch their underdog home team play the college boys from Madison. In addition to the chilly temps, the Badgers also had to contend with playing the game at an exceptionally small ice hockey rink.

The Badgers scored the first goal early in the game to get the attention of all the locals, both on and off the ice. Wisconsin spare, Walter Baumgardt, who wasn't even wearing a Wisconsin Badgers hockey jersey, picked up the puck mid-ice and skated toward the front of the opponents rink when he took a hard shot that snuck past the City Team netminder. After the score, UW coach Thomsen pulled Baumgardt out of the game. His player had been battling the flu, was still weak from recovery and wasn't expected to play at all in this game.

But Eau Claire refused to back down and battled on with the enthusiastic support of their home crowd. Wisconsin went into a strictly defensive mode in an attempt to deny the City Team from scoring at all in this game. UW defenseman, Bill Southworth, who was from Eau Claire, played an excellent match and impressed the crowd. Wisconsin goalie Dave Greeley played an exceptional game and turned away numerous quality chances from the home team. In the final minutes of the third period, the Eau Claire City hockey team scored their first goal and knotted up the score. Fans and players were denied an overtime period to determine a true winner since this game was deemed an exhibition. Coach Thomsen intentionally ruled against the opportunity for OT because he did not want his players to be especially tired for their upcoming game against the Gophers.

Wisconsin Lineup: Mercer (Center), Jansky (Right Wing), Stehr (Left Wing), Fawkes (Right Defense), Southworth (Left Defense) and Greeley (Goalie). Substitutes: captain Kubista, Baumgardt, Halverson, Lyke and Dusley. Referee: Harold Parvar.

Wisconsin met up with their northern rivals, the Minnesota Gophers, at the Eau Claire Wisconsin Winter Carnival for a highly anticipated hockey game Saturday, February 4 at 2:30 p.m. This game would be billed as the main attraction of the annual municipal winter sports show. Last year the University of Minnesota hockey team was the sectional champions during the Olympic tryouts to represent the USA in international competition. They lost the chance to represent America in the Winter Olympic games after being bested by an all-amateur hockey team from Boston.

Both Wisconsin and Minnesota braved the -20 degree weather in Eau Claire and played the game as scheduled even though they were subjected to bone numbing air temps throughout the course of the game at the Teachers College Rink. Thankfully, this rink was regulation size unlike the constrictive size of the much smaller Birch Street Rink from yesterday's game. The players were cold, but the spectators were a lot colder just watching this match. Minnesota scored first just eight minutes after the start and tallied another goal to take a 2-0 lead.

Wisconsin versus Minnesota at the Eau Claire Winter Carnival.

Badger center Bob Mercer put Wisconsin on the board by scoring the first goal of the second period to cut the lead to 2-1. That would be as close as the Badgers would get in this match. The Gophers pounded in three more goals in the middle period to make the score 5-1. Minnesota would add one more tally with five minutes left in the final period. Wisconsin was held to only scoring one goal. The Gophers defeated the Badgers 6-1.

Wisconsin Lineup: Mercer (Center), Jansky (Right Wing), Stehr (Left Wing), Fawkes (Right Defense), Southworth (Left Defense) and Greeley (Goalie). Substitutes: captain Kubista, Halverson, Lyke and Dusley. Referee: Bill Haman of St. Paul.

A pair of games rescheduled between Marquette University and the University of Wisconsin were slated for February 7 and 8 in Madison. This wasn't finalized until Monday, February 6 when UW intramural director and Marquette Athletic Director Connie Jennings finalized the agreement to allow the hockey games to occur. Coach Thomsen had new challenges to face. Star defenseman and UW football captain, Greg Kabat abruptly left the University and notified school officials that he would not return to Wisconsin for the second semester. Instead, he transferred to UW-Milwaukee to complete his studies. Jimmy Lykes, a junior spare from Janeville, was the likely player to fill the void left by Kabat's departure. Robbie Halverson, who had been unable to play since having his ankle deeply cut at practice in January, was now dealing with a serious infection from that injury. His anticipated return to the Badgers lineup this season was doubtful.

Yet again, Mother Nature had other plans as a monsterous snowstorm dropped over 13 inches of snow on southern Wisconsin and temperatures plummeted to 15 below zero. Both of the scheduled hockey games between the UW and the Marquette Hilltoppers were canceled due to the blizzard. The two schools agreed to get a game or two on the calendar as soon as decent weather and schedules allowed. A rematch between Wisconsin and Marquette was tentatively scheduled for February 14. If all went well, the second game in the series would be played at Madison sometime later in the month.

The Badgers were able to get two days of practice in Madison on their home rink prior to their departure for the University of Minnesota. To continue their growing rivalry, Wisconsin traveled to Minnesota for two games February 10 and 11. To date, Minnesota won all six of the hockey games they had played and their sophomore players had racked up 20 of the 27 goals they had scored. All of the Minnesota players were healthy and their roster was rock solid. The Badgers had the odds severely stacked against them and were clearly the underdog.

This first game was scheduled with an 8:15 p.m. start time. Over five thousand fans at the St. Paul Hippodrome watched their Gophers in the first of the final two home stands this season. The first period was a close battle that frustrated the Gophers. Both teams had a few quality shots on net but none got in the net. At least not until just under three minutes remaining in the first period, when the Gophers punched in their first goal to make it 1-0. The Badgers felt thankful to get out of the period down by only one goal.

It was only a minute-and-a-half into the second period when Minnesota scored their second goal. Then the wheels came off for the Badgers as the Gophers registered four more successive goals to take a commanding 6-0 lead by the end of the period. During the third period, the Badgers battled on but it was to no avail. Around the seven minute mark, Minnesota scored their seventh goal of the game. With less than five minutes to play, the Gophers racked another. The University of Minnesota hockey squad easily dispatched the UW and shut them out in the first game by a score of 8-0.

Wisconsin Lineup: Mercer (Center), Jansky (Right Wing), Stehr (Left Wing), Fawkes (Right Defense), Southworth (Left Defense) and Greeley (Goalie). Substitutes: captain Kubista, Halverson and Dusley. Saves: Wisconsin 29, Minnesota 10. Penalties: Wisconsin 1, Minnesota 3. Referee: Bill Haman of St. Paul.

In the second game, the Wisconsin Badgers had their work cut out for them. Their efforts were evident as the first period ended with the score at 0-0. Coach Thomsen adjusted the Wisconsin strategy so that at least three Badger players would be in front of their goalie helping to deny shots on goal and get the puck out of their zone. However in the first period alone, UW goalie Dave Greeley made 21 saves. The Gophers were shelling the Badger net due to the lack of defensive pressure on the perimeter.

Minnesota scored after just one minute of play in the second period. That score would stand as the two teams entered the final frame. It wasn't until five minutes into the third that the Gophers pushed their lead to 2-0. Greeley continued to play well in net for the Badgers, but his teammates were unable to solve the Gopher goalie. With less than six minutes remaining in the game, Minnesota scored their third and final goal, to the delight of their hometown fans.

Wisconsin goalie Greeley was credited with exemplary play making 41 saves, including 21 in the first period! The netninder's extraordinary performance wasn't enough to prevent the inevitable, a 3-0 win for Minnesota and a Big Ten title. The Badgers were sent home angry and furstrated with their performance.

Wisconsin Lineup: Mercer (Center), Jansky (Right Wing), Stehr (Left Wing), Fawkes (Right Defense), Southworth (Left Defense) and Greeley (Goalie). Substitutes: captain Kubista, Halverson and Dusley. Saves: Wisconsin 41, Minnesota 16. Penalties: Wisconsin 1, Minnesota 5. Referee: Bill Haman of St. Paul.

Madison finally got the chilly temperatures needed for quality ice at their outdoor rink, but this time it was too cold. It was a cruel twist in a year that had been unseasonably warm. The Badgers upcoming game against in-state rival Marquette would have to be postponed.

Professor Guy S. Lowman of the Wisconsin Intramural Athletic Department confirmed the Marquette versus Wisconsin matchup would happen in February. On Valentine's Day, the Marquette Hilltoppers hosted the University of Wisconsin for a heartbreaking smakeup game. The rink was surrounded by several hundred enthusiastic spectators that came out on this Tuesday evening in Milwaukee to watch this tilt that would be their only home game of the season.

The doctors cleared Robbie Halverson, although he wasn't 100% after a serious foot infection following a deep ankle laceration that happened during practice in January. He started at right wing and gave the Badgers some much needed offensive talent. The Hilltoppers got on the board under halfway through the first period with a hard shot from just inside the blue line. A scoreless second period demonstrated how evenly these teams played each other. In the third period, the same Marquette forward that scored the first goal was able to bang in a loose puck for their second goal.

The puck enters the Wisconsin net for the Hilltoppers second goal.

Both goals for the Hilltoppers were scored while Wisconsin had players in the penalty box. Despite the best efforts of the Badgers on the Milwaukee rink, the Marquette team was able to shut out the UW squad and earn a 2-0 win. The Badgers were unable to get their offense ramped up before time ran out.

Wisconsin Lineup: Mercer (Center), Halverson (Right Wing), Fawkes (Left Wing), Lyke (Right Defense), Southworth (Left Defense) and Greeley (Goalie). Substitutes: captain Kubista, Jansky, Stehr and Michael. Penalties: Wisconsin 4, Marquette 6. Officials: Jake Thompson and Max Smith from Milwaukee.

The second makeup game between the Badgers and Hilltoppers was scheduled for Tuesday, February 18 at 8 p.m. in Madison. Unseasonably warm weather also forced this game to be canceled. It would not be rescheduled.

Wisconsin had games scheduled with the Wolverines in Ann Arbor on the weekend of February 17 and 18. The UW club made the trip to Michigan using several automobiles. Wisconsin forward Rob Halverson was still hobbled by a bad ankle but made the trip to support his squad. As the players were getting dressed for this contest he informed coach Thomsen that he would play this game. Ignoring the pain in his swollen foot, Halverson taped his ankle tightly so he could compete as best he could. When asked if his ankle hurt, Halverson let the coach know that watching from the stands hurt more.

Michigan was first to score during the opening 20 minutes. They pulled away in the second with three more goals, including a hat trick by their captain. Wisconsin's lone goal was scored in the second period while Michigan was down a man serving a penalty on a nice individual effort by centerman Bob Mercer. He cut across the front of the net and patiently held the puck until the last instant when he slid it past the outstretched foot of the goalie and into the back of the net. It wouldn't be enough as the Wolverines bagged four goals in this period to take a commanding 5-1 lead going into the third period.

Michigan pounded in three more goals in the third. Fortunately for the Badgers, UW goalie Greeley hadn't given up. He made multiple critical saves to stop the score from going into double digits. Wisconsin lost, 8-1.

Wisconsin Lineup: Mercer (Center), Jansky (Right Wing), Stehr (Left Wing), Fawkes (Right Defense), Southworth (Left Defense) and Greeley (Goalie). Substitutes: captain Kubista, Halverson and Dusley. Penalties: Wisconsin 1, Michigan 2. Referee: Fox from Detroit.

The second tilt between these two hockey powerhouses was a lot closer. Michigan scored first at 15 minutes into the opening period. Prior to that, neither team would back down. It looked like a different Wisconsin team showed up for this game. At the end of the first period, the Wolverines were up 1-0.

The second period was a back-and-forth war. Aggressive body checking by both sides was only seperated by rushes up and down the ice. Wisconsin's goaltender Dave Greeley continued to make spectacular saves to keep the Badgers in the game. Michigan's co-captain was chasing after a loose puck as fast as he could in the Wisconsin end when he failed to navigate the upcoming boards. He slammed his skates into the boards at full speed and fell to the ice. He had badly twisted his ankle during the on-ice crash. The player left the game and was physically unable to return.

UW's Billy Southworth took a high stick to the face that opened up a noticeable laceration. His teammates urged him to come to the bench for treatment so that a substitute player could replace him. Southworth ignored his fellow players and stayed on the ice as blood was running down the right side of his face. He told his coach and teammates that he preferred to get stitched up after the game. At the end of the middle period it was still 1-0 Michigan.

Southworth and Greeley on Guard

A scoreless second period set up a tense third period. Wisconsin's winger Rob Halverson tied the score early in the third period when he smashed the puck into Michigan's net during a pileup in front of the Wolverines goalie. His goal at 2:25 into the third period was an inspiration to his teammates since Halverson could barely put any weight on his injured ankle and yet he was out skating and fighting for the Wisconsin Badgers. The score was 1-1.

Not to be outdone on their home ice, the Wolverines strategy was to send four players down at once in formation to attack the Wisconsin net. The strategy worked and Michigan scored an unassisted shot with this unusual player alignment with 30 seconds left in the period to go up by one. For the final moments left in the game, the Wolverines held off the attacking Badgers for the 2-1 win. It was a painful end to the Wisconsin hockey season.

Wisconsin Lineup: Mercer (Center), Jansky (Right Wing), Stehr (Left Wing), Fawkes (Right Defense), Southworth (Left Defense) and Greeley (Goalie). Substitutes: captain Kubista, Halverson and Dusley.

A makeup of the second game with Marquette was scheduled for Tuesday, February 21 but an unplayable ice surface at the Lower Campus Rink caused the cancellation of this game. Wisconsin's hockey season was officially over.

In a first at the University of Wisconsin, the Badger hockey team did not win a single game this year, but they continued to compete and represent the UW. They also continued the storied history for what would one day be a national championship program. The Wisconsin Badgers hockey team would fight on and take the ice next season.

1932-33   Schedule and Results:

Coach Art Thomsen

0-5-0 Last place in the WIHL   0-9-1 Overall

Date	**Result**	**Opponent**
January 13	Loss 5-0	@Michigan College
January 14	Loss 4-0	@Michigan College
January 17	Loss 4-2 OT	Milwaukee*
February 3	Tie 1-1	Eau Claire#
February 4	Loss 6-1	Minnesota#
February 10	Loss 8-0	@ Minnesota
February 11	Loss 3-0	@ Minnesota
February 14	Loss 2-0	@ Marquette (WI)
February 17	Loss 8-1	@Michigan
February 18	Loss 2-1	@Michigan

*Exhibition Game

#Eau Claire Winter Carnival games played in Eau Claire, Wisconsin.

Chapter Fifteen
Car Crash in the Snowstorm

1933–34 UW Hockey Team

Returning Wisconsin hockey players and personnel were optimistic about the upcoming 1933-34 season and were eager to distance themselves from the 1932-33 season in which they collected zero wins and nine straight losses.

Varsity hockey players included co-captain William Southworth, co-captain Robert Halverson, Charles Heyer, Charles Quinn, Jerome Femal, Donald Maxwell, James Gillies, James Fallon, Jim Lyke, Wes Silvian, Don Muther and Robert Mercer. Freshman squad players included Robert Null, Robert Petrie, Donald Gosin, Edward Berry, Wallace Drew, Emerson Vorel, Hugh O'Malley, Alfred Thomsen, Walter Bigford and Ernest Sullivan. Unfortunately, Jim Fallon, the starting right winger was declared academically ineligible. There was a chance that he would return during the second semester and be allowed to play for the varsity hockey team if his grades met the university requirements.

Wisconsin head coach Art Thomsen would experience another extraordinarily rough year. He was repeatedly knocked down by the familiar one-two punch delivered by Mother Nature and the frequently unplayable ice surface of the rink on the lower Madison campus. As a result, numerous hockey practices were held indoors at the Red Gym on the floor without the luxury of ice. Roller skates were used to simulate skating on the gym floor. The UW team conducted daily practice sessions in preparation for the upcoming season but without an indoor ice rink, Wisconsin would remain unable to compete and the survival of the hockey program would remain in jeopardy.

In early November 1933, a sufficient cold spell froze over Lake Wingra for several days. The University of Wisconsin players made their way there to take advantage of the skating surface and had several practice sessions on the lake. The warm weather would return a few days later and eliminate any of the outdoor ice and ruin the opportunity for additional practice sessions before the preseason scrimmage games began. Once the ice was decimated, the players were back in the Red Gym working out.

Thomsen was so desperate for decent ice that he took his entire team to Chicago and rented out the Chicago Colisseum in mid-November just so his boys could practice on an accomodating ice surface to improve their skills for the upcoming hockey season.

Coach Thomsen knew the importance of preseason exhibition games and scheduled eight of them before the regular season began. Up first on November 30 was a Thanksgiving Day contest against the Baby Ruth Hockey Team, an all-star club out of Chicago. They had the luxury of being sponsored by the Curtiss Candy Company and their squad was a marketing ploy created to sell more candy. Each of these players were paid the handsome amount of $25 per week to play for the team. Considering this was in the middle of the Great Depression, when the American economy was in the tank, getting paid a weekly sum of $25 to play hockey was a rich blessing for those players.

Wisconsin's hockey squad would have 11 players selected by coach Thomsen to make the trip to Chicago. The Badger players and staff loaded up their automobiles and headed to the Windy City at their own expense since the University was unable and unwilling to pay the costs associated with the hockey team.

Wisconsin players making the Chicago trip:

Player	Hometown
Westley Silvian	Duluth, MN.
Jim Gillies	Madison, WI.
Bill Southworth	Madison, WI.
Jim Lyke	Janesville, WI.
Jerry Femal	Madison, WI.
Dick Fawkes	Madison, WI.
Bob Mercer	White Plains, NY.
Robert Halverson	Madison, WI.
Chuck Quinn	Madison, WI.
Don Maxwell	La Tuque, QC.
Dick Muther	Boston, MA.

Coach Thomsen decided to go with his "Kid Line" to begin the game against the Baby Ruths. They were given the nickname since the players were all sophomores. Don Maxwell played center, Dick Muther manned right wing and Chuck Quinn was at left wing,. Co-captain Bill Southworth and Jim Gillies started at defense while Wes Silvian was the starting goaltender.

Thomsen's second line of players consisted of Bob Mercer at center, Dick Fawkes at left wing and co-captain Rob Halverson at right wing. At defense on the second line was Jim Lyke and Jerry Femal.

Wisconsin would have its hands full against the team widely regarded as the as one of the best amateur hockey clubs in the country. An overwhelming crowd of six thousand five hundred hockey fans made for an intimidating venue at the iconic Chicago Coliseum.

Although this game was played on the Thanksgiving holiday, the Badger players didn't have a lot to be thankful for in terms of hockey. All of the members of Baby Ruths were advanced hockey players and were clearly in control of the game. The home team scored first on a hard shot in the middle of the opening period. The two teams played even the rest of the period and it was 1-0 going into the second. Another goal for Baby Ruths went in after they made several impressive passes. The home team went up 2-0 in the second period. Several minutes later the Chicago team scored their third goal when a Badger player overskated the puck leaving it for a Baby Ruths player to shoot it past the UW netminder. The home team had a 3-0 lead.

Although Wisconsin had more than two dozen shots on goal, they were unable to beat the Chicago goalie. Both teams were held scoreless in the final period. The Badgers were fortunate to hold them to three goals as they were shut out and lost this ultra fast preseason game by a score of 3-0.

Wisconsin Lineup: Maxwell (Center), Muther (Right Wing), Quinn (Left Wing), Gillies (Right Defense), co-captain Southworth (Left Defense) and Silvian (Goalie). Substitutes: Lyke, Mercer, co-captain Halverson, Femal and Fawkes.

A welcome cold spell arrived in mid-December and gave the Badger hockey team some desperately needed ice for practices. It allowed the UW skaters to get in a week of preparation before they ventured up to Wausau for a couple of games. The Wausau team was presumably in better shape since they were fortunate to have gotten more than three weeks of consistent practice. On Saturday, December 16, the cardinal and white skaters traveled north by automobile to Wausau, Wisconsin for a pair of games against the Wausau Veterans of Foreign War Hockey Club.

From the opening faceoff, the pace of this game was furious as the teams skated end-to-end trying to keep possession of the puck before scoring against their opponents. Wisconsin quickly realized that the Vets team relied a lot on heavy body checking as part of their strategy. Wausau was first to score when one of their wingers skated with the puck behind the UW net before attacking the other side and pushing it into the Badger goal. Several minutes later, Wisconsin tied the game when right winger Dick Muther gave a nice pass to center Donny Maxwell who was able to convert on his scoring attempt. After one period the score was 1-1.

The pace of the game was again exceedingly fast at the start of the second period as both teams tried to get some offense going. A few minutes into the middle period, the Vets were back in the lead after scoring on a nifty attempt. It was now 2-1 in favor of the home team. The period would end without any more goals by either side.

The Badgers mounted several offensive attempts in the third period, but Wausau shut them down time and time again. The Vets continued to be the more physical team. At each opportunity they hit, checked and banged the Wisconsin players into the boards or onto the playing surface. Halfway through the last period, Wausau scored two back-to-back goals within minutes to make the score 4-1. Coach Thomsen used some creative strategy for its time when he pulled UW goalie Westley Silvian in order to play six players with an empty net during the last three minutes of the first game. The Badgers rallied for multiple attacks. but were only able to counter with one more goal to make it 4-2. The Vets defense was impressive and they refused to be dominated by the college boys from Madison. Wausau claimed the 4-2 win when regulation time ended.

Wisconsin Lineup: Maxwell (Center), Muther (Right Wing), Quinn (Left Wing), Gillies (Right Defense), co-captain Southworth (Left Defense) and Silvian (Goalie). Substitutes: Lyke, Mercer, co-captain Halverson, Femal and Fawkes. Penalties: Wisconsin 5, Wausau 0.

The second game on the afternoon of December 17 was a lot more even, but it went very much like the match the day before. In the first period, the Vets were on the board after a nice goal that beat UW goalie Wes Silvian. Several minutes later Donny Maxwell scored for the visiting Badgers to tie the game at 1-1. That score would hold as the period ended.

The Wausau Vets came out flying again during the middle period. Their tentacity paid off as the home team pounded in two goals to give them a 3-1 advantage. It was clear that the Wausau goaltender was superb at his position. He turned away many quality scoring chances from the Badgers.

In the third period, the Wisconsin squad rallied for several offensive chances and defended their own zone admirably. Coach Thomsen again used some creative strategy when he pulled UW goalie Westley Silvian in order to play six players with an empty net during the last nine minutes of this second game. During the six on five, Wausau was completely prevented from getting into a scoring position, as Wisconsin dominated the play with an extra attacker. It was not enough to even up the score. Wausau won 3-1 to take both games from the Badgers this weekend.

Wisconsin Lineup: Maxwell (Center), Muther (Right Wing), Quinn (Left Wing), Gillies (Right Defense), co-captain Southworth (Left Defense) and Silvian (Goalie). Substitutes: Lyke, Mercer, co-captain Halverson, Femal and Fawkes. Penalties: Wisconsin 1, Wausau 1.

Next up, the exhibition games on the schedule had the boys headed into Michigan December 20 for two contests in Houghton against Michigan College. Both the players and coaches were required to caravan on the way to Michigan since they had to make the trip using privately owned automobiles. Budgetary slashes at the University of Wisconsin no longer allowed the hockey team to travel by train. Thursday December 21 was the first game pitting the Wisconsin Badgers against the Michigan College Huskies.

Donald Maxwell, a center for the Badgers, got Wisconsin the early 1-0 lead by scoring late in the first period. Tech came back tied the score less than a minute into the start of the second period. Later in the second, co-captain Robert Halverson was able to put the Badgers up 2-1 with a nifty goal, but the Huskies would not fold and were able to tie the game again before the period ended.

Neither team was able to break the tie and score in the wild third period. After a 10-minute rest, the teams took the ice to play an overtime period. Both the Badgers and Tech were unable to record the game winner after the 10-minute OT and the officials ended the game. It went in the record books as a 2-2 tie.

Wisconsin Lineup: Maxwell (Center), Muther (Right Wing), Quinn (Left Wing), Gillies (Right Defense), co-captain Southworth (Left Defense) and Silvian (Goalie). Substitutes: Lyke, Mercer, co-captain Halverson, Femal and Fawkes.

Friday night's game on December 22, started out with the possibility that Wisconsin would get the better of Michigan College. The two thousand-plus spectators watching this affair were not thrilled with how this game was going. Wisconsin was able to get one goal early in the first period after Donald Maxwell scored for the second night in a row. At the end of the first period, it was 1-0 Wisconsin.

Michigan College scored twice on the Badgers in the middle period to take a 2-1 lead. Wisconsin could not get any goals past the Tech goalkeeper this period but that score would hold up as the period ended. The third period had all the makings of a frenetic finish. Not only was the score close, with the visitors being down by one as the final period started the Badgers were able to get multiple offensive attacks on the Huskies net.

The home team kept battling and were able to net their third goal, which was contested in a heated debate. During hockey games in the 1920s and 1930s, an umpire stood directly behind each net on the ice so that they could help the referee determine whether a goal should be counted or not. In this game, the goal judge signaled Michigan College's third goal was good. Wisconsin's goalie Wes Silvian went berserk arguing that the puck never crossed the goal line. The goal judge began to argue back just as ferociously as the visiting goaltender, and within minutes the judge and goalie were in one hell of a fist fight. It took several players to separate the combatants.

Wisconsin coach Thomsen took the side of his goalie and gathered up his players and told them they were walking out of the game in protest. The couple of thousand people watching the game began loudly booing in disapproval after seeing the Badgers were going to quit the game in protest. Michigan hockey officials were able to convince the UW to complete the game. Wisconsin reluctantly agreed to finish, but by the end of the contest they had lost 3-1.

Wisconsin Lineup: Maxwell (Center), Muther (Right Wing), Quinn (Left Wing), Gillies (Right Defense), co-captain

Southworth (Left Defense) and Silvian (Goalie). Substitutes: Lyke, Mercer, co-captain Halverson, Femal and Fawkes.

Adding insult to injury, the Badgers were forced to drive their automobiles home through a bad winter storm. It was treacherous traveling home from Michigan's upper peninsula back to Madison, Wisconsin while driving through deep snow. The team had a few of their cars slide off into the ditches two different times. In both instances, they had to get assistance to get their vehicles back onto the roadway. One of the sedans packed with six Badger players and their hockey equipment lost control on the snow-covered road and rolled over twice. Every window of the car was broken in the accident and the auto was heavily damaged. Fortunately, the UW players escaped with only cuts and bruises and the car was able to make it back to the Madison campus with the others on the trip.

Christmas Eve day would not be a day of rest for the team. While their fellow students were enjoying the holiday, the players were in Chicago for a 3p.m. game against the Nestor Johnsons. The match was intended to sharpen the skills of the Badgers before they met up with the Queens University team from Kingston, Ont.

The Chicago team was an all-star club sponsored by Nestor Johnson Manufacturing, a major ice skate company based in Chicago, Illois Once again the Chicago Coliseum would be the host venue for this hockey game and some four thousand-plus hockey fans came out to watch. Bill Southwell, the co-captain of the Badgers and star left defenseman would lead his men into this battle. Dickie Fawkes got the scoring going for the Badgers goal after five minutes into the first period. The crowd went crazy in approval of the fine shot and for the fact that this Wisconsin goal was considered an embarassment for the Nestor Johnsons. By the end of the first period it remained 1-0 for the Badgers but the momentum would quickly turn.

At just over five minutes into the second period, the Nestor Johnsons began their scoring onslaught to tie the game. The Chicago club would score their second goal three minutes later to take a 2-1 lead. That score would remain as the period ended but unfortunately for the Badgers their competitors were just getting warmed up. The mighty Nestor Johnson team pounded in four more goals in the third period while holding Wisconsin scoreless. Clearly, the Nestor Johnsons were superior in both offense and defense. In the end the UW squad lost 6-1.

Wisconsin Lineup: Maxwell (Center), Muther (Right Wing), Quinn (Left Wing), Gillies (Right Defense), co-captain Southworth (Left Defense) and Silvian (Goalie). Substitutes: Lyke, Mercer, co-captain Halverson, Thomas, Femal, Fallon and Fawkes. Penalties: Wisconsin 5, Nestor Johnson 1.

Two days later the Badgers returned to the Windy City for a hockey game scheduled against an unfamiliar opponent. On December 26, Wisconsin took to the ice to battle the Egan Shamrocks Hockey Club at the Chicago Coliseum. The Shamrocks belonged to the Junior Division of the Chicago Amateur Hockey Association.

Much to the approval of coach Thomsen, the UW squad was playing better hockey and finally finding success. Wisconsin's defense and stellar goaltending by Silvian held the Shamrocks to one goal while the Badger offense netted three goals. It was a respectable 3-1 victory over a very good opponent and it would be one win the Badgers could savor for a couple of days before their third straight game in Chicago. Next up was the most difficult opponent they'd see all season, the famous hockey squad from Queens University in Canada.

Wisconsin Lineup: Maxwell (Center), Muther (Right Wing), Quinn (Left Wing), Gillies (Right Defense), co-captain Southworth (Left Defense) and Silvian (Goalie). Substitutes: Lyke, Mercer, co-captain Halverson, Femal and Fawkes.

On Thursday, December 28, the Wisconsin Badgers headed back to Chicago for an 8:30 p.m. scrimmage game to be played against the team from the prestigous Queens University based in Kingston, Ontario. It was the first international collegiate game that was ever scheduled in Chicago, Illinois and some twenty five hundred fans were on hand to watch. Hockey players from Queens University took their hockey very seriously. Many experts surmise that the game of ice hockey originated at Queens University and the team Wisconsin would face was considered the best hockey squad on the continent at the time.

Despite the best efforts of the lads from Madison, the Queens University team put on a display that rendered the Badgers helpless and in awe. Even though he was incredibly gifted and mature for his age, 17-year-old Badger defenseman Jimmy Gillies got a crash course in exceptional hockey during this game. He was forced to learn his position very quickly and was doing a phenomenal job during the preseason games against players that were several years older.

The Canadians scored early in the first, folllowed by two more to make it 3-0 heading in to the first intermissioin. The Queens University team pushed their lead to 4-0 in the second period, then scored two more goals in the third. They were able to easily deny the offensive attempts of the UW players and shut out the Badgers 6-0. It would have been much worse if not for the extraordinary play of UW goalkeeper Wes Silvian, along with the efforts of his defensive teammates.

Wisconsin Lineup: Maxwell (Center), Fallon (Right Wing), Quinn (Left Wing), Gillies (Right Defense), co-captain Southworth (Left Defense) and Silvian (Goalie). Substitutes: Lyke, Mercer, Muther, co-captain Halverson, Femal and Fawkes.

Aside from the games against the Baby Ruths and Queens College, the Badgers had been in every game and were even leading as the third period started. All of the breakdowns could be blamed on a lack of sufficient conditioning and ice hockey experience. The exhibition games were also played against serious competition that often included players much older than the collegiate players representing the University of Wisconsin. Coach Thomsen directed his men to essentially disband the hockey team for several days over the rest of the holiday break until after classes resumed at the University in early January.

A home series against the University of Minnesota on January 11 and 12 had to be canceled due to melting ice on the Lower Campus Rink. Weather adverse to skating ice continued to lurk in the area canceling all possible games for the remainder of the month of January. Without explanation, coach Thomsen made a goaltending change. Freshman Charles Heyer would be the goalie for remainder of the season.

It wasn't until February 9 that the Badgers headed to Minnesota for two games against the University of Minnesota Gophers. The games were set to be played at the Hippodrome located in White Bear. Wisconsin went into the foreign arena hopeful for success, but the home team had other plans. In the first game, both were clubs matched up equally on offense and defense, but at the final whistle, the Gophers had edged out the Badgers 1-0.

Wisconsin Lineup: Maxwell (Center), Muther (Right Wing), Quinn (Left Wing), Gillies (Right Defense), co-captain

Southworth (Left Defense) and Heyer (Goalie). Substitutes: Lyke, Mercer, co-captain Halverson, Femal and Fawkes.

The following night, February 10, the Gophers opened up the scoring and pounded the Badgers. This loss was unpreventable as bad luck embraced the UW squad. Both starting defenseman, Billy Southworth and Jerry Femal, succumbed to serious injuries in the first period that would keep them out for the rest of the game. Wisconsin was shut out again. The University of Minnesota schooled the visiting Badgers by outscoring them 8-0 in the pair of games in front of four thousand-plus spectators on both nights.

Wisconsin Lineup: Maxwell (Center), Muther (Right Wing), Quinn (Left Wing), Gillies (Right Defense), co-captain Southworth (Left Defense) and Heyer (Goalie). Substitutes: Lyke, Mercer, co-captain Halverson, Femal and Fawkes.

After a long drive to Ann Arbor, Michigan Friday, February 17, the UW squad played another fierce hockey game against the Michigan Wolverines. Although Wisconsin was able to net the puck three times, it was not enough. Michigan scored two quick goals in the opening minutes of the third period and went on to score three more before the contest ended. Wisconsin lost 5-3 in this opening game.

Wisconsin Lineup: Maxwell (Center), Muther (Right Wing), Quinn (Left Wing), Gillies (Right Defense), co-captain Southworth (Left Defense) and Heyer (Goalie). Substitutes: Lyke, Mercer, co-captain Halverson, Femal and Fawkes.

On Saturday, February 18, the Badgers were out of steam. The Wolverines scored two goals and blanked the Badgers as they were unable to tally a single goal. This match ended the two-game series and the season, with an unsatisfying score of 2-0 for Michigan's win. The Wolverines beat the Badgers in both games and put an end to the anti-climatic season.

Wisconsin Lineup: Maxwell (Center), Muther (Right Wing), Quinn (Left Wing), Gillies (Right Defense), co-captain Southworth (Left Defense) and Heyer (Goalie). Substitutes: Lyke, Mercer, co-captain Halverson, Femal and Fawkes.

The Badgers had only won a game, tied one and lost a total of 10 games by seasons end. They finished dead last in the conference standings after losing all games to Michigan and Minnesota. Without a consistent ice surface at their home rink upon which the UW squad could train and play, they would remain ill prepared to compete. The

University of Wisconsin Athletic Department noticed the challenges and began the difficult process of debating the fate of the program.

A group of University of Wisconsin students began working on informal plans for an indoor hockey arena to be built on the Madison campus. Stipulations included that proceeds earned from hockey game admissions, open skating fees and concessions would provide a revenue stream for the University of Wisconsin Athletic Department. A state of the art facility was also intended to benefit the students, the Uuniversity and the Badger hockey team. In fact, a "modern rink" would not be held hostage by adverse weather and would provide the student body with a place for consistent entertainment during the quirky winter weather months. Most importantly, the Wisconsin Badgers ice hockey team would have a reliable ice surface that would allow for practices, scrimmages and games all year long.

After the 1933-34 season concluded, it was announced that the Marquette Hilltoppers from Milwaukee were dropping ice hockey as a varsity sport due to the unpredictable Wisconsin winter weather that often caused a lack of ice for practices and games.

Co-captain Bill Southworth was named to the All Western Hockey Team as a defenseman, an honor that was bestowed on him by coaches and sportswriters. Southworth was a solid player for the Badgers the past two seasons. Heyer, the UW goalie and Fallon, a UW winger were awarded honorable mention on the All-Western Hockey Team. Charles "Chuck" Heyer, the Badgers hockey goal keeper was quite the athlete and he was also a second baseman on the UW varsity baseball team.

Hockey was canceled as an intercollegiate sport by the University of Wisconsin Athletic Board after the 1933-34 season concluded. Frequently undependable outdoor ice was the main reason behind the cancellation. In addition, costs associated with the sport were significant, especially during The Depression. Director of Intramural Athletics, Guy S. Lowman, devised a last ditch plan to save hockey that was approved by the Student Athletic Board. Hockey would be placed under the umbrella of the Intramural Department and would continue as an extamural sport for the time being.

Wisconsin players and friends enjoy skating at Wingra Lagoon in March 1934.

Wisconsin players and friends enjoy skating at Wingra Lagoon in March 1934.

By this season the rules of hockey had been significantly revised and were followed throughout the United States and Canada. Some of the guidelines established during this period remain in the game today. Other rules seem odd when compared to the current rules of hockey.

As of 1934, rules dictated that the ice surface was to be at least 160 feet by 60 feet and no larger than 250 feet by 100 feet. The boards were to be at least 3 feet high to accommodate play and to provide both players and spectators a bit of safety. Nets placed on both ends of the rink and were to be constructed so that pucks could only enter through the front of the cage. The ice surface had two zone lines marked parallel to the hockey goal, which were intended to divide the rink into three sections: a center zone and two end zones. Hockey equipment was also regulated. Sticks were not allowed to have blades longer than 15 inches, shafts no longer than 54 inches and the width of the stick was not allowed to exceed three-and-a-half inches at any part.

A hockey team consisted of six players: a center, left wing, right wing, right defenseman, left defenseman and a goalie. Clubs were also allowed to have substitute players. Before the start of each game, a referee would toss a coin to determine which team would choose which goal they wanted to defend at the opening faceoff. One point was awarded whenever the puck completely crossed the goal line. A goal was disallowed if the scoring team had more than six players on the ice or if the goal was scored while the scoring team was guilty of a rule infraction. The length of each game was 60 minutes or three 20-minute periods. A 10-minute rest was provided between each period. If the score was tied at the end of regulation play, an extra period was played in its entirety to determine a winner. If the first overtime period failed to determine a clear winner, a second and final, extra period would be played. Unlike the modern rules, substitutions were only allowed when the referee halted play. Action would resume once the referee dropped the puck between two players for a faceoff.

Players were only allowed to pass to their teammates that were skating in the same zone. If a pass was made to a player in another zone the referee promptly whistled the play offside. When the puck was not in a teams' defensive zone, they were not allowed to have more than three players, including the goalie, in their defensive zone. Players were prohibited from kicking the puck into the net for a score. Goalies were severly restricted with what they were allowed to do to stop the puck. They could not hold, carry or throw it forward. They were also not allowed to sit, kneel or lie down on the puck to prevent a goal scoring opportunity anywhere on the ice except immediately in front of the net while the action is underway.

Hockey players were also confined to play within the boundaries of other rules aimed at fair play and safety. Players were not permitted to throw their sticks or prevent a player from having their own stick. Body checking was not allowed within 5 feet of the boards so only open ice hits were allowed during this era. Players were penalized if they were caught by the referee charging, kneeing, elbowing, holding, pushing, cross checking or tripping an opponent.

Any infraction deemed minor received a two-minute penalty with the player required to leave the playing surface. A major penalty received a five-minute consequence and the offending player's team was forced to play with one less player on the ice while the five-minute penalty was served. Any player charged with four infractions was removed from the game. Rule enforcers and officials typically consisted of a referee, two umpires and a timekeeper.

1933-34   Schedule and Results:

Coach Art Thomsen
0-4-0 Last place in the WIHL   1-10-1 Overall

Date	**Result**	**Opponent**
November 30	Loss 3-0	@Baby Ruths*#
December 16	Loss 4-2	@Wausau*
December 17	Loss 3-1	@Wausau*
December 21	Tie 2-2 OT	@ Michigan College*
December 22	Loss 3-1	@ Michigan College*
December 24	Loss 6-1	@Nestor Johnsons*#
December 26	Win 3-1	@Egan*#
December 28	Loss 6-0	@Queens University (Kingston,Ont.)*#
February 9	Loss 1-0	@ Minnesota
February 10	Loss 7-0	@ Minnesota
February 16	Loss 5-3	@ Michigan
February 17	Loss 2-0	@ Michigan

*Exhibition Games

#Played at Chicago Coliseum.

Hockey was dropped as a varsity sport at the UW after the 1933-34 season.

Authors Note: The UW Yearbook, "Badger," makes reference to a 1/3/1934 game that was a 6-1 against the Watertown Hockey Club and a 1/4/1934 game that was a 10-1 win against Madison Hockey Club. It appears neither one of these games happened at the varsity level.

Several 1934 Year-in-Review summaries of the Wisconsin Badgers hockey schedule and game results specifically details the games and scores from this season. However, there is no mention of games against the Watertown Hockey Club or Madison Hockey Club found in any UW publications or statewide news articles. In fact, both the January 9 and January 10, 1934 issues of The Daily Cardinal report Wisconsin Badgers hockey game results to date and future matchups. Again, no mention of Watertown Hockey Club or Madison Hockey Club in varsity competition. It is likely these hockey matches were played against the UW JV squad.

Chapter Sixteen
Rumors

1934–35 UW Hockey Team

Coach Art Thomsen married Olga Kumershek in July of 1934. It would be the highlight of his year. The numerous challenges facing the Wisconsin hockey program were increasing in severity and would cause coach Thomsen a lot of serious challenges. The University halted funding for the program since it was dropped as a Minor sport. Hockey at the University was salvaged under a strategic plan devised by Director of Intramural Athletics, Guy S. Lowman. It was now a part of the UW Athletics Intramural Department and would be allowed to operate as an extramural sport this season.

Weather woes continued to haunt the Wisconsin hockey team along with all other hockey organizations in the Midwest that were forced to rely on outdoor ice. The Lower Campus Rink was usually without ice and as a result the UW was unable to schedule home games. Coach Art Thomsen had no choice but to again have his players meet at the Red Gym for daily practice on roller skates since ice was not available for hockey practices. Prior to their Christmas hockey tour, the Badgers only had a handful of on-ice practices at Lake Wingra to prepare for their scheduled games against northern teams.

A total of six veteran players would make up the core of this seasons varsity roster. These players included: Charles "Chuck" Heyer (Goalie), Jerry Femal (Defense), Hugh O'Malley (Defense), James Gillis (Left Wing), Robert Mercer (Center) and James Fallon (Right Wing). Substitute players were: John Anderson (Center), Wallace Drew (Left Wing), Ed Berry (Right Wing), Robert Null (Right Wing), Jim Fuller (Left Wing), Wayne Lewis (Goalie) Emerson Vorel (Defense), Bob Petrie (Forward) and Al Thomson (Forward).

Former Wisconsin standout hockey player Billy Rahr would take the reigns of the Manitowoc ice hockey club this season. It was his first head coaching position and his experience playing for a Big Ten team was instrumental in landing this job.

Coach Thomsen arranged a schedule that started with a preseason tour against a slew of teams from northern Wisconsin. Since the University of Wisconsin Athletic Department would no longer finance the costs incurred by men's hockey, the team was forced to play on the road all season long. Each opponent would guarantee a certain payment to the UW team to secure their visit and to ensure they had more than enough to cover their costs. This arrangement would allow for a small profit after travel, lodging, equipment and meal expenses were covered. This would explain why the Badger hockey team was referred to by many as "The Orphans." They were without a home this season.

Tentative Preseason Exhibition Schedule:
12/22/34 Wausau, 12/23/34 Wausau, date TBD Milwaukee Rowing Club, 12/23/34 Marinette, 12/30/34 Wisconsin Rapids, 12/30/34 Eagle River, 1/1/35 Eagle River, 1/4/35 Green Bay and 1/5/35 Green Bay.

During the Christmas holiday exhibition matches, the Badgers arrived in Wausau first for two games against the Wausau Veterans of Foreign War, also known as the Lumberjacks, hockey team.

In the first game December 22, both teams met at the First Avenue Rink in Wausau at 9:15 p.m. The ice was in perfect condition after a recent bout of cold weather. The Vets hockey team from Wausau was always a dangerous opponent and this pair of games would be no different.

As luck would have it, this hockey game was during the middle of a bad Wisconsin winter storm. Somehow, both teams played a tight, back and forth game during the blizzard conditions. The Vets came out flying in the first period and scored first against the UW to go up by the score of 1-0. A few minutes later Wisconsin countered when winger spare Al Thomson scored on an individual effort to tie the score at 1-1. Several minutes later Wisconsin spare Reidle scored to give the visitors a 2-1 lead. Jim Lyke, the former Wisconsin Badger hockey player who was playing for the Wausau team scored his team's second goal of the game to tie things at 2-2. Battling through the snowstorm, the Vets got the puck in the UW net again to make it 3-2. Wisconsin's star forward Jimmy Fallon was able to score a goal for the Badgers after a nice individual effort to knot the score at 3-3.

During the second period, Jim Lyke scored his second goal for the Wausau Vets to give his new team the 4-3 lead. Despite numerous scoring attempts, the defenders and goalies stopped all of the rest of the opportunities this period. The score remained 4-3. Without a doubt the winter storm made stickhandling, passing and even skating extremely challenging.

In the third period, spare player Harry Quinn from the UW squad scored his own unassisted goal to knot the score at 4-4. This score would stand at the end of regulation. The weather was still a bear as the heavy snow continued to fall. After a brief rest, the teams took the ice and completed the first 10 minute OT period without scoring. A second overtime period was played and also unable to determine a clear winner in the blizzard, so the referee declared the game a tie at 4-4. After this game the rink was shoveled off and sprayed with water again to put down a new surface in preparation for the second game.

Wisconsin Lineup: Mercer (Center), O'Malley (Right Wing), Fallon (Left Wing), Berry (Right Defense), Femal (Left Defense) and Heyer (Goalie). Substitutes: Anderson, Drew, Gillies, Petrie, Vezina, Reidle, Quinn, Holman, Null, Thomson and Sullivan. Saves: Wisconsin 33, Wausau 35. Penalties: Wisconsin 3, Wausau 2.

During the afternoon of Sunday, December 23, these two teams met again for game two. In the first period, the Wausau team got the scoring going by burying a puck in the Badger net. The score remained at 1-0 when the period ended. Wisconsin had work to do.

In the second period, Wisconsin scored their lone goal when Badger left winger Jimmy Fallon made a nice pass to teammate Reidle who put the puck around the Vet goaltender and tied the game at 1-1. That score would remain as time ran out in the second period.

Several of those in the home crowd expressed their displeasure with Thomson, the Badger substitute right winger, due to what was perceived as extra aggressive use of his hockey stick. Several Vet players were sent sprawling and a star player for Wausau was put out of the game with an injury caused by Thomson's creative stick work. That Wausau player would not be able to play hockey for several weeks due to the injury.

Both teams were stopped after several offensive attempts in the third period. With less than three minutes left in the match, the Wausau squad netted their second goal to go up 2-1. In response, UW coach Art Thomsen put out a line up consisting of only offensive players. With less than one minute left, the Badgers scored what they felt was the game-tying goal. However, the referee ruled that the Wisconsin boys scored after a blue line pass violation was whistled. The goal was waived off to the displeasure of the visting team. The Wausau Veterans team bested the Badgers with a 2-1 win at the end of regulation.

Wisconsin Lineup: Mercer (Center), O'Malley (Right Wing), Fallon (Left Wing), Berry (Right Defense), Femal (Left Defense) and Heyer (Goalie). Substitutes: Drew, Gillies, Petrie, Vezina, Reidle, Quinn, Holman, Thomson and Sullivan. Saves: Wisconsin 22, Wausau 20. Penalties: Wisconsin 1, Wausau 1.

As the Christmas games continued, the Wisconsin road trip included a match against the Milwaukee Rowing Club. Although a game summary of this scrimmage is nonexistent, records indicate the Badgers were victorious.

The next stop of the exhibition tour had the University of Wisconsin team in Wisconsin Rapids for another tuneup game. This match was set for Sunday, December 30 and the game would be played at the Lincoln Field Hockey Rink at 2:30 p.m. Bleachers were added to accommodate the one hundred-plus spectators that were expected to purchase tickets. Canvas sheets were also added around the fencing and encicled the rink to help combat frequent winter breezes.

The Rapids team was composed of former collegiate hockey stars and current standout high school players. The Badgers arrived in town around noon. After putting on their battle gear and lacing up the skates, the Badgers soon found out that the Vikings would be a game opponent.

The home team had a splendid defensive setup and the college boys were forced to take mostly long shots. The Vikings goalie recorded 12 saves in this opening period alone. At one point, two Vikings players smashed a Badger player in front of the Wisconsin Rapids net that resulted in a big pile up. The home crowd jeered with laughter and taunts when a second Badger player was discovered at the very bottom of the stack. Jerry Femal got the UW's first goal with less than two minutes left in the opening period giving the Badgers a 1-0 lead after the first period.

Femal scored his second goal of the game after the second period was only a few minutes old. He deked one way and went the other a couple of times to juke the Rapids defense and goalie out of position so he could score. After two periods, the University of Wisconsin team had a decent 2-0 lead but that score would not last long.

The Badgers demonstrated their superior passing ability and scored four goals in the final period. Wisconsin spare Fallon scored his first of the third period after he skated the puck behind the Rapids net and curled back around the front to shoot the puck past the goalie. Femal got his third goal of the game in the third period, a hat trick! Spare Badger player Bob Petrie scored a goal late in the period. To top off the scoring, Femal cranked a long shot from center ice to score the sixth and final goal for the Badgers. The Wisconsin Badgers had rallied for four unanswered goals in this final period. At the end of regulation, the UW had beat the Vikings by a score of 6-0.

The UW team was considerably bigger and in much better physical condition allowing them to easily defeat their opponents. The team would grab dinner and stay over night in Wisconsin Rapids before heading to Eagle River the next morning.

Wisconsin Lineup: Holman (Center), Berry (Right Wing), Gillies (Left Wing), Femal (Right Defense), Vorel (Left Defense) and Heyer (Goalie). Substitutes: Drew, Fallon, O'Malley, Petrie, Vezina, Reidle, Quinn, Mercer, Holman, Thomson and Sullivan. Saves: Wisconsin 11, Wisconsin Rapids 28. Referee: Art Thomsen - UW Head Coach.

A pair of games were on the schedule on New Years Eve and New Years Day in Eagle River. Both teams were considered to be similar in the level of talent among their skaters. Just over one hundred local spectators were on hand to watch these hockey matches. The Eagle River Falcons hockey squad had control the entire game from start to finish and ultimately defeated the UW team by a score of 4-1 in the first contest.

Wisconsin Lineup: Holman (Center), Berry (Right Wing), Gillies (Left Wing), Femal (Right Defense), Vorel (Left Defense) and Heyer (Goalie). Substitutes: Drew, Fallon, O'Malley, Petrie, Vezina, Reidle, Quinn, Mercer, Holman, Thomson and Sullivan.

New Years Day 1935 was not the start to the year that the Wisconsin Badgers were wishing would happen. The second game against the Falcons was almost identical to the game these two teams had played the day before. Eagle River was in total control and exerted their dominance throughout the entire game. The Badgers were handed another loss from the Eagle River Falcons by the same score of 4-1.

Wisconsin Lineup: Holman (Center), Berry (Right Wing), Gillies (Left Wing), Femal (Right Defense), Vorel (Left Defense) and Heyer (Goalie). Substitutes: Drew, Fallon, O'Malley, Petrie, Vezina, Reidle, Quinn, Mercer, Holman, Thomson and Sullivan.

On January 2, the Badgers made their way to Marinette, Wisconsin They had a two-game series scheduled against the Marinette Shamrocks, a local amateur hockey club that had some talented players. The Ice Palace in Marinette just had its grand opening three days earlier. At the time, it was one of only two enclosed ice rinks in the state of Wisconsin. It had an unobstructed playing surface (no posts or other obstructions to impede skaters) and the ice sheet measured 60 feet by one hundred and 40 feet. The Ice Palace had seating for three hundred spectators and those attending the games were encouraged to bring a blanket while they watched the action. This rink also had a lighting system installed so night games could be played and enjoyed by spectators. A new accommodation appreciated by the skaters was the availability of several heated rooms where they could warm up and change into or out of, hockey equipment and skates. This was at a time when locker rooms were not typical and certainly unusual.

This 8 p.m. game signaled the start of the season for the Marinette Shamrocks. Co-coach Rudy Turk was also a player on the Shamrocks roster. The other Shamrocks Co-coach and former Candian hockey star, Jack Mettner, was the on-ice official for this game.

Once the game started it was a lot closer than Wisconsin had hoped. It was not until nearly 10 minutes into the first period before a goal was scored. Al Thomson gave the Badgers a 1-0 lead. Over the next six minutes, Wisconsin was able to pound in two more goals. Fallon scored to push the UW lead to 2-0. Left defenseman Emerson Vorel would notch the third goal for the Badgers. The Shamrocks were able to tally their first goal with three-and-a-half minutes left in the period. At the end of the first, it was 3-1.

It was a fairly even second period and the defense improved greatly for both teams. It was not until less than a minute left when the

Badgers scored again. Wisconsin was caught off guard in the third period. Just after 36 seconds had ticked off the clock, Shamrocks coach/player Rudy Turk cranked a shot from mid-ice that found the back of the net and got the home crowd on their feet to celebrate the goal. The score was 4-2 once time expired. Wisconsin earned a solid win over the Marinette Shamrocks.

Wisconsin Lineup: Fallon (Center), Berry (Right Wing), Thomson (Left Wing), Femal (Right Defense), Vorel (Left Defense) and Heyer (Goalie). Substitutes: Drew, O'Malley, Gillies, Mercer, Holman, Petrie and Anderson.

Game Two was on Thursday, January 3 and also had an 8 p.m. start at the Ice Palace. Once the match started it didn't take long for the Badgers to start racking up goals. Bob Petrie, the UW centerman, scored the first goal of the evening just two minutes after the game started. Jimmy Fallon put in the second goal of the game 35 seconds later to give the Badgers a 2-0 lead. With four minutes remaining in the first period, Badger left winger Emerson Vorel scored on a long shot that wowed the Marinette crowd. At the end of the period, Wisconsin had a 3-0 advantage.

When the second period was only four minutes old, the Shamrocks scored their first goal. It was now 3-1 in favor of Wisconsin. Some 10 minutes later, Fallon scored again for the Badgers after a nice pass from Petrie, to give the Badgers a nice 4-1 lead. Two minutes later Petrie notched an unassisted goal to push the lead to 5-1 in favor of the college boys. With five seconds left in the middle period, the Marinette squad scored off a desperation shot from mid-ice. Their tally cut the score to 5-2 as the second period ended.

Jimmy Fallon would score his third goal of the game nine minutes into the third period to make it 6-2. Holman, Wisconsin's spare center, would score twice more before time ran out in regulation. The final score was 8-2 in favor of Wisconsin.

Wisconsin Lineup: Petrie (Center), Fallon (Right Wing), Vorel (Left Wing), Femal (Right Defense), Thomson (Left Defense) and Heyer (Goalie). Substitutes: Drew, Berry, O'Malley, Gillies, Mercer, Holman and Anderson.

The UW team arrived in Green Bay January 4 to take on the Green Bay Frigidaires at the Polo-Resto Hockey Rink. A regional Wisconsin alumni club was heavily promoting this game and helped significantly boost attendance. The faceoff was scheduled for 8 p.m. Max Murphy, a former Wisconsin Badger skater was now playing for the Green Bay squad.

A scoreless first period was an embarrassment to the cardinal and white players. The Badgers came out flying in the second and finally opened up the scoring. Jim Gillis scored a hat trick by putting the puck in the net three separate times. Jim Fallon scored two more goals for the UW. Both Jim Fuller and Ed Vorel put together a nice play for the sixth Badger goal. Nearly midway through the third period, Green Bay was able to break the shutout with their own goal. It wouldn't be enough as Wisconsin won this game by a score of 6-1.

Wisconsin Lineup: Holman (Center), Berry (Right Wing), Gillies (Left Wing), Femal (Right Defense), Vorel (Left Defense) and Heyer (Goalie). Substitutes: Drew, Fallon, O'Malley, Petrie, Vezina, Reidle, Quinn, Mercer and Sullivan.

These two teams faced off again at 8 p.m. on Saturday, January 5. It seemed as if Wisconsin was looking past the host team or maybe Green Bay was ready to face the talented college boys.

Green Bay scored what they believed to be the first goal of the heated rematch. At first the goal judge signaled a goal for the home team, but he quickly reversed his decision and stated no goal to the displeasure of the local crowd and home team. The goal judge ruled that the puck entered the net through a hole in the netting on the side of the Badger's goal. After several great offensive chances and plenty of eceptional defensive plays, the score remained 0-0 at the end of the first period.

The body checking in this game was frequent and extremely violent. On two different occasions Green Bay Frigidaire players were knocked completely unconscious after receiving thunderous checks from Wisconsin players. The game was still scoreless at the end of the middle period.

In the third, the game continued to be tightly contested. The defensemen and goalies thwarted multiple offensive attacks. Badger forward Jimmy Fallon scored a nice goal in the final minutes of the period after a hard working individual effort. Green Bay responded by going into an intentional five-man offensive format. The Frididaires were unable to score before time ran out. Wisconsin left town with a second victory over the Green Bay Frigidaires by winning 1-0.

Wisconsin Lineup: Holman (Center), Berry (Right Wing), Gillies (Left Wing), Femal (Right Defense), Vorel (Left Defense)

and Heyer (Goalie). Substitutes: Drew, Fallon, O'Malley, Petrie, Vezina, Reidle, Quinn, Mercer and Sullivan.

Wisconsin earned six wins in matches against hockey teams from Marinette, Wisconsin Rapids, Green Bay and the Milwaukee Rowing Club. They headed into the regular season after finishing their holiday break games with an impressive record of 6-3-1. Jimmy Fallon was the leading scorer with 12 goals and six assists.

As if the challenges this season couldn't get any worse for the UW hockey program, Badgers starting defenseman Al Thomson was declared ineligible on an academic technicality. He was carrying enough class credits and had a sufficient grade-point average, but wasn't carrying enough credits in the agricultural school to support his major.

Before heading to Michigan, the Badgers were badly handicapped by the weather and were without decent practice ice for the week before the Michigan game. Conversely, the Wolverines had the advantage of artificial ice and were able to practice daily. Wisconsin packed their hockey gear and headed to Ann Arbor, Michigan Thursday, January 10.

Wisconsin faced off against the Wolverines on January 11 in conference play. Michigan got on the scoreboard early when they scored two goals before the first period was halfway over. The first goal came just over three minutes after the game started. The second was scored around six later. It was 2-0 for the home team at the end of the first.

The Badgers put up a wall in the second period. Their defensive play was spectacular in this period and so was goalie Chuck Heyer. The UW were unable to counter with any offense and the second period was scoreless as time ran out.

In the final period, Michigan pounded in four more goals. The Wolverines literally scored about every two minutes until the halfway mark. By that time they were up 6-0. Wisconsin goalie Chuck Heyer, also a star second baseman on the Badger baseball team, kept the score from getting worse with his outstanding glove and athleticism. When the time ended, Michigan recorded the 6-0 victory.

Wisconsin Lineup: Anderson (Center), Fallon (Right Wing), Gillies (Left Wing), Femal (Right Defense), Mercer (Left Defense) and Heyer (Goalie). Substitutes: Vorell, Berry and Null. Penalties: Wisconsin 3, Michigan 3. Referee: "Puss" Traub.

In the second of their two games series January 12 the Badgers retooled their strategic approach to playing the Wolverines. At 11:35 into the first period, UW right winger Jimmy Fallon scored on a nifty goal for the 1-0 advantage. Wisconsin decided to fall into a strictly defensive format for the remainder of the game, refusing to attack the Wolverines net even when Michigan was down a player due to a penalty. The strategy was questionable as Wisconsin was nursing a 1-0 advantage going into the second period.

Around three minutes into the middle period, Michigan scored to tie the game at 1-1 when UW right winger Fallon was off the ice serving his penalty. Neither team scored another goal in the middle period and the game remained knotted, 1-1.

In the final period, about seven minutes in, Michigan scored again to take a 2-1 lead. The Wolverines went into a five-man defensive scheme. It worked and the Badgers were unable to penetrate Michigan's defensive stronghold. Once time expired, Michigan had won their second game in a row over the Badgers, this time a score of 2-1.

Wisconsin Lineup: Mercer (Center), Fallon (Right Wing), Anderson (Left Wing), Femal (Right Defense), Vorell (Left Defense) and Heyer (Goalie). Substitutes: Berry, Null and Gillies. Penalties: Wisconsin 2, Michigan 1. Referee: "Puss" Traub.

The Badgers were scheduled to travel to Houghton, Michigan to face the Michigan College hockey team, but that match up was immediately canceled and Wisconsin headed back to Madison. On the long bus ride home, the men that made up the Wisconsin Badgers Hockey Team drafted the numerous reasons, in a document titled Resolutions, supporting their decision to cancel the remainder of the season. Canceling the games with Michigan College was the first formal step the players took to air their grievances and outline their justifications for calling off the remainder of the 1934-35 season for the Badgers hockey program.

The lack of a an indoor practice facility with artificial ice had numerous consequences that handcuffed the players. Facing opponents who had the distinct advantage of artificial ice was an impossible task and, frankly, the Badgers didn't have a shot in hell to pull off many victories in those competitions. The lack of financial support and funding from the University of Wisconsin was another challenging obstacle. There were several more compelling arguments in their justifications to nix the season. Coach Art Thomsen told his players the decision to cancel or continue the season would be solely theirs since it was the players who were required to compete under the adverse conditions.

Once the team was back on campus they set up an emergency meeting with professor Guy Lowman, the Director of Intramural Sports. After much discussion he persuaded the players that completing the season by playing the final two games versus the Gophers in Minnesota next month was the right thing to do. Reluctantly, the players agreed to honor the scheduling commitment. The pair of games in Minnesota would be the only games left against a Big Ten opponent this season. If weather permitted, the Badgers would practice and play some scrimmage games amongst themselves. They would also honor their previous commitment to participate in the Wisconsin state hockey amateur championship tournament in mid-February.

The ongoing need for an indoor hockey facility with artificial ice was a constant argument the entire time Wisconsin had a formal hockey program. Considering Wisconsin was a leader in most winter sports, the university was the target of growing criticism and disdain since the lack of a suitable hockey arena had such severe consequences to the UW hockey program and game outcomes. Frankly, they were at a significant disadvantage in their competitions since they were reliant on decent outdoor ice. Conference rivals like Minnesota and Michigan had hockey arenas with artificial ice. Wisconsin should have had their own hockey rink with artificial ice. In addition, the University of Wisconsin Athletic Department's determination not to fund the UW hockey program was an equally unpopular decision.

A press release from the State of Wisconsin Amateur Hockey Association aimed at elite hockey teams around the state of Wisconsin was issued on January 14. The communication outlined that the state hockey playoffs would be held at the Eagle River stadium on February 16 and 17. Committed entrants into this tournament included the University of Wisconsin, Webster, Wausau Veterans, Chippewa Falls, Oshkosh and Green Bay among other participants from around the state.

In an effort to refute growing sentiment indicating that the UW had canceled the remainder of its hockey schedule this season, Coach Art

Thomsen denied the assertion as an unfounded rumor on January 15. Coach Thomsen was somewhat vague on the topic and refused to acknowledge if the University of Wisconsin was considering an option to cancel remaining games. Thomsen indicated that he would make an official statement only after he was able to have a team meeting.

On January 16, the Director of the University of Wisconsin Intramural and Minor sports, Guy Lowman, was forced to address the rampant rumors suggesting that the University of Wisconsin hockey program would not complete the remainder of its scheduled hockey games. Lowman partially denied the rumors and confirmed that the UW would play the pair of games scheduled against the Gophers at the University of Minnesota to complete the hockey season. As a result of continued poor ice at the Lower Campus Rink, Lowman confirmed that no more hockey games would be scheduled or played at Madison for the remainder of this season.

On Friday, February 8, Wisconsin was in Minnesota to play the Gophers at the Minneapolis Arena for the first of the final two games of the Badgers hockey season. Some two thousand fans were on hand to watch this match. The home team put their first goal into the Badger net just over eight minutes into the first period. They followed up with another goal just eight seconds later to take a 2-0 lead.

Minnesota continued its dominance by scoring their third goal six-and-a-half minutes into the second period. Just over a minute later came goal number four for the Gophers . A penalty-free first period was followed by the Gophers being charged with two penalties while the Badgers were charged with one in the second period. At the end of the period, Minnesota had a commanding 4-0 advantage.

Up until the third period, the game was somewhat civil although tensions were rising noticeably. Minnesota found the back of the Wisconsin net four minutes in to the third period. With the score at 5-0, tensions began nearing a critical point. Wisconsin spare defenseman Al Thomson tried to level a hard check on a Gopher player, but Thomson ended up knocking himself out cold on the attempt. It took several moments to revive him before he regained consciousness. Thomson was unable to return to the game. Several pleasantries had been exchanged between players on both teams by this time. Physical play ramped up as the severity and frequency of fierce body checks was evident. Each team was trying to outdo the other by hitting an opponent harder then their last teammate was hit.

Midway into the third period, a Gopher forward was checked into the Wisconsin crease area after a failed scoring attempt. The Gophers thought the goal should count, but Referee Bill Haman rang the hand bell to signal an infraction and stop the hockey game. Haman informed the players and coaches that it was no goal due to an offside violation on the home team. One would have thought the players confused the ice hockey referee bell that was supposed to stop the game with a boxing bell that signals the start of a fight. Badger goalie Chuck Heyer took exception to the invading Minnesota player and pushed him out of the UW goal crease area. The UM player shoved Heyer back and Wisconsin's Jimmy Fallon grabbed the invading Gopher and punched him in the mouth. Immediately the two players went down to the ice punching each other. Wisconsin defenseman Jerry Femal came into the fray right away and started throwing haymakers into the side of the head of the Gopher player that Fallon was battling.

Players from both sides promptly took issue with perceived violations against their teammates and joined the scrum with more shoving and harsh words. Within seconds, the shoving in front of the Wisconsin net turned into several fist fights as punches were thrown between the battling teams. Both benches emptied as the spare players joined the melee. A hundred or so Minnesota spectators rushed on to the ice and into the various skirmishes happening concurrently. There were nearly 20 simultaneous fistfights happening during the riot. Although some of the Gopher fans who left their seats and went onto the playing surface acted like they were trying to restore order, it was apparent the majority of ticketed participants had less than pure motivations while on the ice. Several fan versus UW player fights were witnessed during the chaos. The disturbance and delay in the hockey game was over five minutes long.

Once the referee was able to separate the battling gladiators to restore order and get the teams separated, it was time to dole out penalties. Each team was charged with three match penalties for their respective roles in the hockey brawl. The players charged with the match penalties were kicked out for the remainder of the game. The Badgers and Gophers were only allowed three aside for the final six minutes of the period. That meant two players and a goalie on the ice for both teams to complete the game. The fans got a chuckle out of watching the rare three-on-three hockey game.

Unfortunately for Wisconsin, Minnesota captain Spencer Wagnild decided to put on a clinic and scored three goals within thirty-seven seconds to add insult to injury. Minnesota scored their final and ninth goal, with less than a minute remaining in the third period. Wisconsin was trounced and shut out by a final score of 9-0.

Wisconsin Lineup: Mercer (Center), Fallon (Right Wing), Anderson (Left Wing), Femal (Right Defense), Vorell (Left Defense) and Heyer (Goalie). Substitutes: Gillies, Drew, Thomson and Berry. Saves: Wisconsin 42, Minnesota 21. Penalties: Wisconsin 7 (4 minors and 3 majors), Minnesota 5 (2 minors and 3 majors). Referee: Bill Hamas.

These two teams met again the next night. As expected, the rough stuff and big body checking started up as soon as the game began. While it never got to the point of resembling a turf war as it did the previous night, the game was not short of willing combatants dishing big hits all game long.

Both teams were back and forth for the first 17 minutes of the first period and no one was able to register a goal. Minnesota finally scored at the 18 minute mark for a 1-0 lead. Not even 40 seconds later, the Gophers put in another goal to make it 2-0.

In the second period, Wisconsin tried to stack players into a defensive scheme to slow the Minnesota scoring machine. Around six minutes in to the middle period, Minnesota knocked in another to make it 3-0. At the eleven-and-a-half minute mark, Badger center Bob Mercer had a good look at the Gopher net and put Wisconsin on the scoreboard. No one at the time knew it would be the last goal for Wisconsin this season. The score was 3-1 in favor of the home team. The score would remain the same as the middle period ran out.

The Gophers got back to scoring in the third period. Just under four minutes in, UM made it 4-1. Another four minutes later they tallied their fifth of the game. The Gophers were able to easily outscore the Badgers and control the game. In the end, the Badgers lost by an anticlimatic score of 5-1.

Wisconsin Lineup: Mercer (Center), Fallon (Right Wing), Anderson (Left Wing), Femal (Right Defense), Vorell (Left Defense) and Heyer (Goalie). Substitutes: Gillies, Drew, Thomson and Berry. Saves: Wisconsin 41, Minnesota 10. Penalties: Wisconsin 3, Minnesota 4. Referee: Bill Hamas.

Contrary to earlier reports, the University of Wisconsin Hockey Team disbanded during the week of February 10 and was not allowed to play in any additional games. Their application to participate in the Wisconsin State Hockey Amateur Tournment on February 16 and 17 was rescinded.

Jimmy Fallon

Jerry Femal

Two members of the varsity hockey team were recognized with selections to the All-Midwest Hockey Team. Jimmy Fallon, a standout winger was named to the second team. Badger defenseman Jerry Femal was named to the third squad. This was a huge accomplishment considering the hockey team played very few regular season games.

Player-turned-coach Art Thomsen made incredible contributions to hockey at the University of Wisconsin in the 1920s and 1930s. During his playing days he was a star performer on both the Wisconsin swimming and hockey teams and at times competing for both teams on the same day! After graduating in 1931, he returned to coach the Badger hockey team until 1935. He also taught at the University of Wisconsin for 42 years.

When the Wisconsin hockey program was revived years later, he would return to co-coach the men's hockey team from 1963 through 1966 when Badger Bob Johnson would take over at the helm. Thomsen also had a couple of famous grandchildren, Beth and Eric

Heiden, who were accomplished athletes like their Grandpa. Beth was a bronze medalist at the 1980 Winter Olympics in speedskating. She also won numerous other medals at various World Championships in both speedskating and road cycling. Her brother, Eric Heiden, won a a record five gold medals at the 1980 Winter Olympics in speedskating. He won multiple medals before those Olympics as well. Over the course of his career, Eric set a total of 15 World Records in the sport of speedskating.

1934–35   Schedule and Results:
Coach Art Thomsen
0-4-0   6-7-1 Overall

Date	**Result**	**Opponent**
December 22	Tie 4-4 2OT	@ Wausau*
December 23	Loss 2-1	@ Wausau*
December #	Win #	@ Milwaukee*
December 30	Win 6-0	@ Wisconsin Rapids*
December 31	Loss 4-1	@ Eagle River*
January 1	Loss 4-1	@ Eagle River*
January 2	Win 4-2	@ Marinette*
January 3	Win 8-2	@ Marinette*
January 4	Win 6-1	@ Green Bay*
January 5	Win 1-0	@ Green Bay*
January 11	Loss 6-0	@ Michigan
January 12	Loss 2-1	@ Michigan
February 8	Loss 9-0	@ Minnesota
February 9	Loss 5-1	@ Minnesota

* Exhibition Games

Unknown date and score.

Chapter Seventeen
Timeout – UW Hockey Program Canceled

In the spring of 1935 the University of Wisconsin Athletic Department made the difficult decision to end the Wisconsin Hockey Program. Hockey was discontinued as both a formal and informal intercollegiate sport at the University.

At the UW Athletic Board Meeting in May 1935, a motion was made by professor Goodnight that would end the sport of ice hockey as a recognized varsity sport at the University of Wisconsin.

**MINUTES OF THE ATHLETIC BOARD
SATURDAY, MAY 11, 1935
9 a.m.
UNIVERSITY CLUB**

Moved by Goodnight seconded by Hobson that the Board accept the recommendation of the Director and of the Hockey Coach that Hockey be discontinued as a competitive sport until such time as it can provide adequate facilities for practice and play. The Board endorses Hockey as a fine game and will endeavor to reestablish Hockey on an Intercollegiate basis as soon as possible. Carried.

Consequently, varsity ice hockey at the University of Wisconsin would be dormant for the next 28 years. Ice hockey at the UW refused to completely die and simply reverted back to a club sport as it previously existed from 1892 through 1921 on the Madison campus.

Going forward, the spirit of the game at Wisconsin was kept alive by club teams, fraternity teams and local amateur teams (The Madison Cardinals) comprised of former Badger players and coaches. Hockey around the UW campus had a faint pulse and would not be formally revived until 1962…

Cover of the March 9 1938, <u>The Wisconsin Octopus</u> showing Badger hockey players standing in water on a melted hockey rink. The University of Wisconsin hockey program was formally canceled as a varsity sport in 1935 since hockey at the UW was played outdoors and reliant on weather cold enough to maintain a frozen ice surface. <u>The Wisconsin Octopus</u> was a student humor magazine that ran from 1919 to 1959.

University of Wisconsin Badgers
Men's Hockey
1912 - 1935
Schedule & Results

1912-13   **Schedule and Results:**
Coach Joe Steinauer
<u>Date</u>   <u>Result</u>   <u>Opponent</u>

No Games Played

1913-14   **Schedule and Results:**
Coach Joe Steinauer
1-0-0 Overall
<u>Date</u>   <u>Result</u>   <u>Opponent</u>
February 22   Win 5-1   Milwaukee

1914-15   **Schedule and Results:**
Coach Joe Steinauer
<u>Date</u>   <u>Result</u>   <u>Opponent</u>

No Games Played

1915-16   **Schedule and Results:**
Coach Joe Steinauer
1-0-0 Overall
<u>Date</u>   <u>Result</u>   <u>Opponent</u>
February 22   Win 3-0   St. John's

1916-17   Schedule and Results:
Coach Joe Steinauer
3-1-0 Intercollegiate Champions

Date	Result	Opponent
January 27	Loss 4-3	@Northwestern
February 17	Win 3-2	Northwestern
February 24	Win 1-0	Milwaukee
March 3	Win 5-3	@Northwestern

1917-18   Schedule and Results:
Coach Joe Steinauer
0-1-1 Overall

Date	Result	Opponent
February 2	Tie 2-2	@Culver
February 19	Loss 10-5	@Illinois
February 22	6-2	UW Interfraternity*

*Scrimmage Game

1918-19   Schedule and Results:
Coach Joe Steinauer
0-1-0 Overall

Date	Result	Opponent
February 8	Loss 10-1	Milwaukee

1919-20   Schedule and Results:
Coach Joe Steinauer

Date	Result	Opponent

No Games Played

1920-21   Schedule and Results:
Coach Tom Jones

Date	Result	Opponent

No Games Played

1921-22   Schedule and Results:
Coach Dr. A.K. Viner
0-7-0 Third in WIHL   0-8-0 Overall

Date	Result	Opponent
January 14	Loss 4-2	Milwaukee*
January 20	Loss 3-0	Minnesota
January 21	Loss 3-1	Minnesota
February 3	Loss 12-2	@Minnesota
February 4	Loss 7-0	@Minnesota
February 13	Loss 6-3	Michigan
February 18	Loss 3-0	@ Notre Dame
February 21	Loss 5-1	@ Michigan

*Exhibition Game

First year hockey was a varsity sport at the University of Wisconsin.

1922-23   Schedule and Results:
Coach Dr. A.K. Viner
2-6-3   Third in WIHL

Date	Result	Opponent
January12	Loss 2-1 2OT	@ Michigan
January 13	Loss 1-0	@ Michigan
January 19	Loss 1-0	Michigan
January 20	Win 1-0	Michigan
February 9	Loss 4-1	Minnesota
February 10	Tie 1-1 2OT	Minnesota
February 17	Win 3-1	Marquette (WI)
February 26	Loss 1-0 OT	@ Minnesota
February 27	Loss 4-0	@ Minnesota
March 2	Tie 1-1 2OT	@ Marquette (WI)
March 3	Tie 2-2 2OT	@ Marquette (WI)

1923-24   Schedule and Results:
Coach Robert Blodgett
0-10-1 Third in the WIHL 2-11-1 Overall

Date	Result	Opponent
January 12	Loss 4-1	Marquette (WI)

January 18	Loss 3-0	@ Michigan
January 19	Tie 2-2 3OT	@ Michigan
January 25	Loss 4-0	Minnesota
January 26	Loss 5-0	Minnesota
February 9	Win 3-1	@ Janesville*
February 13	Win 3-1	Janesville*
February 15	Loss 3-0	Michigan
February 16	Loss 3-1	Michigan
February 22	Loss 3-0	@ Marquette (WI)
February 23	Loss 2-1 2OT	@ Marquette (WI)
February 28	Loss 8-7 OT	Carleton*
February 29	Loss 4-0	@ Minnesota
March 1	Loss 4-0	@ Minnesota

*Exhibition Games

1924-25   Schedule and Results:
Coach Kay Iverson
0-6-0 Third in WIHL   1-7-1 Overall

Date	Result	Opponent
January 15	Win 3-0	@ Janesville*
January 16	Tie 0-0	@ Janesville*
February 13	Loss 5-1	Minnesota
February 14	Loss 1-0 2OT	Minnesota
February 20	Loss 2-1	Carleton*
February 27	Loss 2-0	Michigan
February 28	Loss 1-0	Michigan
March 4	4-3 3OT	Portage**
March 13	Loss 1-0	@ Minnesota
March 14	Loss 1-0	@ Minnesota

*Exhibition Games

**Intrasquad Scrimmage Game

1925-26   Schedule and Results:
Coach Kay Iverson
4-3-3 Tied for first in WIHL and second in Big Ten   9-6-4 Overall

Date	Result	Opponent

December 26	Loss 2-0	@ Duluth*
December 31	Loss 7-0	@ Eveleth Cubs*
January 1	Loss 2-0	@ Eveleth Junior College*
January 2	Win 3-2	@ Virginia*
January 8	Win 11-0	Marquette (WI)
January 9	Win 3-0	Marquette (WI)
January 15	Tie 0-0 OT	Minnesota
January 16	Tie 1-1 OT	Minnesota
January 22	Win 3-0	Janesville*
January 23	Win 5-0	Janesville*
February 6	Tie 1-1	Notre Dame*
February 12	Tie 1-1 OT	@ Michigan
February 13	Loss 2-1	@ Michigan
February 19	Win 2-0	Carleton*
February 20	Win 4-2	Carleton*
March 4	Win 2-1	Michigan
March 5	Win 2-0	Michigan
March 10	Loss 4-2	@Minnesota
March 11	Loss 2-1	@Minnesota

* Exhibition Games

1926-27   Schedule and Results:
Coach "Rube" Brandow
0-8-0 Third in WIHL   1-9-0 Overall

Date	Result	Opponent
January 7	Win 4-1	Janesville*
January 14	Loss 1-0	Minnesota
January 15	Loss 3-1	Minnesota
January 21	Loss 7-0	Manitoba*#
February 14	Loss 4-0	@ Minnesota
February 15	Loss 2-1	@ Minnesota
February 19	Loss 1-0	Michigan
March 5	Loss 2-1	Michigan**
March 7	Loss 1-0 OT	Michigan**
March 9	Loss 1-0	Michigan**

*Exhibition Games

#First ice hockey game against international opponent played at the University of Wisconsin (Exhibition Game).

**First American intercollegiate ice hockey games held outside of the U.S.A and were played in Windsor, Ontario.

1927-28   Schedule and Results:
Coach John Farquhar
3-5-2 Second in WIHL/Big Ten   5-7-4 Overall

Date	Result	Opponent
December 27	Loss 3-2	@ Marquette (MI)*
December 29	Loss 6-0	@ Michigan College*
December 30	Tie 0-0	@ Michigan College*
December 31	Tie 1-1	@ Wausau*
January 2	Win 4-0	@ Oshkosh*
January 6	Loss 3-2	Marquette (WI)
January 7	Win 2-1	Wausau*
February 3	Win 2-1 2OT	Minnesota
February 4	Tie 1-1 4OT	Minnesota
February 16	Win 3-1	Michigan
February 17	Win 2-1 2OT	Michigan
February 20	Loss 1-0	@ Minnesota
February 21	Loss 4-1	@ Minnesota
February 24	Loss 6-2	@ Marquette (WI)
February 27	Tie 0-0 OT	@ Michigan#
February 28	Loss 3-1	@ Michigan#

*Exhibition Games

#Played at Olympia Stadium.

1928-29   Schedule and Results:
Coach John Farquhar
3-6-1 Tied for second in WIHL   11-7-2 Overall

Date	Result	Opponent
December 27	Tie 1-1 OT	@ Michigan College*
December 28	Win 3-1	@ Marquette (MI)*
January 1	Win 4-1	@ Wausau*
January 3	Win 3-1	@ Chicago*

January 11	Win 4-2	North Dakota*
January 12	Win 8-4	North Dakota*
January 18	Loss 9-0	@Marquette (WI)
February 7	Win 6-1	Wausau**
February 8	Win 1-0	Marquette (MI)**
February 10	Loss 2-0	Eveleth Junior College**
February 13	Win 2-1	Minnesota
February 14	Loss 2-0	Minnesota
February 18	Loss 3-2 OT	Michigan
February 19	Win 3-0	Michigan
February 21	Win 1-0	Marquette (WI)
February 23	Win 1-0	Chicago*
March 1	Loss 3-1	@ Michigan
March 2	Tie 2-2 2OT	@ Michigan
March 4	Loss 2-0	@ Minnesota
March 5	Loss 4-0	@ Minnesota

*Exhibition Games

**Winter Frolic Tournament in Wausau, Wisconsin.

1929-30   Schedule and Results:

Coach John Farquhar

4-4-1 Second in WIHL   5-6-1 Overall

Date	Result	Opponent
December 19	Win 3-1	@ Michigan College*
December 20	Loss 3-2	@ Michigan College*
January 6	Loss 3-1	@ Chicago*
January 10	Win 2-0	Minnesota
January 11	Win 4-3	Minnesota
January 17	Loss 2-1 2OT	Michigan
January 18	Win 3-2	Michigan
January 25	Loss 4-0	Marquette (WI)
February 15	Loss 2-1 2OT	@ Minnesota
February 17	Win 2-1 OT	@ Minnesota
February 27	Loss 5-1	@ Michigan
March 1	Tie 0-0 2OT	@ Michigan

*Exhibition Games

1930-31 Schedule and Results:

Coach Spike Carlson

4-4-1 Tied for second in WIHL   4-7-1 Overall

Date	Result	Opponent
December 22	Loss 4-2	@ Hibbing*
December 23	Loss 5-3	@ Hibbing*
December 25	Loss 2-1	@ Fort Frances (Ont.)*
January 9	Win 3-1	Minnesota
January 16	Win 2-0	Michigan
January 17	Win 1-0 OT	Michigan
January 20	Win 2-1 OT	Marquette (WI)
February 11	Loss 1-0	@ Marquette (WI)
February 13	Loss 2-1	@ Minnesota
February 14	Loss 4-1	@ Minnesota
February 19	Tie 0-0 2OT	@ Michigan
February 21	Loss 3-0	@ Michigan

*Exhibition Games

1931-32 Schedule and Results:

Coach Art Thomsen

0-3-0   2-5-1 Overall

Date	Result	Opponent
December 5	Loss 1-0	@ Wausau*
December 31	Loss 3-2	Michigan College*#
January 1	Tie 2-2 OT	Michigan College*#
January 9	Win 5-1	Milwaukee*
January 19	Loss 10-1	@ Minnesota
February 13	Win 5-2	@ Wausau*
February 19	Loss 7-1	@ Michigan
February 20	Loss 5-0	@ Michigan

*Exhibition Games

#Played at Eagle River, Wisconsin.

1932-33 Schedule and Results:

Coach Art Thomsen

0-5-0 Last place in the WIHL   0-9-1 Overall

Date	**Result**	**Opponent**
January 13	Loss 5-0	@Michigan College
January 14	Loss 4-0	@Michigan College
January 17	Loss 4-2 OT	Milwaukee*
February 3	Tie 1-1	Eau Claire#
February 4	Loss 6-1	Minnesota#
February 10	Loss 8-0	@ Minnesota
February 11	Loss 3-0	@ Minnesota
February 14	Loss 2-0	@ Marquette (WI)
February 17	Loss 8-1	@Michigan
February 18	Loss 2-1	@Michigan

*Exhibition Game

#Eau Claire Winter Carnival games played in Eau Claire, Wisconsin.

1933-34   Schedule and Results:
Coach Art Thomsen
0-4-0 Last place in the WIHL   1-10-1 Overall

Date	**Result**	**Opponent**
November 30	Loss 3-0	@Baby Ruths*#
December 16	Loss 4-2	@Wausau*
December 17	Loss 3-1	@Wausau*
December 21	Tie 2-2 OT	@ Michigan College*
December 22	Loss 3-1	@ Michigan College*
December 24	Loss 6-1	@Nestor Johnsons*#
December 26	Win 3-1	@Egan*#
December 28	Loss 6-0	@Queens University (Kingston,Ont.)*#
February 9	Loss 1-0	@ Minnesota
February 10	Loss 7-0	@ Minnesota
February 16	Loss 5-3	@ Michigan
February 17	Loss 2-0	@ Michigan

*Exhibition Games

#Played at Chicago Coliseum.

Hockey was dropped as a varsity sport at the UW after the 1933-34 season.

1934–35   Schedule and Results:
Coach Art Thomsen
0-4-0   6-7-1 Overall

Date	**Result**	**Opponent**
December 22	Tie 4-4 2OT	@ Wausau*
December 23	Loss 2-1	@ Wausau*
December #	Win #	@Milwaukee*
December 30	Win 6-0	@ Wisconsin Rapids*
December 31	Loss 4-1	@ Eagle River*
January 1	Loss 4-1	@ Eagle River*
January 2	Win 4-2	@ Marinette*
January 3	Win 8-2	@ Marinette*
January 4	Win 6-1	@ Green Bay*
January 5	Win 1-0	@ Green Bay*
January 11	Loss 6-0	@ Michigan
January 12	Loss 2-1	@ Michigan
February 8	Loss 9-0	@ Minnesota
February 9	Loss 5-1	@ Minnesota

*Exhibition Games

#Unknown date and score.

Photo Credits/Publications

Special Thank You to The Board of Regents of the University of Wisconsin System

Courtesy of UW-Madison Archives.
The Wisconsin Athletic Review magazine
Feb. 1924 and Dec. 1927

Courtesy of UW-Madison Archives.
The Wisconsin Octopus magazine
March 1938

Courtesy of UW-Madison Archives.
Glass Plate Negatives Collection:
3980C, 3981C, 3982C, 3983C, 3984C, 3985C, 3986C, 3987C and 3988C

Courtesy of University of Minnesota Archives.
The Gopher Yearbook 1933 P. 218 Vol. 46
(P. 251)

Courtesy of Marquette University-Department of Special Collections and University Archives, Raynor Memorial Libraries.
Hilltop Yearbook 1931 P. 247 Vol. 17 (P. 228)
Hilltop Yearbook 1933 P. 177 Vol. 19 (P. 254)

The Badger (1914). Edited by Arthur Hallam. Vol. 28. Published by the junior class of the University of Wisconsin, 1913.
The Badger (1915). Edited by Stanley Hollen. Vol. 29. Assembled and Published by the class of 1915 of the University of Wisconsin, 1914.
The Badger (1916). Edited by G.L. Broadfoot and A W Powell. Vol. 30. published by the junior class of the University of Wisconsin, 1915.
The Badger (1917). Edited by R.L. Wadsworth. Vol. 31. Published by the junior class of the University of Wisconsin, 1916.

PHOTO CREDITS/PUBLICATIONS

The Badger (1918). Edited by Frank V. Birch. Vol. 32. Published by the junior class of the University of Wisconsin, 1917.

The Badger (1919). Edited by Harry H. Scott. Vol. 33. Assembled and published by the class of 1919 of the University of Wisconsin, 1918.

The Liberty Badger (1920). Edited by Lincoln A. Quarberg. Vol. 34. Assembled and published by the class of 1920 of the University of Wisconsin, 1919.

The Badger (1921). Edited by C. Wesley Travers. Vol. 35. Assembled and published by the class of 1921 of the University of Wisconsin, 1920.

The Badger (1922). Edited by Thomas T. Coxon. Vol. 36. Assembled and published by the class of 1922 of the University of Wisconsin, 1921.

The Badger (1923). Edited by Horace Breese Powell. Vol. 37. Assembled and published by the class of 1923 of the University of Wisconsin, 1922.

The Badger (1924). Edited by Gamber F. Tegtmeyer. Vol. 38. Annual publication of the junior class of the University of Wisconsin, 1923.

The Badger (1925). Edited Ellis Giles Fulton. Vol. 39. Annual publication of the junior class of the University of Wisconsin, 1924.

The Badger (1926). Edited by Otis L. Wiese. Vol. 40. Published by the junior class of the University of Wisconsin, 1925.

The Badger (1927). Edited by Ewart L. Merica. Vol. 41. Published by the junior class of the University of Wisconsin, 1926.

The Badger (1928). Edited by Harry C. Thoma. Vol. 42. Published by the junior class of the University of Wisconsin, 1927.

The Badger (1929). Edited by William K. Grube. Vol. 43. Published by the junior class of the University of Wisconsin, 1928.

The 1930 Badger. Edited by Stuart Higley. Vol. 44. Published by the junior class of the University of Wisconsin, 1929.

The 1931 Badger. Edited by S. Braymer Sherman. Vol. 45. Published by the junior class of the University of Wisconsin, 1930.

The Badger 1932. Edited by Jack Thompson. Vol. 46. Published by the junior class of the University of Wisconsin, 1932.

The 1933 Badger. Edited by Arthur Churchill Benkert. Vol. 48. Published by the 1933 senior class of the University of Wisconsin, 1933.

The 1934 Badger. Edited by Owen D. Nee. Vol. 49. Published by the 1934 senior class of the University of Wisconsin, 1934.

The 1935 Badger. Edited by Richard S. Bridgman. Vol. 50. Published by the senior class of the University of Wisconsin, 1935.

The 1936 Badger. Edited by Victor S. Falk. Vol. 51. Published by the senior class of the University of Wisconsin, 1936.

PHOTO CREDITS

Courtesy of UW Madison Archives
Wm. J.Meuer PhotoArt - Images

Image	UW Archives Info
S17098	Hockey Squad, 1927-1927, Meuer vol. 14 p. 85
S17099	Hockey players: Kreuger, Meiklejohn & Getz, Meuer vol. 14 p. 85
S17100	Hockey goalie: Mitchell, Meuer vol. 14 p. 85
S17101	Hockey team: Fry & Peare (Manager)
S17102	Hockey Coach Farquhar
S17103	Hockey players: McCarter, Mitchell, and Mason, Meuer vol. 14 p. 86
S17104	Hockey players posed before goal: McCarter, Mitchell, and Mason, Meuer vol. 14 p. 86
S17105	Hockey player: Farquhar, Meuer vol. 14 p. 86
S17106	Hockey player: Thompson, Meuer vol. 14 p. 86
S17107	Hockey team: Fry, Meuer vol. 14 p. 86
S17108	Hockey player: Don Meiklejohn, Meuer vol. 14 p. 86
S17109	Hockey player: Farquhar, Meuer vol. 14 p. 87
S17110	Hockey player: McCarter, Meuer vol. 14 p. 87
S17111	Hockey player: Farquhar, Meuer vol. 14 p. 87
S17112	Hockey player: Kreuger, Meuer vol. 14 p. 87
S17113	Hockey player: Murphy, Meuer vol. 14 p. 88
S17114	Hockey player on Library Mall: Don Meiklejohn, Meuer vol. 15 p. 49
S17115	Hockey player on Library Mall: Metcalf, Meuer vol. 15 p. 49
S17116	Hockey players face off on Library Mall, Meuer vol. 15 p. 49
S17117	Hockey player on Library Mall: Don Meiklejohn, Meuer vol. 15 p. 49
S17118	Hockey player on Library Mall: Metcalf, Meuer vol. 15 p. 49
S17119	Hockey player on Library Mall: Don Meiklejohn, Meuer vol. 15 p. 49
S17120	Hockey player on Library Mall: Metcalf, Meuer vol. 15 p. 49
S17121	Hockey players face off on Library Mall, Meuer vol. 15 p. 49
S17122	Hockey player: Meiklejohn, Meuer vol. 15 p. 50
S17123	Hockey player: Metcalf, Meuer vol. 15 p. 50
S17124	Hockey team: Coach Farquar in suit, Meuer vol. 15 p. 50
S17125	Hockey player: Metcalf, Meuer vol. 15 p. 50
S17126	Hockey player: Meiklejohn, Meuer vol. 15 p. 50
S17127	Wisconsin vs. Michigan Hockey Game (January 18, 1930): Hockey players and spectators, Meuer vol. 15 p. 60
S17128	Wisconsin vs. Michigan Hockey Game (January 18, 1930): View of Red Gym during game, Meuer vol. 15 p. 60
S17129	Players on the ice during Wisconsin vs. Michigan Hockey Game (January 18, 1930), Meuer vol. 15 p. 60

S17130	"Thompson's Quick Change," Wisconsin vs. Michigan Hockey Game (January 18, 1930), Meuer vol. 15 p. 60
S17131	Spectators in stands at Wisconsin vs. Michigan Hockey Game (January 18, 1930), Meuer vol. 15 p. 60
S17132	View of scoreboard during Wisconsin vs. Michigan Hockey Game (January 18, 1930), Meuer vol. 15 p. 60
S17133	Players on the ice during the Wisconsin vs. Michigan Hockey Game (January 18, 1930), Meuer vol. 15 p. 60
S17134	Varsity Hockey Squad, Meuer vol. 15 p. 78
S17135	Varsity Hockey Squad, Meuer vol. 15 p. 78
S17136	Freshman Hockey Squad, Meuer vol. 15 p. 78
S17137	Hockey players Swiderski, Frisch, and Metcalf, Meuer vol. 15 p. 78
S17138	Hockey player: Krueger, Meuer vol. 15 p. 78
S17139	Hockey player: Gallagher, Meuer vol. 15 p. 78
S17140	Hockey player: Meiklejohn, Meuer vol. 15 p. 78
S17141	Hockey player: Swiderski, Meuer vol. 15 p. 78
S17142	Hockey players: Meiklejohn & Krueger, Meuer vol. 15 p. 79
S17143	Hockey Coach Farquhar, Meuer vol. 15 p. 79
S17144	Hockey players: Swiderski, Frisch, and Metcalf, Meuer vol. 15 p. 79
S17145	Hockey players on Library Mall, Meuer vol. 16, p. 64
S17146	Hockey players on Library Mall, Meuer vol. 16, p. 64
S17147	Unid. Man on ice (Coach Carlsen?), Meuer vol. 16, p. 64
S17148	Hockey players on Library Mall, Meuer vol. 16, p. 64
S17149	Hockey players on the ice at Library Mall: Rebholz, Frisch, Gallagher, Meuer vol. 18 p. 83
S17150	Hockey goalie Art Frisch, Meuer vol. 18 p. 83
S17151	Hockey players on Library Mall, Meuer vol. 18, p. 83
S17152	Hockey players on Library Mall, Meuer vol. 18, p. 83
S17153	Hockey player on Library Mall, Meuer vol. 18 p. 84
S17154	Hockey player Hal Rebholz, Meuer vol. 18 p. 84
S17155	Hockey coach or manager, Meuer vol. 18 p. 84
S17156	Hockey player Carl Pederson, Meuer vol. 18 p. 84
S17157	Hockey player on Library Mall, Meuer vol. 18 p. 84
S17158	Hockey player on Library Mall, Meuer vol. 18 p. 84
S17159	Hockey player on Library Mall, Meuer vol. 18 p. 84
S17160	Hockey player Jos. Gallagher, Meuer vol. 18 p. 85
S17161	Hockey coaches Johnny Farquhar and Spike Carlson, Meuer vol. 18 p. 85

S17162	Hockey player on Library Mall, Meuer vol. 18 p. 85
S17163	Hockey player on Library Mall, Meuer vol. 18 p. 85
S17164	Hockey player on Library Mall, Meuer vol. 18 p. 85
S17165	Hockey players in protective masks, Meuer vol. 18 p. 85
S17166	Hockey player on Library Mall, Meuer vol. 18 p. 85
S17167	Hockey players (incl. Meiklejohn & Kreuger) on Library Mall, Meuer vol. 15 p. 100
S17168	Hockey team, Meuer vol. 18 p. 119
S17169	Hockey team, Meuer vol. 18 p. 119
S17170	Varsity Hockey Squad, 1917, Meuer vol. 23 p. 64
S17171	Varsity Hockey Squad, 1917, Meuer vol. 23 p. 64
S17172	Hockey players on Lake Mendota during Ice Carnival, Meuer vol. 23 p. 96
S17173	Hockey players on Lake Mendota during Ice Carnival, Meuer vol. 23 p. 96
S17174	Hockey players on Lake Mendota during Ice Carnival, Meuer vol. 23 p. 96
S17175	Hockey players taking a break during Ice Carnival, Meuer vol. 23 p. 96
S17176	Hockey players on Lake Mendota during Ice Carnival, Meuer vol. 23 p. 96
S17177	Joe Steinauer at Ice Carnival, 1920
S17178	Skaters and their friends at Ice Carnival
S17223	Ice rink on Lake Mendota, February 1919 (Meuer Vol. 3, p. 23)
S17224	Hockey game on Library Mall (Meuer Vol. 8 p. 49)
S17225	Hockey game on Library Mall (Meuer Vol. 8 p. 49)
S17226	Hockey game on Library Mall (Meuer Vol. 8 p. 49)
S17227	Hockey game on Library Mall (Meuer Vol. 8 p. 49)
S17228	Hockey game on Library Mall (Meuer Vol. 8 p. 49)
S17229	Hockey game on Library Mall (Meuer Vol. 8 p. 49)
S17230	Hockey game on Library Mall (Meuer Vol. 8 p. 49)
S17231	Hockey game on Library Mall (Meuer Vol. 9 p. 72)
S17232	Michigan vs. Wisconsin Hockey Game (Meuer Vol. 9 p. 72): Wisconsin 1, Michigan 0
S17233	Hockey game on Library Mall (Meuer Vol. 9 p. 72)
S17234	Hockey game on Library Mall (Meuer Vol. 9 p. 72)
S17235	Hockey game on Library Mall (Meuer Vol. 10, p. 54)
S17236	Chester A. Gross outfitted in his hockey gear (Meuer Vol. 10, p. 75)
S17237	G. R. McLean outfitted in his hockey gear (Meuer Vol. 11, p. 78)
S17238	Hockey game on Library Mall (Meuer Vol. 11, p. 79)
S17239	Hockey game on Library Mall (Meuer Vol. 11, p. 79)

S17240	Hockey Team (Varsity?) (Meuer Vol. 12 p. 69)
S17241	Hockey Team (Freshmen?) (Meuer Vol. 12 p. 69)
S17242	Hockey Team (JV?) (Meuer Vol. 12 p. 69)
S17243	Hockey Team portraits: Chamberlain (Meuer vol. 12 p. 81)
S17244	Hockey Team portraits: Lidiker (Meuer vol. 12 p. 81)
S17245	Hockey Team portraits: Coach Iverson (Meuer vol. 12 p. 81)
S17246	Hockey Team portraits: Whiteside (Meuer vol. 12 p. 81)
S17247	Hockey Team portraits: Jansky (Meuer vol. 12 p. 81)
S17248	Hockey Team portraits: McLean posing in the goal (Meuer vol. 12 p. 83)
S17249	Minnesota Hockey Squad (Meuer vol. 12 p. 83)
S17250	Hockey Team portraits: Unidentified (Meuer vol. 12 p. 83)
S17251	Hockey Team portraits: Emil & Kay Iverson (Meuer vol. 12 p. 83)
S17252	Hockey Team portraits: Unidentified (Meuer vol. 12 p. 83)
S17253	Hockey Team playing on library mall (Meuer vol. 11 p. 97)
S17254	Varsity Hockey Squad assembled on Library Mall (Meuer vol. 12 p. 87)
S17255	Hockey player, Kneebohm (Meuer vol. 12 p. 87)
S17256	Hockey player, Morehead (Meuer vol. 12 p. 87)
S17257	Hockey player, Murphy (Meuer vol. 12 p. 87)
S17258	Hockey player, Moorhead (Meuer vol. 13 p. 74)
S17259	Hockey player, Rahr (Meuer vol. 13 p. 74)
S17260	Hockey player, Moelk (Meuer vol. 13 p. 74)
S17261	Hockey player, Boyer (Meuer vol. 13 p. 74)
S17262	Hockey player, Lidicker (Meuer vol. 13 p. 74)
S17263	Hockey player, Jansky (Meuer vol. 13 p. 74)
S17264	Hockey player, Drummond (Meuer vol. 13 p. 74)
S17265	"Hockey Squad" pictured on Library Mall (Meuer vol. 13 p. 74)
S17266	Hockey player, Brandow (Meuer vol. 13 p. 75)
S17267	Hockey player, Cahoon (Meuer vol. 13 p. 75)
S17268	Hockey player, Silverthorn (Meuer vol. 13 p. 75)
S17277	Hockey Squad pictured on Library Mall (Meuer vol. 12 p. 90)
S17278	Hockey player on Library Mall: Jansky (Meuer vol. 12 p. 104)
S17279	Hockey player on Library Mall: Lidicker (Meuer vol. 12 p. 104)
S17280	Hockey player on Library Mall: Whiteside (Meuer vol. 12 p. 104)
S17281	Hockey player on Library Mall: McCarter (Meuer vol. 12 p. 104)

S17282	Hockey player on Library Mall: Carriere (Meuer vol. 12 p. 104)
S17283	Hockey player on Library Mall: Carlson (Meuer vol. 12 p. 104)
S17284	Hockey player on Library Mall: Ruf standing in the goal (Meuer vol. 12 p. 104)
S17285	Hockey player on Library Mall: Ruf standing in the goal (Meuer vol. 12 p. 104)

Notes

(1) The Capital Times (Madison, WI) 28 Feb. 1925 Page 6.   P. 104
(2) Portage Daily Register (Portage, WI) 5 March 1925 Page 2. P. 108
(3) Wisconsin State Journal (Madison, WI) 5 Jan. 1926 Page 12. P. 117
(4) The Capital Times (Madison, WI) 17 March 1926 Page 8. P. 137
(5) Wisconsin Alumnus Vol. 49 No. 3 Dec. 1947.   P. 137
(6) The Capital Times (Madison, WI) 3 Feb 1928.   P. 165
(7) The Wisconsin Athletic Review May 1928 Page 15.   P. 176
(8) The Capital Times (Madison, WI) 23 Feb 1929 Page 5.   P. 195
(9) The Capital Times (Madison, WI) 26 Dec 1930 Page 11.   P. 241
(10) College Humor May 1930 Page 87.   P. 256
(11) The Capital Times (Madison, WI) 11 Mar 1931 Page 13. P. 257

If you have any Wisconsin Badgers hockey jerseys, equipment or collectibles you may be willing to sell, please send an email to: uwjersey@gmail.com.

Additional Thanks

Some of my friends and Wisconsin Badger hockey heroes; Pat Ethier, Marc Behrend, Bob Suter, Mark Johnson, Mike Dibble, John Newberry, Rob Malnory, Theran Welsh, Gary Suter, Ron Vincent, Gary Engberg, Pat Johnson, Alex Rigsby-Cavallini, Shane Connelly, Jessie Vetter, Nancy Olson, Paul Houston, Chris Chelios, Steve Alley, Julian Baretta, Pete Johnson, Matt Walsh, John Taft, Kelly Nash, Norm Cherrey, Chuck Ellis, Dean Talafous, Brian Englbom, Craig Norwich, Nate LaPoint, Gary Bunz, Stan Hinkley, Tony Granato, Brianna Decker, Max Bentley, Ian Perrin, Trent Frederic, Mark "Greeny" Greenhalgh, Ryan Suter, Mike Hastings, Dave Maley, Bruce Driver, Mark Osiecki, Sis Paulsen, Tarek Baker, Jessie Vetter-McConnell, Hillary Knight, Rob Vega, Blake Geoffrion and Cole Caufield. Huge thank you to all current and former men and women from the Wisconsin Badgers hockey program.

Boomer, Holly and the gang at Boomer's 5th Quarter. "The House that Jack built."
Bruce "Dok" Meyer from the Klassik & KK.
Spencer & Vito from Avantis
Leo, Mark/Vee/Lurch and the crew from the Village Bar

Special thanks to my friends and classmates at Madison West. Go Regents! RIP: Dan "Z" Zanoya, Chris "Ole" Olson, Vince "Vito" Gandolph, Karl Roeber, Billy Jackson and the other fallen brothers and sisters.

For all my cool teammates and friends from the former Madison Westmorland youth hockey association in Madison, WI. West HS hockey and the Men's Roller Hockey League at Fast Forward. Especially; Jamie Kruger, Jeff Jorenby, Eric Schunke, Andy Cripps, Glen & Eddie Matsushima, Justin Ailing, Rob Jorenby, Shayne Meyer, Tyler Wright, Blake Jorenby, Lou Clark and Joe Mack (RIP). + others.

Mike O'Brien and family. Especially Jingles O'Brien, a true hockey pioneer and hero.

Jimmy, Jeff & Joel Marshall… Heck, the entire Marshall dynasty.

Jerry Heinrichs, Madison Cardinals legend. Wife Jean plus children Beth, Lisa, Tony & Amy.

The Nelson and Meharg families. Aunt Pat & Uncle Duke "Gary" Doucette, Aunt Ginny Meharg, Aunt Mary & Uncle Joe Purcell, Aunt Katie, Uncle Mike, Aunt Ginny Nelson and Aunt Sue Meharg. Kevin & Lori Tebrinke plus all the cousins and other relatives. Love you.

Scott "Douds" Doudna, BJ "Pos" Jordan, Bob "BC" Corliss and the rest of the Piper Park Crew (aka All-Stars); Wiley (RIP) Timmy V (RIP), Feegs, Jay, Colonel, Nigel, Sweet Dreams, KC, Lurch, Chadley, BA, Guam, Jason, Brooksie, Clumpy, Weez, JD and Purse.

All of the special friends that make up the Chicks and Fellas at UWRF. Jase, Joc, Rich, Jed, Beav, Catness, Omar, Flea, Hankes, Huge, Karl, Sweet Lew, Dogger, Cris, Bets, Molly, Amy, Heidi, Jennifer, Murph, Jakeus the Fracas, GK, Satre and the other chosen ones. Especially the gone, but not forgotten, Legends: Trevor "Sam" "Trev Cat" Smeby, Eric "Poy" Gensen, Cyrus "My Friend, My People" Irani, Kent Wosepka and Milka "Silk" Miller. RIP Brothers.

Some of my home town friends; Troy Parkos, Robert Hass, ScottyGuy, Larry Quakenbush, Jamie Kruger, Dave Schachte, Luke Doubler, Justin & Sally Temple, Dan Langlois, Nate Klaas, Ken Waller, Ben Cowan, Amy & Robert White, Dr. Butch Lalik, Paul Zweifel, Mike McKersie, Rob Mizelle, Dave Lombardo, Damien Heckelsmiller, Jim & Bill Schmitt, Dan Odegard, Dave Crowe, Chris Reidel, Scott & Margaret Watson, Tony Heinrichs, Derek Terrian, Jason Kripps, Craig & Bobbi Fey, Joel Fonseca, Brian Larson, Greg Schroeder, Jay Jurrens, Rob Hudson, Jason Geiger, Tom Grosse, Mike Bakalars, Rick Roth, Dr. Greg Matzke, Emily Pelletter, John Hebgen, Bill Snow, Jeff Herberger, Paul Pilof, Adetayo Dina, Josh Biser, Joe Borelli, Jim Dawson, Lance Langer, Brad Gould, Tim Mahaffey, Shawn Dugan, Mike Sullivan, Dave Lohrei, Earl Tollefson, Bill Brotzman, Randy Blaisdell, Pat Toner, Lane Manning, Scott Mirwald, Curt Beilman, Ron Hoffman and Todd Carlson. Many others, can't list them all.

My Corporate friends; Fernando Rivera, Jeff Kuhl, Larry Quackenbush, Arlington Davis III, Brad Trudell, Susan Caldwell, Randy Harmon, Gary Wilhelm, Cheryl Lutz, Gary Brendemuehl, Jim Febus, Herb Held III, Chris Crow, Kent Nauman, Kim Richmond, June Meier, Steve Rohde, Linda Hebard, Amanda Natvig, Dan Foster, Tom Olson, Kathy Topp, Mike Hacker, Geoff Engel, Lynne Johnson, Barbara Zabawa, John O'Laughlin, Alisha Kraus, Brandie Hiller Greenwood, Hedi LaMarr Rudd, Ann & Cindi Gonzagowski, Sue Webber, Jaime Gogola, Jerry Barbian, Dan Damon, Karl Johnson, Gianna Showers, Bryan Loney, Craig Hammerling, Brian Brugger, Shane Kellar and Rick Page. There's so many more and can't list them all. You know who you are.

Jason "Jase," Sheila, Nick, Luke, and Drew Goetz.
Scott and Kris Sumbler
Paul, Christine, Evan and Nick Senty
Scott, Kelli, Sam and Harry Seid.
Troy, Tammy, Jack and Grace Parkos & Ted.
Robert, Paula, Maria and Carly Hass.
Marty, Mary Anne and Tim Kennedy
Bob Cattelino & Nina
Dr. Randy Heidel & Dr. Donald Tipple
Father T – Pastor Tafadzwa Kushamba

Please consider helping grow the game of hockey in Wisconsin.

Jingles O'Brien Hockey Scholarship Fund

https://www.jinglesobriensf.com/

Coach Jeff Sauer Foundation

https://www.coachsauerfoundation.org/

"It's a great day for hockey."

"Badger" Bob Johnson

Wisconsin Badgers Hockey Coach
1966-1982

About the Author

Craig P. Nelson is a longtime hockey enthusiast from Madison, Wisconsin. He grew up playing the game on the west side of town and continued playing in various beer leagues as an old man.

As a youth hockey player, his coach once told the team to be sure to give back to the sport of hockey when you are an adult. Nelson took that to heart as he coached youth hockey for over two decades, served on a variety of hockey related Boards and has helped numerous hockey events earn desperately needed funds to help countless kids and hockey rinks around the Midwest.

After some twenty plus years working in the insurance industry, Nelson elected to depart corporate America and began working on his vision of completing a book covering the UW Hockey programs little known initial era from over 100 years ago. His efforts and contributions with this book, *Seasons on Ice – The Birth of Wisconsin Badgers Hockey,* on the history of hockey at the University of Wisconsin has literally rewritten the record books and cemented the storied legacy.

These days he is still enjoying following his son around the Midwest to watch him play lacrosse. On weekends you can find Nelson on a field watching his sons' teams, at a rink catching a local amateur game or downtown cheering on the Wisconsin Badgers teams.